Conifers

**Compiled by
Aljos Farjon and Christopher N. Page**

IUCN/SSC Conifer Specialist Group

with contributions from:
M.J. Brown, P. Dogra, M.F. Doyle, He X., R.S. Hill, Hu Y., S. Khuri, Lin J., J. A. Pérez de la Rosa, N. Schellevis, R. Schmid, J. Schouten, S. N. Talhouk, Tang Y., A. Watt, C. Williams, & T. A. Zanoni

IUCN
The World Conservation Union

SPECIES SURVIVAL COMMISSION

Sultanate of Oman

Chicago Zoological Society

WWF

DETR
ENVIRONMENT
TRANSPORT
REGIONS

ROYAL
BOTANIC
GARDEN
EDINBURGH

ROYAL
BOTANIC
GARDENS
KEW

Published by: IUCN, Gland, Switzerland and Cambridge, UK

Copyright: © 1999 International Union for Conservation of Nature and Natural Resources

Reproduction of this publication for educational or other non-commercial purposes is authorized without prior written permission from the copyright holder provided the source is fully acknowledged.

Reproduction of this publication for resale or other commercial purposes is prohibited without prior written permission of the copyright holder.

Citation: Farjon, A. and Page, C.N.(compilers). (1999). *Conifers. Status Survey and Conservation Action Plan*. IUCN/SSC Conifer Specialist Group. IUCN, Gland, Switzerland and Cambridge, UK. ix + 121 pp.

ISBN: 2-8317-0465-0

Cover photo: Monkey-puzzle trees (*Araucaria araucana*) in a natural stand in Chile are examples of ancient conifers still holding out, little changed since the age of the dinosaurs. Photograph C. N. Page.

Layout by: Conservation Education Consultants, Cheltenham, UK.

Produced by: International Centre for Conservation Education, Brocklebank, Butts Lane, Woodmancote, Cheltenham, Gloucestershire, GL52 4QH, UK.

Printed by: Cotswold Printing Company, Stroud, Gloucestershire, UK.

Available from: IUCN Publications Services Unit
                   219c Huntingdon Road, Cambridge CB3 ODL, United Kingdom
                   Tel: +44 1223 277894, Fax: +44 1223 277175
                   E-mail: info@books.iucn.org
                   WWW: http://www.iucn.org

                   A catalogue of IUCN publications is also available.

Contents

Foreword iv

Compilers v

Acknowledgements v

Executive Summary vi

     Resúmen (trad.) Ma. de Lourdes Rico Arce & Mariano Gimenez-Dixon vii

     Résumé (trad.) Paul Strahm & Denis Landenbergue viii

Summary Table of Recommended Actions ix

Chapter 1 Global Assessment of Conifer Diversity and Threats 1

Introduction 1

Conifer diversity and distribution 2

     Global diversity 2

     Regional diversity 6

Major threats to conifer survival 7

Global Red List of Conifers 11

Chapter 2 Conservation Issues **27**

Conservation 27

     Conservation incentives 27

     Conservation priorities 27

Recommendations for conservation action 31

     Guidelines for *in situ* strategies 31

     Strategies for *ex situ* conservation 32

Integration of *in situ* and *ex situ* strategies 36

     The role of botanic gardens in conifer conservation 36

Summary of action recommendations 37

References 39

Chapter 3 Regional Accounts **40**

Introduction 40

New Caledonia Action Plan 41

Himalayas Action Plan 50

Mexico: Nueva Galicia Action Plan 55

Caribbean Action Plan 59

Tasmania Action Plan 63

Southwest Pacific oceanic islands Action Plan 72

Californian Floristic Province Action Plan 75

Chapter 4 Species Accounts **89**

Clanwilliam Cedar *Widdringtonia cedarbergensis* J. A. Marsh 90

Giant Sequoia *Sequoiadendron giganteum* (Lindl.) J. Buchholz 92

Alerce *Fitzroya cupressoides* (Molina) I.M. Johnston 95

Sicilian Fir *Abies nebrodensis* (Lojac.) Mattei 97

Fiji Acmopyle *Acmopyle sahniana* J. Buchholz and N.E. Gray 99

Bigcone Pinyon Pine *Pinus maximartinezii* Rzed 101

Dawn Redwood *Metasequoia glyptostroboides* Hu and W.C. Cheng 103

Krempf's Pine *Pinus krempfii* Lecomte 105

White Berry Yew *Pseudotaxus chienii* (W.C. Cheng) W.C. Cheng 106

Cedar of Lebanon *Cedrus libani* A. Rich 108

Appendix 1 Conifer Specialist Group members and contributing authors 112

Appendix 2 IUCN Red List Category Summaries 114

Appendix 3 IUCN Protected Area Management Categories 121

Foreword

Conifers, that is pines, spruces, firs, and, oh yes...cypresses, and larches, are these endangered? Most people, when they think of conifers in nature, conjure up images of vast forests in Canada, Scandinavia, Siberia, perhaps in the Alps or the Rocky Mountains, built of spruces, firs, and pines. Surely these species are not in danger of extinction? Some years ago, there was much concern about the effects of acid rain in such forests near industrial centres in Europe and the USA. With the reduction of emissions of SO_2, these problems are in many areas gradually being overcome. Forests (both planted and natural) may have been badly affected, but species were not because they commonly occurred outside the affected regions. Yet conifers, as species, are threatened with extinction globally. To appreciate this, we will have to adjust the common perceptions indicated above and realise that the majority of conifer species do not occur in the northern lands but are scattered on all continents except Antarctica, mostly in small areas, often with very few individuals in a population.

There are about 630 species of conifers world-wide. Despite the much smaller total land mass, nearly 200 of these are restricted to the Southern Hemisphere, where extensive conifer forests are virtually non-existent. Many conifers, notably in the family Podocarpaceae, but also in Araucariaceae, are restricted to the tropics, often in mountains but also in lowlands. The fringes of deserts and desert mountains, as well as the high and arid plateaus of continents are home to yet other conifers, mostly unheard of in more temperate or boreal latitudes. The relatively small tropical Pacific island of New Caledonia has 43 species, all restricted to the island. And in many cases, these conifers have only relict populations that were historically much larger and more widespread. In this Action Plan, evidence shows that an astonishingly high proportion of conifer species are threatened with extinction. The main causes have nothing to do with air pollution, but are the common litany of ills accompanying the overpopulation of this planet with humans and their impact on the natural environment: exploitation, conversion of woods to farmland and urbanisation, degradation of woodland vegetation by excessive gathering of firewood, grazing of livestock, burning etc. What little is left after large-scale exploitation by the affluent portion of humankind is further deteriorated and destroyed by the larger and less well-off resident populations. The situation is bleak in many parts of the world. Yet conifers are highly important ecologically, economically, scientifically and, not least, aesthetically. They have existed in various forms for over 250 million years, twice as long as the flowering plants.

This Action Plan is the first attempt to address the conservation issues of conifers on a global scale, focusing on species (taxa), not forests as such, although the two aspects are intricately connected. It is neither complete, as important gaps in its coverage remain to be filled, nor does it 'solve' all of the problems identified. But the Conifer Specialist Group, whose combined expertise this document represents, believes that it has taken an important first step in presenting what we know of this difficult subject to a wider audience of conservationists and policy makers, whose awareness and subsequent help will bring us closer to the protection of this fascinating type of plant life.

Aljos Farjon
Chair, IUCN/SSC Conifer Specialist Group

Compilers

Mr. ALJOS FARJON is Senior Scientific Officer and Curator of Gymnosperms in charge of conifer research at the Royal Botanic Gardens, Kew. Before he came to Kew he had studied the systematics of conifers (since 1983) at the Universities of Utrecht and Oxford and he published several major works and numerous papers on the subject from all three institutions. His research has concentrated on species, their taxonomic and phytogeographic circumscription and ecological adaptations to their natural environments. He has undertaken several major expeditions to Australia, Asia and North America to study certain genera more closely in the field. In 1994, he replaced Christopher Page as chair of the IUCN/SSC Conifer Specialist Group and organised the compilation of this Action Plan as well as the assessment of categories of risk using the new IUCN criteria for all conifers. He continues his research on conifers at Kew as well as his responsibility for the Conifer Specialist Group and its ongoing efforts to promote conservation of these highly important biological resources.

Dr. CHRISTOPHER N. PAGE has, for 25 years, been Principal Scientific Officer in charge of conifer research at the Royal Botanic Garden, Edinburgh. He is an evolutionary biologist, and believes that much of the scientific knowledge related to evolution can be usefully applied to conservation problems. He has travelled in every continent but Antarctica in the study of the field biology and ecology of conifers in the wild, and has reared material of most genera through their life-cycles in experimental cultivation. He was moved to take up conservation issues because so often he found he was 'just in time' to see some of the last remaining natural forests of many of the rarer species. He has been active in developing scientific strategies for tree species conservation, and is primarily concerned with the integration of *in-situ*, *ex-situ* and re-introduction approaches with living material, and with gaining and applying to this process knowledge of the genetic basis and field biology of the species concerned. He is founder (in 1976) of the Conifer Conservation Programme of the Royal Botanic Garden, Edinburgh and (in 1986) of the Conifer Specialist Group of IUCN-SSC, and its first chair (1986-1994). He now works as a freelance author and environmental consultant and is a Member Emeritus of SSC.

Acknowledgements

The preparation of this Species Survival Commission (SSC) Action Plan, which has taken several years, has been a collaborative and largely voluntary undertaking to which several members have given freely of their expertise and time. It represents the accumulated knowledge on conifer conservation, not only of individual members, but also of all those with whom they have consulted or collaborated, to all of whom the compilers offer their thanks. For a period of over three years during the preparation of this Action Plan, we worked closely together with the team responsible for the compilation of the World List of Threatened Trees under the project *Conservation and Sustainable Management of Trees* jointly undertaken by IUCN/SSC and the World Conservation Monitoring Centre (WCMC). We thank in particular Sara Oldfield and Charlotte Lusty at WCMC at Cambridge, UK and Wendy Strahm, Robin Sears, Elise Blackburn, and Michael Weh at IUCN/SSC at Gland, Switzerland, for all their encouragement, help, and support. The compilers also acknowledge with gratitude the support for conifer conservation and the taxonomic basis presented here from the Royal Botanic Gardens, Kew and Edinburgh.

Executive Summary

Conifers are one of the world's most important resources of timber. Especially in the Northern Hemisphere, these resources are vast and will, if managed wisely and used sustainably, provide wood for a multitude of purposes virtually indefinitely. Other functions, not the least of which are ecological ones provided by these vast conifer forests, are equally important. Unsustainable exploitation of these forests, while not yet banned, is gradually giving way to better forestry in many countries with substantial populations of this invaluable resource. Why then this Action Plan? Why an IUCN/SSC Conifer Specialist Group?

Globally, there are some 630 species of conifers, plus c. 170 taxa at infraspecific ranks (subspecies and varieties), totalling 800 taxa. Of these, 355 are listed as of conservation concern. The total number of taxa **threatened with extinction (CR, EN, VU) is 200 (c. 25%)**. Seventy of these are likely to become extinct in the foreseeable future if current trends continue.

Conifers occur on all continents except Antarctica, but their abundance is unevenly distributed both in terms of individuals and taxa. Where the vast boreal conifer forests stretch across continents and contain billions of trees, they sustain no more than a handful of species. In contrast, more southerly latitudes in the Northern Hemisphere and all of the Southern Hemisphere have either scattered conifer forests, or mixed conifer/hardwood forests in which conifers occur in low densities, dispersed among other trees or shrubs. Many species occupy very small areas, often as relict populations of once greater abundance. Some areas have a high diversity of species, but hardly any of these species are abundant enough to form forests of any appreciable size. A good example is New Caledonia in the Southwest Pacific, an island with 43 species of conifers, all endemic, in an area about the size of Wales. Mexico has 42 species and 18 varieties of pines (*Pinus*), compared with eight species and one variety in all of Canada and Alaska. Unknown to many, c. 200 species of conifers are restricted to the Southern Hemisphere, where vast conifer forests are unknown. It is this scattered diversity that is most threatened with extinction.

This Action Plan assesses conifer diversity and its threats in Chapter 1. Endemic genera are particularly important since they represent taxa of high genetic distinction often represented by a single species. We have indicated where these genera are concentrated. In Chapter 2 we return to this theme and analyse the data to indicate '**conifer hot spots**' or areas where there is a combination of high conifer diversity and threats. Conifer conservation in such areas should be a priority. While a generalised assessment of threats in Chapter 1 and general conservation recommendations in Chapter 2 often apply to such hot spots and may help to identify the action that is needed, more detailed **regional accounts** are provided for several of these hot spots in Chapter 3. In addition, this Action Plan is unique among IUCN's Plant Action Plans so far published in that it gives the complete **Global Red List of Conifers** using the 1994 IUCN Red List Categories and criteria. Since this list includes distribution of the taxa, any country can tally from this list its conifers which are threatened globally. We have also developed a formula for prioritising at the taxonomic level, resulting in a **short-list of threatened species**. We think that we have chosen objective criteria to do this, but since conservation action often will be taken at regional or local levels, taxa which are not short-listed remain important targets. We encourage priority Action Plans to be undertaken for the short-listed species. This Action Plan presents ten species accounts. These accounts should be used both as models for more such reports which need to follow and as first steps towards species Action Plans. In these species accounts, we have included examples of 'success stories' to encourage conservationists to begin work on other species.

With threats to conifers so multifarious and widespread, the three groupings developed in the Conifer Action Plan (Global Red List of Conifers, hot spots, and short-list of threatened species) provide focus for further assessment and conservation action. In a **summary of recommendations** we call for:

Conservation of existing diversity through nine action points focusing on *in situ* strategies supported where necessary by *ex situ* conservation;

Reduction of pressure on conifers as a resource through four action points focusing on timber management and market strategies.

Resúmen

Las coníferas conforman uno de los recursos madereros mas importantes del mundo. Especialmente en el Hemisferio norte, este vasto recurso puede, si se maneja con conciencia y de manera sustentable, proporcionar indefinidamente maderas para múltiples usos. Igualmente importantes son las otras funciones que proveen los bosques de coníferas, entre las que se encuentran las ecológicas. El manejo no sustentable de estos bosques, que aun no ha sido prohibido, esta gradualmente dando lugar a una mejor forestería en muchos países con considerables poblaciones de este recurso invaluable. Entonces ¿por qué este Plan de Acción? ¿Por qué un grupo de especialistas de coníferas de la IUCN/SSC?

Existen unas 630 especies de coníferas, más aproximadamente 170 taxones de rango infraespecífico (subespecies y variedades), en total se trata de 800 taxones. De estos, 355 son considerados de interés para la conservación. El numero total de taxones **amenazados de extinción (CR, EN, VU) es de 200 (cerca del 25%)**. Setenta de estos probablemente se extingan en un futuro previsible si persisten las tendencias presentes.

Las coníferas se encuentran en todos los continentes con la excepción de la Antártica, pero su abundancia, tanto en individuos como taxones, no esta equitativamente distribuida. Mientras que los vastos bosques de coníferas boreales atraviesan continentes y contienen billones de arboles, estos no mantienen mas que un puñado de especies. En contraste, en las latitudes bajas del Hemisferio Norte y todo el Hemisferio Sur poseen, ya sea bosques de coníferas esparcidos o bosques mixtos de coníferas/latifoliadas, donde las coníferas se encuentran en bajas densidades, dispersas entre los arboles y arbustos de otras especies. Muchas especies ocupan áreas muy pequeñas, frecuentemente como relictos de poblaciones que antiguamente eran muy abundantes. Algunas áreas presentan gran diversidad de especies, sin embargo casi ninguna de estas especies son suficientemente abundantes para formar un bosque de tamaño apreciable. Un ejemplo se da en Nueva Caledonia, en el sudeste del Pacifico; una isla con 43 especies de coníferas, todas endémicas, en una área del tamaño de Gales. México tiene 42 especies y 18 variedades de pinos (*Pinus*), comparadas con 8 especies y una variedad en Canadá y Alaska juntos. Desconocido para mucha gente, cerca de 200 especies de coníferas son restringidas al Hemisferio Sur donde se desconocen grandes bosques de coníferas. Esta diversidad esparcida es la mas amenazada de extinción.

Este Plan de Acción señala, en el capitulo 1, la diversidad las coníferas y las amenazas que sufren. Son particularmente importantes los géneros endémicos ya que en ellos esta representada una alta diferenciación genética que frecuentemente se refleja en una sola especie. Hemos indicado donde se concentran estos géneros. En el Capitulo 2, regresamos a este tema y analizamos los datos indicando las **sitios críticos ('hot spots') para coníferas**; áreas donde hay una combinación de alta diversidad, así como de especies amenazas. La conservación de coníferas en estas áreas debe ser prioritaria. Mientras que las evaluaciones generales de las amenazas del Capitulo 1 y las recomendaciones para la conservación del Capitulo 2 suelen ser aplicables a los sitios críticos y pueden ser útiles para identificar las actividades que sean necesarias, el Capitulo 3 provee **informes regionales** más detallados para varios de estos sitios críticos. Además, este Plan de Acción es único entre los Planes de Acción de la IUCN hasta ahora publicados sobre plantas ya que da la **lista Roja Global de coníferas** completa, utilizando las Categorías de las Listas Rojas de la UICN de 1994. Puesto que esta lista incluye la distribución de los taxones, para cualquier país se puede hacer un recuento de sus coníferas globalmente amenazadas. También hemos desarrollado una formula para priorizar al nivel taxonómico, resultando en una **lista selecta de especies amenazadas**. Pensamos que para ello hemos usado criterios objetivos, mas debido a que la acción de conservación generalmente se lleva a cabo a nivel regional o local, hay taxones que no fueron incluidos en la lista selecta que siguen siendo importantes. Instamos a que se desarrollen Planes de Acción para estas especies selectas. Este Plan de Acción presenta 10 informes de especies. Estos informes deben ser empleados tanto, como modelos para informes de otras especies que deben seguirles, como lineamientos iniciales hacia Planes de Acción por especies. En estos informes de especies hemos incluido ejemplos de 'casos exitosos' a fin de alentar a los conservacionistas a comenzar a trabajar con otras especies.

Como las peligros de las coníferas son tan variados y amplios, los tres grupos desarrollados en el Plan de Acción (Lista Roja Global de coníferas, sitios críticos y lista selecta de especies amenazadas) proporcionan un enfoque para ulteriores evaluaciones y actividad en la conservación. **Resumiendo, las recomendaciones** que proponemos son:

Conservación de la diversidad existente a través de 9 puntos de acción enfocados a estrategias *in situ* apoyando donde es necesario la conservación *ex situ*.

Reducción de la presión sobre las coníferas como un recurso a través de 4 puntos de acción enfocados en la gestión y estrategias de mercado de especies maderables.

Résumé

Les conifères constituent une des plus importantes ressources mondiales de bois de construction. Particulièrement abondants dans l'hémisphère nord, ils fournissent du bois pour une grande variété d'utilisations et ceci pratiquement d'une façon illimitée à condition d'être gérés de manière avisée et durable. D'autres rôles remplis par ces vastes forêts de conifères, parmi lesquels les fonctions écologiques ne sont pas les moindres, sont tout aussi importants. Bien que n'étant pas encore interdite, la gestion non durable de ces forêts se voit progressivement remplacée, dans de nombreux pays et sur d'importantes surfaces, par un meilleur type d'exploitation de cette ressource d'une valeur inestimable. Alors pourquoi ce plan d'action? Pourquoi un Groupe de spécialistes des conifères à la Commission de la sauvegarde des espèces de l'UICN?

Globalement, il existe environ 630 espèces de conifères et quelque 170 taxons à l'échelon infraspécifique (sous-espèces et variétés) totalisant 800 taxons. Parmi eux, 355 provoquent des inquiétudes quant à leur protection. En tout, **200 taxons - soit 25 % - sont menacés d'extinction (CR, EN, VU).** Septante d'entre eux sont susceptibles de disparaître dans un proche avenir si la tendance actuelle se poursuit.

On trouve des conifères sur tous les continents à l'exception de l'Antarctique; cependant, leur abondance est inégalement répartie tant en termes de quantité que de taxons. Alors que les vastes forêts boréales de conifères contenant des milliards d'arbres s'étendent sur plusieurs continents, elles sont composées d'un nombre limité d'espèces. En revanche, les latitudes plus méridionales de l'hémisphère nord et l'hémisphère sud dans son ensemble hébergent des forêts de conifères beaucoup plus dispersées, ou alors des forêts mixtes de feuillus et de conifères où ceux-ci n'atteignent que de faibles densités. De nombreuses espèces ne se trouvent que dans des zones très restreintes, souvent sous la forme de populations reliques. Certains secteurs présentent une grande diversité d'espèces mais très peu de celles-ci sont suffisamment abondantes pour constituer des forêts de taille conséquente. Un bon exemple de ce phénomène se trouve en Nouvelle-Calédonie, île du sud-ouest du Pacifique qui recèle 43 espèces de conifères - toutes endémiques - sur une superficie équivalente à celle du Pays de Galles. Le Mexique héberge 42 espèces et 18 variétés de pins (*Pinus*), à comparer avec 8 espèces et une variété pour l'ensemble du Canada et de l'Alaska. Fait beaucoup moins connu, environ 200 espèces de conifères sont confinées à l'hémisphère sud où de vastes forêts demeurent inconnues. C'est le caractère éparpillé de cette diversité qui est le plus menacé.

Ce plan d'action traite dans son premier chapitre de la diversité des conifères et des menaces qui pèsent sur elle. Les genres endémiques revêtent une importance particulière du fait qu'ils constituent des taxons génétiquement très distincts, souvent représentés par une seule espèce. Les endroits où se concentrent ces genres sont indiqués. Le second chapitre approfondit ce thème et analyse les données afin d'indiquer les "**hot spots**" (zones dans lesquelles on relève à la fois une grande diversité de conifères et l'existence de graves menaces). La protection des conifères dans ces zones devrait constituer une priorité. L'évaluation des menaces pesant sur ces arbres - traitée dans le chapitre 1 - et les recommandations relatives à leur protection - contenues dans le chapitre 2 - s'appliquent souvent à de tels "hot spots" et peuvent contribuer à définir les actions à entreprendre. Quant au chapitre 3, il aborde de manière plus détaillée et à l'échelle régionale plusieurs de ces "hot spots". De plus, de tous les plans d'actions publiés à ce jour par l'UICN sur les plantes, celui-ci est unique dans le sens où il fournit la *Liste Rouge globale des Conifères*, sur la base des catégories et critères de la Liste Rouge de l'UICN de 1994. Comme cette liste rouge considère la distribution des taxons, chaque pays a la possibilité d'identifier grâce à elle les conifères existant sur son territoire et qui sont également menacés à l'échelle globale. Nous avons aussi développé une formule de détermination des priorités à l'échelon taxonomique avec pour résultat l'établissement d'une "short list" d'espèces menacées. Nous pensons avoir choisi des critères objectifs dans cette démarche, mais puisque les actions de protection seront souvent entreprises aux niveaux régional ou local, les taxons ne figurant pas dans la "short list" demeurent parmi les objectifs importants. Nous encourageons le lancement de plans d'actions prioritaires pour les espèces comprises dans la "short list". Ce plan d'action présente dix résumés prenant chacun pour thème une espèce particulière. Ces résumés devraient être utilisés à la fois comme modèles pour tout rapport de ce genre nécessaire à l'avenir et en tant que première étape pour l'établissement de futurs plans d'actions par espèce. Nous avons intégré dans ces résumés des exemples de projets couronnés de succès afin d'encourager les protecteurs de la nature à initier des travaux sur d'autres espèces.

Compte tenu de la large répartition et de la multiplicité des menaces qui pèsent sur les conifères, les trois catégories développées dans le Plan d'Action pour les conifères, (liste rouge globale des conifères, "hot spots" et "short list" d'espèces en danger) fournissent des priorités pour les évaluations et les actions de protection à venir. Dans une **synthèse de recommandations,** nous lançons un appel pour :

Le maintien de la diversité existante, par la mise en oeuvre de neuf types d'action mettant l'accent sur des stratégies *in situ* assorties, en cas de besoin, de mesures de protection *ex situ*;

La réduction de la pression subie par les conifères en tant que ressource naturelle, par le biais de quatre types d'action ciblées sur la gestion du bois de construction et sur les stratégies du marché.

Summary Table of Recommended Actions

	Manage fire regimes using suppressions(s) or controlled burns (b)	Ex situ Propagation	Additional Research	New or expanded reserves	Improve management of current reserves	Restore and reintroduce seedlings *in situ*	Prevent forest degradation from logging (l) mining (m) grazing (g) and pests (p)	Enhance legal protection	Involve local residents	Undertake Development of Protection Plans	Maintain species diversity	Coordinate efforts of NGOs and government
Regional Accounts												
New Caledonia	x(s)	x		x	x			x	x			
Eastern Himalayas			x			x	x(l)		x			
Nueva Galicia, Mexico	x(s)	x	x	x	x	x	x(g,l)	x	x			
Caribbean Islands	x(s)	x	x	x							x	
Tasmania	x(s)											
SW Pacific islands						x						
California Floristic Province	x(b)	x		x			x(g,l,p)					
Species Accounts												
Clanwilliam cedar	x(s)											
Giant sequoia	x(s)	x	x	x		x						
Alerce	x(s)	x										
Sicilian fir	x(s)	x				x				x		
Fiji acmopyle							x(m)	x				
Bigcone pinyon pine	x(s)	x	x				x(g)		x			
Dawn redwood												
Krempf's pine		x	x									
White berry yew		x										
Cedar of Lebanon			x	x						x		x
Total	10	9	7	6	2	5	5	3	4	2	1	1

Chapter 1

Global Assessment of Conifer Diversity and Threats

Introduction

The conifers are one of the world's most important resources of timber. Several well-known genera have species that grow rapidly, develop into tall trees, and occur over wide ranges (especially in the cool regions of the Northern Hemisphere). Prime producers of softwood timber include the pines (*Pinus*), spruces (*Picea*), larches (*Larix*), silver firs (*Abies*), Douglas firs (*Pseudotsuga*), and hemlocks (*Tsuga*), all in the family Pinaceae. Other families yield important amounts of excellent timber in the Northern Hemisphere as well as in the Southern Hemisphere, and even in the tropics (e.g. various kauris (*Agathis*) and species of *Dacrydium*).

Conifers can also grow exceedingly slowly and to a great age; sometimes as gigantic trees and sometimes only as short, stocky trees or even shrubs. Hard, often durable and fine-grained, conifer wood is often highly prized for special uses. The wood of certain species is almost indestructible (decay-resistant). Many species are considered excellent trees for afforestation, and even more are used in horticulture, where several species have yielded valuable cultivars. Additional products include resins and their derivatives, such as terpene and essential oils, and even medicinal extracts. An example of the latter is the chemical compound taxol found in yews (*Taxus*) which is now used in treating certain forms of cancer. Conifers, thus, display an amazing array of unique potentials.

Globally there are some 630 species of conifers, distributed over c. 70 genera and 8-9 families (Page 1990a, Farjon 1998). Some genera have a relatively large number of species, such as *Pinus* (c. 110), *Podocarpus* (c. 105 or more, probably several still to be discovered), *Juniperus* (c. 55), *Abies* (c. 50), *Picea* (c. 35), *Dacrydium* (21), and *Araucaria* (19). Many more genera are poorly represented with only a few or even only a single species. Many species seem to belong to old evolutionary lineages, within their genus or even among conifers as a whole, reflecting the ancient origin of the group or the relictual nature of the species.

On the other hand, several of the larger genera contain species that are highly advanced and adapted to a wide variety of habitats. Many conifers are tolerant of adverse climatic or edaphic conditions unsuitable for other trees. These range from frequent fires in tropical 'pine savannas' to extreme climatic conditions at the tree line or beyond in high mountains, from temperate evergreen rain-forests on ocean shores to semi-deserts in the interior of continents. Soils can be sandy, rocky, peaty, dry or wet, and even toxic with heavy metals. This tolerance of such a wide range of climatic and edaphic conditions is unique amongst trees and cannot be achieved by most broad-leaved trees. For these reasons, conifers are very important ecologically as they provide forest cover or other permanent or periodic vegetation to animals and humans in all these habitats.

Natural old growth conifer forests, in which conifers can attain great size and age, are ecosystems sustaining a high level of biodiversity. Many species of plants and animals depend on them. Successional cycles in such forests are long and complex. In other systems conifers are pioneers capable of establishing a quick forest cover to be supplanted later by broad-leaved trees. There are many intermediate forest types between these extremes in which conifers have an important role, and much is still to be learned about these forests.

Exploitation of these resources is as old as civilisation: the Old Testament of the Bible mentions the extensive use of the Lebanon cedar (*Cedrus libani*) for temple building; the Chinese made similar use of conifer wood millennia ago. Shipbuilding depended for centuries on the tallest conifers for masts, while the Polynesians used various conifers for their canoes with which they explored the Pacific. In many areas such use proved to be unsustainable. Yet, with a few exceptions, this did not lead to serious threat to the survival of species on a global scale.

This century, and especially the latter half of it, has seen a dramatic increase in the exploitation of timber resources on every continent where conifer forests occur. Primary old-growth forest is being rapidly destroyed outside nature reserves. Coastal regions and forested islands, due to proximity of ports, are especially exploited, but interior regions are by no means excluded. The rate of exploitation usually far exceeds natural regeneration. Even if the constituent timber species are being grown in managed (plantation) forests *in situ*, this does not equate to sustainability.

For these reasons, such 'harvesting' as it is commonly called, is often an inappropriate term, as one cannot reap more than one sows. Where reforestation occurs, it is almost invariably with species alien to the site and most often in monoculture, or with a monoculture of one of the original constituents, usually the fastest-growing species. In many countries, changes in land use after cutting of forests preclude reforestation altogether. This development often leads to virtually irreversible changes in the environment, notably affecting the soil, often making it unfit for tree growth. In other instances, woodland is degraded by continued selective removal of trees. In all of these cases, such exploitation and transformation has led to decreasing conifer ranges or popu-

1

lations. For species with restricted distributions or scattered populations combined with slow regeneration and growth to maturity, this has led to an increased rarity. Some species are now at the brink of extinction, and a great deal of genetic diversity has been lost, especially in the cases of selective cutting or depletion of separated populations.

More localised environmental changes brought about by human activity are also spreading. These include frequent burning, grazing of domestic animals, mining operations, and urbanisation. Each one of these activities can seriously threaten local conifer species. When undertaken in various combinations and in conjunction with logging, the results can be disastrous. All these activities, but especially their increase in recent decades, pose an accelerating threat to a substantial proportion of conifer biodiversity.

This Action Plan aims to identify the species currently under threat of extinction, using the Red List Categories and criteria developed by IUCN in 1994 to assess threat for all plants and animals. This assessment results in an amended Global Red List of Conifers which forms the core of this document. It is the latest edition of a preliminary list published in 1993 (Farjon et al. 1993), which has been a major source for the compilation of the 1997 IUCN Red List of Threatened Plants (Walter and Gillett 1998). The amended list, compiled using the new IUCN categories, has also been incorporated into the recently published World List of Threatened Trees (Oldfield et al. 1998) and the World Checklist and Bibliography of Conifers (Farjon 1998). As a result, there are two recently published Red Lists of conifers 'endorsed' by IUCN that differ quite substantially from each other: the IUCN Red List of Threatened Plants, which used the 'old' categories, and the present one in this Action Plan. The latter supersedes the former wherever the two appear to differ. In addition, the various threats to conifer survival are identified. Prioritisation leads to the identification of special target species as well as conifer 'hot spots' in the world. For these, separate species accounts and regional plans serve as examples for a more local approach.

The issue of conifer conservation is diverse and complex, and its peculiarities vary from region to region across the globe. In detail, they are therefore best addressed regionally. General proposals for conifer conservation are, however, outlined in this Action Plan. Case studies of several threatened conifers are presented to indicate ways to proceed in individual species action. Individual countries can select their taxa from the list and use these case studies as examples to further develop conservation strategies for threatened conifers. In all these cases, what is brought forward should be seen and read as proposals for conservation action. Amendments are necessary and are likely to be made with more feedback from the regions concerned and with increased knowledge of the conservation status of individual species and the forests in which they occur. The analysis presented of priority species and 'hot spots' has so far resulted in a number of valuable reports by various members, which are presented in this Action Plan. However, largely due to

lack of detailed knowledge of several of these regions as well as species, and to limited resources of personnel to carry them out, more reports are needed. It is hoped that this Action Plan will stimulate the production of these.

A database, developed in close collaboration with the WCMC/SSC Conservation and Sustainable Use of Tree Project at Cambridge, UK, has been updated with these conifer data and will be continuously updated.

Conifer diversity and distribution

Global diversity

Conifer forests include those of the vast boreal regions of high latitudes in Europe, Asia, and North America, where relatively few species in few genera, such as spruces (*Picea*), firs (*Abies*), larches (*Larix*), and pines (*Pinus*) are widespread. The sheer numbers of individuals of each species in these forests ensure that they are not threatened with extinction. However, large-scale exploitation has regionally depleted these forests and the long-term future of the boreal conifer forests may be threatened if the focus of wood extraction on a massive scale were to be diverted from Pacific coastal forests (where conservation issues have become politically sensitive) to, for example, the Russian Far East or Siberia.

Mixed conifer-broadleaved forest, with *Abies mariesii*, in Honshu, Japan.

More diverse are the montane to subalpine zones of mid-latitude major mountain ranges of the northern hemisphere, such as the Alps, Himalayas, mountains of SW China, and Rocky Mountains in the USA. Here we find many more species of the boreal genera, but in addition more restricted genera, e.g. true cedars (*Cedrus*), Douglas firs (*Pseudotsuga*), and junipers (*Juniperus*). Most have relatively wide distributions, but there are notable exceptions, especially in centres of diversity, such as the eastern Himalayas, SW China, the Sierra Nevada of California, and the mountains of northern Mexico.

Other conifers, especially pines, cypresses (*Cupressus*), and junipers, occur in more Mediterranean climates of the

Mixed conifer-broadleaved forest in South Island, New Zealand.

(such as 'pine savannas' extending from the SE United States to Central America). Such areas are generally unsuitable for the development of angiosperm forest largely due to unfavourable soil conditions. These conditions can include extreme deficiency of nutrients and the presence of heavy metal contaminants (such as on the ultramafic soils of New Caledonia). Only a few genera of conifers (e.g. *Podocarpus* and *Agathis*) are able to compete with angiosperm trees by maintaining dominance through attaining great size and age.

While conifers are limited in number of genera and species (approximately 70 and 630) and are, in many respects, a relictual group of plants (whose true heyday was the Mesozoic era), they are widely distributed across the globe. The only major distribution gaps occur in large areas of Africa, parts of South America, and the deserts of Asia, Australia, Antarctica, and the Arctic. In Figure 1.1 the global distribution of conifers is illustrated, while further maps show conifer regions (Figure 1.2) and the distribution of conifer 'hot spots' (Figure 2.1). Table 1.1 outlines the distribution of all genera in major regions.

northern hemisphere. Cypress pines (*Callitris*) occupy similar habitats in Australia, while *Widdringtonia* occupies similar habitats in a similar climate in southern Africa as does *Austrocedrus* in South America. Some of these also have wide distributions, but restricted ranges are more common, and those restricted species are often most threatened. Some species in these genera occur in the interior of continents on mountains and plateaus with semi-arid climates, where they are often the only trees. As with other trees in such climatically difficult conditions, regeneration in relation to life span is often precariously balanced and easily disturbed e.g. by grazing pressures from livestock.

Conifers also form the dominant elements of almost all of the earth's temperate rainforests. These occur mostly around the Pacific Rim, on isolated high mountains within tropical latitudes, and on islands near the southern continents. All conifer families and many genera are represented in these biologically rich forests. It is especially in these temperate rainforests that most of the surviving evolutionary ancient and relictual genera are found, and their number of species is typically small.

In tropical lowland to submontane forests, conifers are generally rare and scattered, occupying restricted habitats

How slow some conifers grow: a slab of the Great Basin Bristlecone pine (*Pinus longaeva*) has several thousand annual rings.

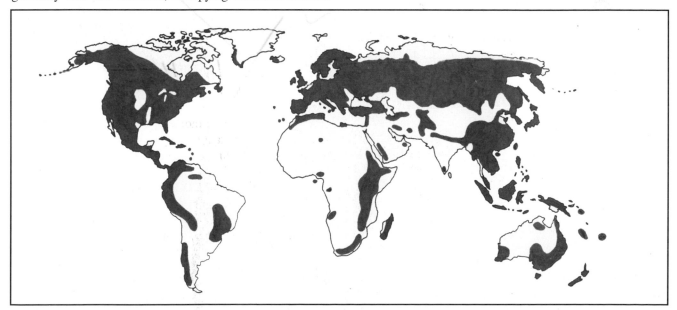

Figure 1.1. Worldwide distribution of conifers.

3

Table 1.1. Distribution of conifer genera by major regions[1].

	BOR	WNA	CAL	MEX	FLO	SAM	MED	AFR	SIN	JAP	MAL	AUS	PAC
Araucariaceae													
Agathis	.	.	.	.	.	.	.	.	.	.	x	x	x
Araucaria	.	.	.	.	.	x	.	.	.	.	x	x	x
Wollemia	.	.	.	.	.	.	.	.	.	.	.	m	.
Cephalotaxaceae													
Cephalotaxus	.	.	.	.	.	.	.	.	x	x	.	.	.
Cupressaceae[2]													
Actinostrobus	.	.	.	.	.	.	.	.	.	.	.	s	.
Austrocedrus	.	.	.	.	.	m	.	.	.	.	.	.	.
Callitris	.	.	.	.	.	.	.	.	.	.	.	x	x
Calocedrus	.	.	s	.	.	.	.	.	s	.	.	.	.
Chamaecyparis	.	x	.	.	x	.	.	.	x	x	.	.	.
Cupressus	.	.	x	x	.	.	x	.	x	.	.	.	.
Diselma	.	.	.	.	.	.	.	.	.	.	.	m	.
Fitzroya	.	.	.	.	.	m	.	.	.	.	.	.	.
Fokienia	.	.	.	.	.	.	.	.	m	.	.	.	.
Juniperus	x	x	x	x	x	.	x	x	x	x	.	.	.
Libocedrus	.	.	.	.	.	.	.	.	.	.	.	.	s
Microbiota	.	.	.	.	.	.	.	.	.	m	.	.	.
Neocallitropsis	.	.	.	.	.	.	.	.	.	.	.	.	m
Papuacedrus	.	.	.	.	.	.	.	.	.	.	m	.	.
Pilgerodendron	.	.	.	.	.	m	.	.	.	.	.	.	.
Platycladus	.	.	.	.	.	.	.	.	m	.	.	.	.
Tetraclinis	.	.	.	.	.	.	m	.	.	.	.	.	.
Thuja	s	s	.	.	.	.	.	.	s	s	.	.	.
Thujopsis	.	.	.	.	.	.	.	.	.	m	.	.	.
Widdringtonia	.	.	.	.	.	.	.	s	.	.	.	.	.
Phyllocladaceae													
Phyllocladus	.	.	.	.	.	.	.	.	.	.	s	s	s
Pinaceae													
Abies	x	x	x	x	.	.	x	.	x	x	.	.	.
Cathaya	.	.	.	.	.	.	.	.	m	.	.	.	.
Cedrus	.	.	.	.	.	.	s	.	s	.	.	.	.
Keteleeria	.	.	.	.	.	.	.	.	s	.	.	.	.
Larix	x	x	.	.	.	.	.	.	x	x	.	.	.
Nothotsuga	.	.	.	.	.	.	.	.	m	.	.	.	.
Picea	x	x	.	x	.	.	x	.	x	x	.	.	.
Pinus	x	x	x	x	x	.	x	.	x	x	.	.	.
Pseudolarix	.	.	.	.	.	.	.	.	m	.	.	.	.
Pseudotsuga	.	s	s	s	.	.	.	.	s	s	.	.	.
Tsuga	x	x	.	.	.	.	.	.	x	x	.	.	.
Podocarpaceae													
Acmopyle	.	.	.	.	.	.	.	.	.	.	.	.	s
Afrocarpus	.	.	.	.	.	.	.	s	.	.	.	.	.
Dacrycarpus	.	.	.	.	.	.	.	.	x	.	x	.	x
Dacrydium	.	.	.	.	.	.	.	.	.	.	x	.	x
Falcatifolium	.	.	.	.	.	.	.	.	.	.	s	.	s
Halocarpus	.	.	.	.	.	.	.	.	.	.	.	s	.
Lagarostrobus	.	.	.	.	.	.	.	.	.	.	.	s	.
Lepidothamnus	.	.	.	.	.	.	.	.	.	.	.	m	.
Manoao	.	.	.	.	.	.	.	.	.	.	.	.	m
Microcachrys	.	.	.	.	.	.	.	.	.	.	.	m	.
Microstrobos	.	.	.	.	.	.	.	.	.	.	.	s	.

	BOR	WNA	CAL	MEX	FLO	SAM	MED	AFR	SIN	JAP	MAL	AUS	PAC
Nageia	.	.	.	.	.	.	.	.	s	s	s	.	.
Parasitaxus	.	.	.	.	.	.	.	.	.	.	.	.	m
Podocarpus	.	.	.	x	.	x	.	x	x	.	x	x	x
Prumnopitys	.	.	s	.	.	s	.	.	.	.	.	s	.
Retrophyllum	.	.	.	.	.	s	.	.	.	.	.	.	s
Saxegothaea	.	.	.	.	.	m	.	.	.	.	.	.	.
Sundacarpus	.	.	.	.	.	s	.	.	.	.	s	.	s
Sciadopityaceae													
Sciadopitys	.	.	.	.	.	.	.	.	.	m	.	.	.
Taxaceae													
Amentotaxus	.	.	.	.	.	.	.	.	x	.	.	.	.
Austrotaxus	.	.	.	.	.	.	.	.	.	.	.	.	m
Pseudotaxus	.	.	.	.	.	.	.	.	m	.	.	.	.
Taxus	x	x	.	x	x	.	x	.	x	x	x	.	.
Torreya	.	.	x	.	x	.	.	.	x	.	.	.	.
Taxodiaceae[2]													
Athrotaxis	.	.	.	.	.	.	.	.	.	.	.	s	.
Cryptomeria	.	.	.	.	.	.	.	.	.	m	.	.	.
Cunninghamia	.	.	.	.	.	.	.	.	s	.	.	.	.
Glyptostrobus	.	.	.	.	.	.	.	.	m	.	.	.	.
Metasequoia	.	.	.	.	.	.	.	.	m	.	.	.	.
Sequoia	.	.	m	.	.	.	.	.	.	.	.	.	.
Sequoiadendron	.	.	m	.	.	.	.	.	.	.	.	.	.
Taiwania	.	.	.	.	.	.	.	.	m	.	.	.	.
Taxodium	.	.	.	s	s	.	.	.	.	.	.	.	.
TOTAL	**8**	**10**	**9**	**10**	**6**	**9**	**8**	**4**	**30**	**16**	**11**	**15**	**16**
total small genera	1	2	2	3	1	3	1	2	7	3	4	7	6
total monotypics	0	0	2	0	0	4	1	0	9	4	1	4	3

(x = genera > 5 recognised species; s = 2-5 recognised species; m = single species (monotypic))

[1] BOR= Boreal zone in North America and Eurasia, incl. northern Rocky Mountains, Alps and mountains of Central Asia.
WNA= Western North America (NW Pacific region and Rocky Mountains in USA).
CAL= California, including parts of Oregon, Nevada and Arizona.
MEX= Mexico and Central America.
FLO= SE USA and Caribbean Islands.
SAM= South America.
MED= Mediterranean region, Turkey and Middle Eastern countries.
AFR= Sub-Saharan Africa, including Madagascar.
SIN= China, Himalayas, Taiwan, mainland SE Asia excl. Malay Peninsula.
JAP= Japan, Korea and Maritime Provinces of Russia.
MAL= 'Malesia' as defined in Flora Malesiana. AUS=Australia.
PAC= SW Pacific islands, including New Caledonia, Fiji and New Zealand.

[2] The families Cupressaceae and Taxodiaceae are kept separate for the purpose of this Action Plan for reasons of convenience. Increasingly, taxonomic and phylogenetic evidence suggest that these families should be merged under the older name Cupressaceae. Generic delimitations in some families, notably Podocarpaceae, are still in a state of flux while further research is ongoing. Likewise, we have adhered to established, but modern views on classification supported by published monographic research.

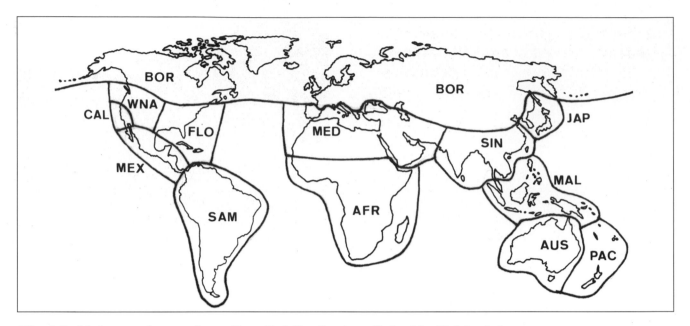

Fig 1.2. Major regions of conifer distribution as listed in Table 1.1.

Regional diversity

Although not strictly comparable for reasons of differences in size, topographical variation, and climate, the 13 regions vary widely in generic diversity of conifers (Figure 1.2). China, with the Himalayas and parts of Indochina, clearly stands out with 30 genera. This region (SIN) has seven small (2-5 species) and nine monotypic genera, representing 53% of all genera in the area. Hence, it is a region that has a higher than average conifer diversity value. Two other regions with high diversity at the genus level are Japan, with Korea and the Maritime Provinces of Russia (JAP, 17 genera, three small and four monotypic = 41%) and the islands of New Caledonia, Fiji, and New Zealand in the Pacific Southwest (PAC, 15 genera, six small and three monotypic = 65%). As is often noted in biodiversity assessments, there is a major distinction between oceanic islands and those nearer to a continent. This difference is largely a reflection of the long-term geological isolation of the islands concerned, for which the surviving conifer diversity acts as a valuable biotic archive. However, there are almost no conifers on mid-oceanic islands, and presumably there never have been many. Most of the other regions average nine genera, with the exception of sub-Saharan Africa, which has only four conifer genera. The paucity of conifers in this vast and diverse continent is striking; it is matched in other tree groups, such as palms (Johnson 1996) and probably has its causes mainly in climatic fluctuations which occurred long before the present man-made decline of biodiversity began. Unlike the palms, conifers display no particular diversity on the large and phytogeographically distinct island of Madagascar.

Many of the genera presented in Table 1.1 are endemic to the regions as defined, and no genera have an estimated extent of occurrence greater than 20% of the territory in each region (extent of occurrence is defined by IUCN (1994) as "the area contained within the shortest continuous imaginary boundary which can be drawn to encompass all the known, inferred, or projected sites of present occurrence of a taxon, excluding cases of vagrancy"). These endemic genera are listed in Table 1.2.

As Fig. 1.3 shows, the diversity of endemic conifer genera is very unevenly distributed among regions. The three regions SIN, AUS and PAC collectively contain 25 of the 39 endemic genera (=64%). At the other extreme, the large continent of Africa contains only two endemic genera (=5%) and the vast boreal region has none. Fossil evidence (Beck 1988) strongly indicates a much wider distribution from the Mesozoic to the Late Tertiary of many of these now endemic genera, both in the Northern and the Southern Hemisphere. It is therefore of primary importance to conserve species belonging to these endemic genera.

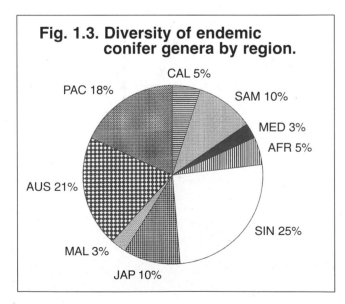

Fig. 1.3. Diversity of endemic conifer genera by region.

CAL 5%
SAM 10%
MED 3%
AFR 5%
SIN 25%
JAP 10%
MAL 3%
AUS 21%
PAC 18%

Table 1.2. Regional distribution of endemic genera of conifers, with an estimate of the extent of occurrence for each as a percentage of its region.

Genus	Family	Region[1]	Estimated extent of occurrence
Sequoia	Taxodiaceae	CAL	<15%
Sequoiadendron	Taxodiaceae	CAL	<10%
Austrocedrus	Cupressaceae	SAM	<5%
Fitzroya	Cupressaceae	SAM	<5%
Pilgerodendron	Cupressaceae	SAM	<10%
Saxegothaea	Podocarpaceae	SAM	<5%
Tetraclinis	Cupressaceae	MED	<10%
Widdringtonia	Cupressaceae	AFR	<5%
Afrocarpus	Podocarpaceae	AFR	c. 10%
Fokienia	Cupressaceae	SIN	<10%
Platycladus	Cupressaceae	SIN	c. 10%
Cathaya	Pinaceae	SIN	<5%
Nothotsuga	Pinaceae	SIN	<5%
Pseudolarix	Pinaceae	SIN	<5%
Pseudotaxus	Taxaceae	SIN	<10%
Taiwania	Taxodiaceae	SIN	<5%
Cunninghamia	Taxodiaceae	SIN	c. 20%
Glyptostrobus	Taxodiaceae	SIN	<5%
Metasequoia	Taxodiaceae	SIN	<5%
Microbiota	Cupressaceae	JAP	<5%
Thujopsis	Cupressaceae	JAP	c. 10%
Sciadopitys	Sciadopityaceae	JAP	<10%
Cryptomeria	Taxodiaceae	JAP	c. 20%
Papuacedrus	Cupressaceae	MAL	<10%
Wollemia	Araucariaceae	AUS	<5%
Actinostrobus	Cupressaceae	AUS	<10%
Diselma	Cupressaceae	AUS	<5%
Halocarpus	Podocarpaceae	AUS	<5%
Lagarostrobus	Podocarpaceae	AUS	<5%
Lepidothamnus	Podocarpaceae	AUS	<5%
Microcachrys	Podocarpaceae	AUS	<5%
Microstrobos	Podocarpaceae	AUS	<5%
Athrotaxis	Taxodiaceae	AUS	<5%
Libocedrus	Cupressaceae	PAC	c. 20
Neocallitropsis	Cupressaceae	PAC	<5%
Acmopyle	Podocarpaceae	PAC	<5%
Manoao	Podocarpaceae	PAC	<5%
Parasitaxus	Podocarpaceae	PAC	<10%
Austrotaxus	Taxaceae	PAC	<5%

[1] As defined in Table 1.1

J. Mitchell/WWF

Clearcutting of conifer forest in Ontario, Canada.

Major threats to conifer species survival

Because conifers are mostly constituents or dominants of forests, factors that negatively influence forests also threaten conifer populations and ultimately species. The pressures that a rapidly growing human population and an expanding economy are bringing to bear on the remaining natural forests are alarming. A history of deforestation which took millennia in the old centres of civilisation such as the Middle East, Europe, and Eastern China now is being repeated globally at an accelerating rate. This development is the fundamental threat to the survival of species that depend on natural forests. However, the environmental problems, when looked at more closely, are complex and often appear to be interrelated. Below, under seven separate headings, we attempt to identify the major threats in some detail.

1. **Direct exploitation through logging operations aimed at the removal of whole trees from natural, non-managed or minimally-managed wild forest stands.**

Considered as a natural resource of timber available for 'harvest,' and in principle renewable, the world's remaining natural forests are under ever-increasing exploitation pressure. The plight of the tropical rainforests, widely publicised, is well known; however, many conifer-dominated forests,

J. Thorsell/WWF

Loaded logging trucks hauling conifers in British Colombia, Canada.

especially those known as the temperate rainforests, are equally threatened. These forests occur along the coasts of oceans, on islands especially around the Pacific Rim outside the tropical latitudes, and in parts of the tropics on high mountains. They usually contain a mixture of conifer and broad-leaved species, in which several of the conifers attain great size and age. Natural regeneration of these is dependent on episodic disturbances over very long intervals. Typically, regeneration occurs from seed dispersed by large individual trees that survived the disturbance (Enright and Hill 1995). The high timber volume and value of these often centuries-old trees has been the cause of and continues to result in their selective removal. Neither selective timber extraction, removing these 'parent' trees, nor forest management with shorter rotations are sustainable in the case of these slower-growing conifer species. Where such species occur as scattered large individuals, these practises have resulted in substantial population reductions and have made several species either rare or genetically depleted or both. The likely result of such management over time is the total removal of these species from the forest.

A variant of this is the wholesale clearance of natural forest for industrial manufacture of timber derived products ('wood chipping'). In this type of exploitation, usually carried out in less 'heavy' timber stands, no species' selection is made. Where rare species occur in such forests they are removed with the rest. Substantial areas are exploited in this way: where reforestation is attempted (by no means everywhere), indigenous species are seldom used and the rare ones are always excluded. In regions like California, Tasmania, and southern Chile, to mention but three examples, large scale exploitation has or will soon lead to the confinement of several conifer species to a limited number of protected areas.

2. Uncontrolled forest fires, combined with grazing of seedlings and saplings by domestic or introduced wild animals.

Fires are an integral part of many ecosystems in which conifers occur. There is, however, usually a delicate balance between regeneration time, relatively undisturbed succession, growth, and recurrence of the disturbance. An increase in this frequency, caused by human action, will lead to forest degradation and in extreme cases eventually to the disappearance of the forest. Such has been the history of many of Europe's and China's forests in past millennia. Increasing population pressures in rural areas around the world, especially in tropical and subtropical latitudes, are causing this process to repeat itself on a geographically larger and often temporally shorter scale. While conifer species can show varied adaptability to this process, it is certain that several are threatened by fire, often in addition to logging. For example, regeneration of *Fitzroya cupressoides* in Chile is greatly impaired by increased frequency of forest fires. In other regions, such as southern Africa, initial removal of forest trees has led to vegetation types that burn much more fre-

Forest fire destroying Scots pine (*Pinus sylvestris*) in Ukraine.

quently (Pauw and Linder, 1997). Here fire presents a real threat for *Widdringtonia cedarbergensis*, an Endangered species. Additionally, and especially on islands, the grazing of introduced livestock allows regeneration of (rare) conifers only in inaccessible places, such as *Juniperus cedrus* on the Canary Islands. Frequent burning is often carried out purposefully to get rid of shrubby understorey vegetation in (degraded) conifer woodland and to stimulate grasses for livestock grazing. A variant of this, especially of concern in the USA, is the alteration of the fire-adapted conifer forest ecosystem either by livestock grazing, fire prevention (causing fuel build-up), or a combination of these. As a result of this fuel build-up, fires, which under natural conditions prepared a seedbed for the largest, fire-resistant conifers, now threaten to turn into destructive conflagrations which kill all the trees along with the underbrush over vast areas.

3. Conversion of forested ecosystems to pasture, arable land, and human habitation.

Often a 'natural' development following a fire disturbance, such land conversion, though unavoidable in an agriculturally based society, has increased exponentially with the sharp rise in world population during the 20th century. China is estimated to have lost 24% of its forested area between 1950-1980, mostly due to conversion for agriculture. In New Zealand, natural forest once covered 70% of the land area,

8

Mixed conifer-broadleaved forest in the Caucasus, Georgia, as it should be . . .

but this has been reduced to 22% in a period of 150 years. In both countries, many rare conifer species (such as *Metasequoia glyptostroboides* in China) have been negatively affected by this threat and sometimes brought to the brink of extinction.

4. Exploitation of non-timber resources involving conifers.

Many conifers yield non-timber products such as resin and its derivatives, edible seeds, and medicines, such as taxol in yews. Discovery of as yet unknown chemicals with medicinal properties is a prospect especially likely in the lesser known species of the family Podocarpaceae, many of which occur in the tropics. Firewood use is often substantial, especially in rural areas of poorer countries where many forests are being exploited for this purpose as well as for timber. With a market largely in the wealthier countries, many conifers are considered ornamentals, and their seed, as well as sometimes live plants, are collected for sale abroad.

In principle, most of these uses should be sustainable. Yet there are several instances where this is not the case. One factor in this unsustainability may be the rarity of a species combined with slow or poor regeneration. In such cases, harvest levels must remain very low and careful atten-

tion must be paid to population regeneration. Another contributing factor to unsustainable harvest can be the increase in the level of exploitation through growing population pressure, which, for example, may cause an increase in firewood collection. This increase in exploitation can also be caused by increased individual demand both for personal use and for sale. A sudden increase in demand resulting in unsustainable use threatened to occur with *Taxus brevifolia*, which recently was discovered to contain the effective anti-cancer chemical taxol. Large quantities of bark were required to extract this chemical. To supply the burgeoning market for this new drug, over vast tracts of its range in the Pacific Northwest of North America, this boom has led to stripping of the larger trees and their consequent demise. Previously, this tree was estimated to be of little value to foresters, and either left alone, or considered 'weedy' in forests managed for timber. In the quest for anti-cancer drugs, similar exploitation was reported in several other parts of the world where species of *Taxus* occur. Other taxa, such as *Cephalotaxus,* are now found to yield similar medicinally-promising compounds, and natural populations are suddenly being exploited, often unsustainably. The path leading from extraction to purification to trial to medicinal use is usually long and costly. There is therefore no incentive to add to the costs by investment in propagation and large scale cultivation, unless and until a substantial profit is made from the end product, by which time it may be too late for the wild populations.

5. Destruction or disturbance of forests by large scale strip-mining or hydroelectric projects, reclamation of swamps, or other development.

Obviously when such projects are planned and carried out on the sites of (rare) conifer species they will usually lead to direct destruction or severe damage. A case in point is a hydroelectric project that flooded a forested valley in Tasmania with important populations of the rare and slow growing podocarp *Lagarostrobos franklinii*. Mining operations on the island of New Caledonia are threatening various rare conifers there. Disturbance of water tables and pollution

. . . and what it threatens to become outside national parks, Caucasus, Georgia.

usually extend far beyond the actual locations of these operations. Drought stress can make populations of conifers that are not directly affected by the development susceptible to pathogens. Sometimes the general disturbance and accessibility through roads tips the balance, as is the case with the remaining 'untouched' stands of *Chamaecyparis lawsoniana* in northern California and Oregon, which are now so infested with a pathogenic fungus transported along these roads that their survival is threatened. Another case, involving drought stress and pathogens, is the near demise of *Juniperus bermudiana* (Challinor & Wingate, 1971), while similar reports are now being made for populations of *Pinus halepensis* and *P. pinea* in the Mediterranean. Often cause and effect are complex and not easy to unravel, as with the 'blight' that nearly wiped out *Torreya taxifolia* along the Florida/Georgia border in the south-eastern United States.

6. Risks of extinction by natural causes increased by human-induced reduction in the size of populations or restriction of natural range.

In many forests and woodlands (co-)dominated by conifer species, natural 'episodal' disturbances leading to destruction of the vegetation occur. Indeed, many species have become dependent on such large-scale occasional disturbances to clear away competitive growth in order to establish a new generation from seed. In some cases, such as with fire-adapted species of pines (*Pinus*), the trees from which the seeds are dispersed themselves are destroyed in the catastrophe. However, in many other instances reseeding occurs from mature trees left untouched in or adjacent to the area of destruction. Where species are confined to small reserves, the lack of adequate seed sources in buffer zones can jeopardise the chances of their survival in the event of a large-scale disturbance in the reserve. Such is now the situation in large parts of the range of *Araucaria araucana* in Chile, where the major stands are confined to the slopes of active or semi-dor-

mant volcanoes, due to encroachment of agriculture and forestry. In addition, some species have obviously declined due to climatic change. A notable example is *Cupressus dupreziana* in the Sahara, restricted to about 230 living trees and at present without natural regeneration. Other cases are *Pinus balfouriana* and *P. longaeva* in California and Nevada. Climatic change due to 'greenhouse gas' (mainly CO_2) accumulation has unpredictable effects; it could hasten 'natural' extinction for these species, especially if it causes greater aridity in these regions.

7. Genetic depletion through selective removal of individual trees and genetic drift.

Selective cutting of conifer trees over large areas and/or long periods of time tends to remove certain genotypes from the population. In slow-growing species, where old growth stands are exploited, these are the large trees, often many centuries old, which proved to be resistant to adverse environmental effects such as pests, pathogens, and storms. Genetic drift especially occurs when populations fall below a critical size or when individuals become very scattered. Although little is known about the effects of genetic depletion to species survival of conifers or, for that matter, even to what extent such depletion may have occurred in individual cases, it should certainly be a matter of concern. Genetic variation in the face of climatic change could be a necessary safeguard ensuring species survival in the future.

There is little doubt that several of the above-mentioned threats often operate synergistically, causing severe rates of decline in extent of occurrence and/or area of occupancy, populations, and fitness or health of remaining individuals. Consequently, in our attempt to apply the criteria for threat, as defined by IUCN (1994), to what is known about geographical range, population sizes, trends in these, and pressures on them, a very substantial proportion of the world's conifer taxa were found to be under some category of threat.

A dead forest of Alerce (*Fitzroya cupressoides*) in the National Parc Alerce Costero, Chile.

M. Gardner

10

Global Red List of Conifers

The Red List of Conifers presented in this Action Plan is a second edition. The first edition, published in 1993 (Farjon *et al.* 1993), appeared as a preliminary world list of threatened conifer taxa in the journal *Biodiversity and Conservation*. This edition was preliminary in several ways. First, its assessment was based on interpretation of the "old" categories of threat, which had been in use by IUCN and conservationists for many years but with little precedent regarding their application to trees. Second, for numerous taxa nothing was known about precise distribution and rates of decline. This edition was also published with the intention that comments obtained from anyone well-informed about a species would be used to update it. The present list has been revised using much new information, including reports sent in by regional members, e.g. from Chile, China, Himalayas, Japan, New Caledonia, and Taiwan. The first edition aroused much interest if judged on the basis of requests for reprints, but very little response when it came to the comments that had been solicited. The authors would like to stress the point that such input is important. Far from being the last word, lists like this should be constantly updated and revised with better information, if only because the conservation status, even if correctly assessed, is likely to change with time. The most important cause of differences between the previous and the present list has undoubt-edly been the application of the new IUCN Red List Categories and criteria (IUCN 1994). In addition, while assessing each taxon, we have used the forms for data collecting on trees developed by the WCMC/SSC Conservation and Sustainable Use of Trees Project. This means that, besides the IUCN criteria, a large amount of other relevant information was gathered and has been considered. This information has been filed on a database at WCMC, while the Conifer Specialist Group (CSG) has filed the forms for future updating. This means that any suggestions to change the status of a listed taxon shall only be considered if accompanied by data (minimally IUCN criteria) which will be compared with the existing information for that taxon. An IUCN Red List Programme has been established with procedures for amending Red List data.

Below, the full list is presented, with distribution and the IUCN Red List Categories and criteria for each taxon. For full explanation of the category and criteria codes see the summary of IUCN Red List Categories (IUCN 1994) in Appendix 2. Taxa which may warrant listing as Threatened (CR, EN, VU) or Lower Risk, but for which adequate information was unavailable, are listed as DD (Data Deficient). All taxa on the list are thought to be of conservation concern. Conifers that we think are under no threat at all are not listed: **this list is a Red List of Conifers, not a checklist of conifers.**

Agathis ovata, New Caledonia.

Araucaria araucana, Southern Chile.

Taxon	Distribution	Status	Criteria
ARAUCARIACEAE			
Agathis atropurpurea B. Hyland	Queensland	LRnt	
Agathis australis (D. Don) Loudon	New Zealand (North Island, North Auckland Peninsula)	LRcd	
Agathis corbassonii de Laub.	New Caledonia	VU	B1+2c
Agathis dammara (Lamb.) Rich. & A. Rich.	W Malesia	VU	A1cd
Agathis endertii Meijer Drees	Borneo (central) (VU; A1c); Malaysia, Sabah, Sarawak	LRnt	
Agathis flavescens Ridl.	Malaysia (Gunong Tahan)	VU	D2
Agathis kinabaluensis de Laub.	Malaysia, Sabah (Mt. Kinabalu)	VU	D2
Agathis lanceolata (Lindl. ex Sebert & Pancher) Warb.	New Caledonia	LRcd	
Agathis lenticula de Laub.	Malaysia, Sabah (Mt. Kinabalu) (VU) (Crocker Range) (E?)	VU	D2
Agathis macrophylla (Lindl.) Mast.	Fiji Is.; Santa Cruz Island; Vanuatu	LRnt	
Agathis microstachya J. F. Bailey & C. T. White	Northern Queensland	LRcd	
Agathis montana de Laub.	New Caledonia (Mt. Panié)	LRcd	
Agathis moorei (Lindl.) Mast.	New Caledonia	VU	B1+2c
Agathis orbicula de Laub.	Malaysia, Sabah, Sarawak	VU	B1+2c
Agathis ovata (C. Moore ex Veillard) Warb.	S New Caledonia	LRcd	
Agathis philippinensis Warb.	Phillipines; Moluccas, Sulawesi	VU	A1cd
Agathis silbae de Laub.	Vanuatu (Santo Peak)	VU	D2
Agathis spathulata de Laub.	P.N.G. (eastern highlands)	LRnt	
Araucaria angustifolia (Bertol.) Kuntze	Argentina, S Brazil, Paraguay	VU	A1, B1+2c
Araucaria araucana (Molina) K. Koch	Argentina; S Chile	VU	B1+2c
Araucaria bernieri J. Buchholz	New Caledonia	LRcd	
Araucaria biramulata J. Buchholz	New Caledonia	LRcd	
Araucaria heterophylla (Salisb.) Franco	Norfolk Island	VU	B1+2c
Araucaria humboldtensis J. Buchholz	New Caledonia	LRcd	
Araucaria hunsteinii K. Schum.	P.N.G.	LRnt	
Araucaria laubenfelsii Corbasson	New Caledonia	LRcd	
Araucaria luxurians (Brongn. & Gris) de Laub.	New Caledonia	EN	B1+2c
Araucaria muelleri (Carrière) Brongn. & Gris	New Caledonia	LRcd	
Araucaria nemorosa de Laub.	New Caledonia (Port Boisé)	CR	B1+2c
Araucaria rulei F. Muell.	New Caledonia	EN	C1
Araucaria schmidii de Laub.	New Caledonia (Mt. Panié)	VU	D2
Araucaria scopulorum de Laub.	New Caledonia (local on coast)	EN	B1+2c
Araucaria subulata Vieill.	New Caledonia	LRcd	
Wollemia nobilis W. G. Jones, K. D. Hill & J. M. Allen	Australia, N.S.W. (Wollemi National Park)	CR	D

Wollemia nobilis, New South Wales, Australia.

A. Farjon

Callitris monticola, New South Wales, Australia.

A. Farjon

CEPHALOTAXACEAE

Cephalotaxus fortunei Hook. f. var. *fortunei*	China, Sichuan, Yunnan, eastward to Zhejiang; N Myanmar	LRnt	
Cephalotaxus griffithii Hook. f.	India, Assam (Mishmi Hills, Manipur, Naga Hills)	LRnt	
Cephalotaxus hainanensis H. L. Li	China, Guangdong (Hainan Island)	EN	A2d
Cephalotaxus lanceolata K. M. Feng	China, Yunnan (Gongshan)	VU	D2
Cephalotaxus mannii Hook. f.	China, Guangdong (Xingyi), Guangxi, Yunnan, SE Xizang Zizhiqu (CR); Vietnam (VU); N Myanmar (Meghalaya) (EN); E India (Naga Hills)	VU	A1d
Cephalotaxus oliveri Mast.	China, Guangdong, Guangxi, Hubei, Hunan, Jiangxi, Sichuan, Yunnan	VU	A1d
Cephalotaxus wilsoniana Hayata	Taiwan	EN	C2a

CUPRESSACEAE

Actinostrobus acuminatus Parl.	SW Australia	LRnt	
Actinostrobus pyramidalis Miq.	SW Australia	LRnt	
Austrocedrus chilensis (D. Don) Pic. Serm. & Bizzarri	S Chile (Antuco, Valdivia); SW Argentina (Questrihue)	VU	A1c
Callitris baileyi C. T. White	SE Queensland, NE N.S.W.	VU	A1c
Callitris drummondii (Parl.) F. Muell.	SW Australia	VU	A1c
Callitris monticola J. Garden	SE Queensland, NE N.S.W.	VU	A1c
Callitris neocaledonica Dummer	New Caledonia	LRcd	
Callitris oblonga Rich. & A. Rich.	NE Tasmania, N.S.W.	VU	A1c
Callitris roei (Endl.) F. Muell.	SW Australia	VU	A1c
Callitris sulcata (Parl.) Schltr.	New Caledonia	EN	B1+2c
Calocedrus formosana (Florin) Florin	N Taiwan	EN	B1+2b
Calocedrus macrolepis Kurz	NE Myanmar; Thailand; China, SE Yunnan, Guizhou, Guangxi, Guangdong (Hainan Island); Vietnam	VU	B1+2b
Chamaecyparis formosensis Matsum.	Taiwan (Mt. Morrison)	EN	A1c
Chamaecyparis lawsoniana (A. Murray bis) Parl.	U.S.A., SW Oregon, NW California (mainly coastal)	VU	A1de+2e
Chamaecyparis obtusa (Siebold & Zucc.) Endl. var. *formosana* (Hayata) Hayata	Taiwan	VU	A1d
Chamaecyparis obtusa Siebold & Zucc. var. *obtusa*	Japan, S Honshu, Shikoku, Kyushu	LRnt	
Chamaecyparis thyoides (L.) Britton, Sterns & Poggenb. var. *henryae* (H. L. Li) Little	U.S.A., Gulf Coast from Florida to Mississippi	LRnt	

Chamaecyparis thyoides var. *henryae*, Florida, USA.

Cupressus dupreziana, Sahara, Algeria.

Species	Distribution	Status	Criteria
Cupressus arizonica Greene var. *montana* (Wiggins) Little	Mexico, Baja California Norte	VU	D2
Cupressus arizonica var. *nevadensis* (Abrams) Little	California (Piute Mts. and vicinity)	VU	D2
Cupressus arizonica var. *stephensonii* (C. B. Wolf) Little	California (Cuyamaca Mts.)	VU	D2
Cupressus atlantica Gaussen (a ssp. of *C. dupreziana*?)	S Morocco (Oued n'fiss Valley)	EN	A1b,B1+2b
Cupressus bakeri Jeps.	N California, S Oregon	VU	B1+2b-d
Cupressus cashmeriana Royle ex Carrière (syn.: *C. corneyana* auct., non Carrière)	Buthan; India?, Arunachal Pradesh?	VU	B1+2c
Cupressus chengiana S. Y. Hu var. *chengiana*	China, NW Sichuan, S Gansu (Min River drainage)	VU	A1c
Cupressus chengiana var. *jiangeensis* (N. Chao) C. T. Kuan	China, Sichuan	CR	D
Cupressus duclouxiana Hickel	China, Yunnan (EW?), SW Sichuan, SE Xizang Zizhiqu	DD	
Cupressus dupreziana A. Camus	SE Algeria (Sahara, Tassili Plateau, Tamrit)	CR	A2c,C1
Cupressus gigantea W. C. Cheng & L. K. Fu	China, S Xizang Zishiqu (Tsangpo River valley)	VU	A1d
Cupressus goveniana Gordon var. *goveniana*	California, Monterey Co. (near coast)	VU	D2
Cupressus goveniana var. *abramsiana* (C.B. Wolf) Little	California (Santa Cruz Mts.)	EN	C2a
Cupressus guadelupensis S. Watson var. *guadelupensis*	Mexico, Baja California Norte (Guadelupe Island)	CR	B1+2c
Cupressus guadelupensis var. *forbesii* (Jeps.) Little	SW California; Mexico, Baja California Norte (near U.S. border)	VU	D2
Cupressus lusitanica Mill. var. *benthamii* (Endl.) Carrière	Mexico, Puebla, Hidalgo, Veracruz	LRnt	
Cupressus macrocarpa Hartw. ex Gordon	California (near Monterey)	VU	D2
Cupressus sempervirens L.	Mediterranean (probably not wild); S Turkey (LRnt); W Iran (VU)	LRnt	
Cupressus torulosa D. Don	W Himalaya, SW Xizang Zizhiqu (Himalaya)	LRnt	
Fitzroya cupressoides (Molina) I. M. Johnst.	S Chile (Region X); Argentina, W Patagonia	EN	A1cd+2cd
Fokienia hodginsii (Dunn) A. Henry & H. H. Thomas	S China, from Zhejiang to SE Yunnan (along Vietnamese border); Vietnam; N Laos	LRnt	
Juniperus barbadensis L.	BWI, St. Lucia (Petit Piton); Bahamas (VU); Cuba	CR	D
Juniperus barbadensis var. *lucayana* (Britton) R. P. Adams	(Sierra de Nipe, Isla de Pinos) (CR); Haiti (EW); Jamaica (VU)	VU	B1 +2c
Juniperus bermudiana L.	Bermudas	CR	B1+2c
Juniperus blancoi Martínez	Mexico, NE Sonora, Durango (El Salto), México (Carmona)	VU	D2
Juniperus brevifolia (Seub.) Antoine	Azores	EN	B1+2c
Juniperus cedrus Webb & Berthel.	Canary Is., Tenerife, Palma; Madeira	EN	B1+2c, D
Juniperus comitana Martínez	Mexico, Chiapas (Comitán) (EN); N Guatemala	VU	B1+2c
Juniperus convallium Rehder & E. H. Wilson var. *convallium*	China, NW Sichuan, E Xizang Zizhiqu	LRnt	
Juniperus convallium var. *microsperma* (W. C. Cheng & L. K. Fu) Silba	China, SE Xizang Zizhiqu	DD	

Juniperus bermudiana, dead tree on Nonsuch Island, Bermuda.

Juniperus deppeana Steud. var. *patoniana* (Martínez) Zanoni	Mexico, Durango	VU	B1+2ce
Juniperus deppeana var. *robusta* Martínez	Mexico, Durango	VU	B1+2ce
Juniperus deppeana var. *zacatecensis* Martínez	Mexico, W Zacatecas, Durango	VU	B1ı2cc
Juniperus durangensis Martínez	Mexico, Sonora, Durango, Chihuahua, Jalisco, Zacatecas, Aguascalientes	VU	B1+2c
Juniperus gamboana Martínez	Mexico, Chiapas; Guatemala, Huehuetenango	VU	B1+2c
Juniperus gaussenii W. C. Cheng	China, Yunnan	LRnt	
Juniperus gracilior Pilg. var. *gracilior*	Dominican Rep. (near Constanza, Valle del Jaque)	EN	B1+2c
Juniperus gracilior Pilg. var. *ekmanii* (Florin) R. P. Adams	Haiti (Morne la Selle, Morne la Visite (EW?))	CR	D
Juniperus gracilior var. *urbaniana* (Pilg. & Ekman) R. P. Adams	Haiti (Pic la Selle)	EN	B1+2c
Juniperus jaliscana Martínez	Mexico, NW Jalisco, S Durango	EN	B1+2c
Juniperus komarovii Florin	China, N Sichuan	LRnt	
Juniperus martinezii Pérez de la Rosa	Mexico, Jalisco	LRnt	
Juniperus pingii W. C. Cheng ex Ferré	China, W Sichuan, NW Yunnan	LRnt	
Juniperus przewalskii Kom.	China, E Qinghai, S Gansu, N Sichuan	LRnt	
Juniperus recurva Buch-Ham. ex D. Don var. *coxii* (A. B. Jacks.) Melville	N Myanmar; China, NW Yunnan	VU	A1c
Juniperus saxicola Britton & P. Wilson	Cuba (Granma, Sierra Maestra, Pico Turquino)	VU	D2
Juniperus standleyi Steyerm.	Mexico-Guatemala (Volcan Tacana); Guatemala (highlands)	EN	B1+2b

Libocedrus austrocaledonica Brogn. et Gris	New Caledonia	LRcd	
Libocedrus chevalieri J. Buchholz	New Caledonia (Mt. Humboldt, Mt. Kouakoué)	EN	B1+2de
Libocedrus plumosa (D. Don) Sarg.	New Zealand	LRnt	
Libocedrus yateensis Guillaumin	New Caledonia (Yaté River, Ouinné River)	VU	B1+3d, C2a
Microbiota decussata Kom.	Russian Fed., Sikhote Alin Prov. (near Suchan River)	DD	
Neocallitropsis pancheri (Carrière) de Laub.	New Caledonia (SE part)	VU	A1c, B1+2b
Pilgerodendron uviferum (D. Don) Florin	S Chile (VU); Argentina (Andes to Tierra del Fuego)	VU	A2cd
Platycladus orientalis (L.) Franco	NE-Central & SW China, Hebei, Shanxi, Henan, S Shaanxi, S Gansu; Far East of Russian Fed. (VU)	LRnt	
Tetraclinis articulata (Vahl) Mast.	S Spain (EN; D); Malta (CR; D); N Morocco (VU); N. Algeria (LR)	LRnt	
Thuja koraiensis Nakai	North Korea, South Korea; NE China, Jilin (EN; B1,2c)	DD	
Thuja sutchuenensis Franch.	China, NE Sichuan (near Chengkou)	EW	
Widdringtonia cedarbergensis J.A. Marsh	South Africa, Western Cape Prov., Cedarberg Mts.	EN	A1cd
Widdringtonia schwarzii (Marloth) Mast.	South Africa, Cape Prov. (Willowmore District)	VU	A1cd,D2
Widdringtonia whytei Rendle	Malawi (Mt. Mulanje)	EN	A1a-d, B1+2a-e

PINACEAE

Abies beshanzuensis M. H. Wu	China, Zhejiang (Mt. Bai-shan-zu NE of Qingyuan)	CR	D
Abies bracteata (D. Don) A. Poit.	California (Santa Lucia Mts.)	LRcd	
Abies cephalonica Loudon	Greece, Cephalonia, Euboea, Pelopónnisos	LRnt	
Abies chengii Rushforth	China, NW Yunnan?	DD	
Abies chensiensis Tiegh. ssp. *chensiensis*	China, S Shaanxi, W Hubei, SE Gansu, Henan (Nexiang), W Sichuan?	VU	A2d
Abies chensiensis ssp. *yulongxueshanensis* Rushforth	China, Yunnan (Lijiang Shan)	VU	D2
Abies cilicica (Antoine & Kotschy) Carrière ssp. *isaurica* Coode & Cullen	Turkey (Isaurian Taurus)	LRnt	
Abies durangensis Martínez var. *coahuilensis* (I. M. Johnston) Martínez	Mexico, Coahuila	VU	D2

Neocallitropsis pancheri, juvenile foliage, New Caledonia.

C. N. Page

Abies squamata, in cultivation at Dawyck (Royal Botanic Garden, Edinburgh, Scotland).

C. N. Page

Taxon	Distribution	Status	Criteria
Abies fanjingshanensis W. L. Huang *et al.*	China, NE Guizhou (Fanjing Shan, near langkou)	EN	D
Abies forrestii var. *georgei* (Orr) Farjon	China, NW Yunnan, SW Sichuan, SE Xizang Zizhiqu	VU	A1cd+2cd
Abies fraseri (Pursh) Poir.	U.S.A., SW Virginia, W North Carolina, E Tennessee	VU	D2
Abies guatemalensis Rehder var. *guatemalensis*	S Mexico; W Guatemala; Honduras; El Salvador	VU	A1d
Abies guatemalensis var. *jaliscana* Martínez	Mexico, Jalisco	VU	A1d
Abies guatemalensis var. *tacanensis* (Lundell) Martínez	Mexico, N Chiapas	VU	A1d
Abies hickelii Flous & Gaussen var. *hickelii*	Mexico, Guerrero, Oaxaca, Chiapas	VU	A1d
Abies hickelii var. *oaxacana* (Martínez) Farjon & Silba	Mexico, Oaxaca, Guerrero	VU	A1d
Abies kawakamii (Hayata) T. Itô	Taiwan (central mts.)	LRnt	
Abies koreana E. H. Wilson	South Korea	LRnt	
Abies nebrodensis (Lojac.) Mattei	Italy, Sicily (Monti Nebrodi, Monte Scalane, Polizzi Generosa)	CR	D
Abies nordmanniana (Steven) Spach ssp. *equi-trojani* (Asch. & Sint. ex Boiss.) Coode & Cullen	W Turkey (Kaz-Dagh, Ulu-Dagh)	LRnt	
Abies numidica de Lannoy ex Carrière	N Algeria (Mts. Babor, Tababor)	VU	D2
Abies pinsapo Boiss. var. *pinsapo*	S Spain, Prov. Malaga, Granada	VU	D2
Abies pinsapo var. *marocana* (Trab.) Ceballos & Bolaño	N Morocco (Rif Mts.)	LRnt	
Abies pinsapo var. *tazaotana* (S. Côzar ex Villar) Pourtet	N Morocco (Mt. Tazaot)	VU	D2
Abies recurvata Mast. var. *recurvata*	China, Sichuan (Songpan)	VU	D2
Abies sachalinensis (F. Schmidt) Mast. var. *gracilis* (Kom.) Farjon	Russian Fed., Kamchatka	VU	D2
Abies sibirica Ledeb. ssp. *semenovii* (B. Fedtsch.) Farjon	Kirgizstan (Talasskij Ala Tau)	VU	D2
Abies squamata Mast.	China, E Xizang Zizhiqu, W Sichuan, S Gansu, S Qinghai	VU	A1d
Abies veitchii Lindl. var. *sikokiana* (Nakai) Kusaka	Japan, Shikoku	LRnt	
Abies vejarii Martínez ssp. *mexicana* (Martínez) Farjon	Mexico, SE Coahuila, Nuevo León (Sierra Santa Catarina)	VU	D2
Abies yuanbaoshanensis Y. J. Lu & L. K. Fu	China, N Guangxi (Rongshui Xian, Yuanbao Shan)	CR	B1+2c
Abies ziyuanensis L. K. Fu & S. L. Mo	China, NE Guanxi (Ziyuan), SW Hunan (Xingni, Chenbu)	CR	B1+2c
Cathaya argyrophylla Chun & Kuang	China, NE Guangxi (Longsheng, Jingxiu), SE Sichuan (Nanchuan, Wulong), Hunan (Luohandong), Guizhou (Daozheng, Tongxing)	LRcd	
Cedrus brevifolia (Hook. f.) A. Henry	Cyprus (Mt. Triphylos)	VU	D2
Cedrus libani A. Rich. var. libani	Lebanon (EN; A1d); Syria (Lebanon Mts.); Turkey (Taurus and Anti-Taurus Ranges)	LRnt	
Keteleeria fortunei (A. Murray bis) Carrière	China, SE Yunnan, Guangxi, Guizhou, N Guangdong, S Hunan, SW Jiangxi, Fujian, Zhejiang, Hong Kong	LRnt	
Larix decidua var. *polonica* (Wóycicki) Ostenf. & Syrach	Poland (headwaters of Wista, Carpathians?)	VU	B1+2c
Larix griffithiana Hook. f. var. *speciosa* (W. C. Cheng & Y. W. Law) Silba	China, NW Yunnan, SE Xizang Zizhiqu (Himalaya)	LRnt	

Larix mastersiana Rehder & E. H. Wilson	China, W Sichuan, Guanxian	VU	A1c
Larix potaninii Batalin var. *himalaica* (W. C. Cheng & L. K. Fu) Farjon & Silba	China, S Xizang Zizhiqu (Himalaya); Nepal (Langtang Khola)	VU	D2
Nothotsuga longibracteata (W. C. Cheng) Hu ex C. N. Page	China, NE Guizhou, SW Hunan, N Guangdong, NE Guangxi, S Fujian, Jiangxi	EN	A1c
Picea alcoquiana (Veitch ex Lindl.) Carrière var. *acicularis* (Maxim. ex Beissn.) Fitschen	Japan, central Honshu, Yatsugadake Mts.	VU	D2
Picea alcoquiana var. *reflexa* (Shiras.) Fitschen	Japan, central Honshu, Akaishi Range	VU	D2
Picea aurantiaca Mast.	China, W Sichuan, SE Xizang Zizhiqu?	EN	B1+2a-c
Picea brachytyla (Franch.) E. Pritz. (incl. var. *rhombisquamea* Stapf)	China, S Gansu, Henan (Xixia), S Shaanxi, NW Hubei, W Sichuan, NW Sichuan, NW Yunnan, SE Xizang Zizhiqu	VU	A1cd
Picea brachytyla var. *complanata* (Mast.) W. C. Cheng ex Rehder	China, W Sichuan, NW Yunnan; N Myanmar; NE India	VU	A1cd
Picea breweriana S. Watson	U.S.A., SW Oregon, NW California, Siskiyou Mts.	LRnt	
Picea chihuahuana Martínez	Mexico, SW Chihuahua, S Durango, Nuevo León	EN	B1+2e
Picea engelmannii Parry ex Engelm. ssp. *mexicana* (Martínez) P. A. Schmidt	Mexico, S Chihuahua, Nuevo León	EN	A1a, B1+2c
Picea farreri C.N. Page & Rushforth	Myanmar (Fen-Shui-Ling Valley); China, W Yunnan	EN	B1+2a-c
Picea koraiensis Nakai var. *pungsanensis* (Uyeki ex Nakai) Schmidt-Vogt ex Farjon	North Korea	VU	D2
Picea koyamae Shiras.	Japan, Honshu, Yatsugadake Mts.	EN	D
Picea likiangensis (Franch.) E. Pritz. var. *hirtella* (Rehder & E. H. Wilson) W. C. Cheng	China, W Sichuan, SE Xizang Zizhiqu	VU	B1+2c
Picea likiangensis var. *montigena* (Mast.) W. C. Cheng	China, SW Sichuan	EN	B1+2a
Picea martinezii T. F. Patt.	NE Mexico, Nuevo León	CR	B1+2c
Picea maximowiczii Regel ex Mast. var. *maximowiczii*	Japan, central Honshu (Mt. Yatsugadake, Mt. Senjyodake)	VU	B1+2c
Picea maximowiczii var. *senanensis* Hayashi	Japan, central Honshu (Azusa-yama)	VU	B1+2c
Picea morrisonicola Hayata	Taiwan, central mountains	VU	A2c
Picea neoveitchii Mast.	China, NW Hubei, S Shaanxi, Sichuan, S Gansu, Shanxi (Wutai Shan), Henan (Neixiang) (CR; B2a-b)	EN	B1+2ab
Picea omorika (Pancic) Purk.	Bosnia-Herzegovina; Yugoslavia (Tara Mts., Drina River drainage)	VU	D2
Picea retroflexa Mast.	China, W Sichuan	VU	B1+2a-c
Pinus albicaulis Engelm.	W Canada; NW U.S.A.	VU	A1c
Pinus amamiana Koidz.	Japan, Kyushu (Yakushima, Tanegashima)	EN	C1
Pinus aristata Engelm.	U.S.A., Colorado, New Mexico, Arizona	LRnt	
Pinus armandii Franch. var. *mastersiana* (Hayata) Hayata	Taiwan	EN	A1c
Pinus ayacahuite Ehrenb. ex Schldtl. var. *veitchii* (Roezl) Shaw	Mexico	LRnt	
Pinus balfouriana Jeffrey ex Balf. ssp. *balfouriana*	N California (Klamath Mts.)	LRcd	

Species	Distribution	Status	Criteria
Pinus balfouriana ssp. *austrina* R. Mastrog & J. Mastrog.	S California (Tulare, Fresno & Inyo Counties)	LRcd	
Pinus brutia Ten. var. *eldarica* (Medw.) Silba	Azerbaijan (near border with Georgia); Georgia (EN); Iran?; Afghanistan?	DD	
Pinus brutia var. *pityusa* (Steven) Silba	Ukrainian Rep., Crimea; Russian Fed.; Georgia (eastern coast of Black Sea); Syria?	VU	A1c+2c
Pinus caribaea Morelet var. *caribaea*	W Cuba (Pinar del Rio, Isla de Pinos)	VU	A1c+2c
Pinus cembroides Zucc. ssp. *lagunae* (Rob.-Pass.) D. K. Bailey	Mexico, Baja California Sur (Sierra de la Laguna)	VU	A1c
Pinus cembroides ssp. *orizabensis* D. K. Bailey	Mexico, Tlaxcala, Puebla, Veracruz	LRnt	
Pinus clausa (Chapm. ex Engelm.) Sarg.	U.S.A., Florida, Alabama (Baldwin Co.)	LRnt	
Pinus contorta Douglas ex Loudon var. *bolanderi* (Parl.) Koehne	California (Mendocino Co.)	LRnt	
Pinus culminicola Andresen & Beaman	Mexico, Coahuila, Nuevo León	EN	B1+2bc
Pinus dabeshanensis W. C. Cheng & Y. W. Law	China, Anhui (Yuexi, Jingzhai), Henan (Shangcheng), Hubei (Yingshan, Luotian)	VU	B1+2c
Pinus dalatensis Ferré	Vietnam, prov.: Dac Lac, Lâm Dông, Binh Tri Thiên Gia Lai-Công Tum	VU	B1+2c
Pinus densiflora Siebold & Zucc. var. *funebris* (Kom.) T. N. Liou & Q. L. Wang ex Silba	North Korea	DD	
Pinus fenzeliana Hand.-Mazz.	S China, Guangdong (+ Hainan Island), Guangxi, S Hunan; Vietnam	LRnt	
Pinus gerardiana Wall. ex D. Don	India, Jammu-Kashmir; N Pakistan; E Afghanisan; China, S Xizang Zizhiqu (Himalaya)	LRnt	
Pinus greggii Engelm. ex Parl.	E Mexico	DD	
Pinus henryi Mast.	China, Hubei, Hunan, Shaanxi, Sichuan	LRnt	
Pinus jaliscana Pérez de la Rosa	Mexico, W Jalisco	LRnt	
Pinus krempfii Lecomte	S Vietnam (between Dalat and Nhatrang)	VU	B1+2c
Pinus latteri Mason	China, Guangdong (Hainan Island), Guangxi; E Myanmar; N Vietnam	LRnt	
Pinus longaeva D. K. Bailey	U.S.A., E California, S Nevada, Utah	VU	B1+2e
Pinus massoniana Lamb. var. *hainanensis* W. C. Cheng & L. K. Fu	China, Guangdong (Hainan Island, Yajiadaling)	EN	B1+2b
Pinus maximartinezii Rzed.	Mexico, S Zacatecas (Sierra de Morones, Pueblo Viejo)	EN	B1+2bc
Pinus merkusii Jungh. & de Vriese	N Sumatra; Philippines	VU	B2c-e
Pinus muricata D. Don (incl. var. *borealis* Axelrod ex Farjon)	California, Pacific coast, Santa Cruz & Santa Rosa Is.; Mexico, Baja California Norte	LRnt	
Pinus nelsonii Shaw	NE Mexico, Nuevo León, Tamaulipas, San Luis Potosí, Coahuila (Mont. del Carmen)	VU	C2a
Pinus nigra J. F. Arnold ssp. *dalmatica* (Vis.) Franco	Croatia, Dalmatia	VU	B1+2c
Pinus occidentalis Sw.	(Hispaniola) Dominican Rep.; Haiti	LRnt	
Pinus palustris Mill.	SE U.S.A., from Virginia to E Texas	VU	A1c-e
Pinus peuce Griseb.	Albania; Serbia; W Bulgaria; extreme N Greece	LRnt	

Pinus pinceana Gordon	Mexico, Coahuila, Zacatecas, San Luis Potosí, Querétaro, Hidalgo	LRnt	
Pinus radiata D. Don var. *radiata*	California (San Mateo, Santa Cruz, Monterey & San Luis Obispo Co.)	LRcd	
Pinus radiata var. *binata* (Engelm.) Lemmon	Mexico, Guadalupe Island (CR), Cedros Island (EN)	EN	C1
Pinus rzedowskii Madrigal & M. Caball.	Mexico, W Michoacán (Cerro de Chiqueritas, Cerro Ocotoso, Puerto del Pinabete)	EN	D
Pinus squamata X. W. Li	China, Yunnan (Qiaojia Xian)	CR	D
Pinus strobus L. var. *chiapensis* Martínez	S Mexico; Guatemala	VU	B1+2b
Pinus taiwanensis Hayata var. *damingshanensis* W. C. Cheng & L. K. Fu	China, Guizhou, Guangxi (Daming Shan)	LRnt	
Pinus tecunumanii Eguiluz & J. P. Perry	Belize (EN); Guatemala (EN); Honduras; Nicaragua; El Salvador; Mexico, Chiapas, Oaxaca	VU	A2c
Pinus torreyana Parry ex Carrière ssp. *torreyana*	S California (Pacific coast N of San Diego)	EN	C2b
Pinus torreyana ssp. *insularis* J. R. Haller	S California (Santa Rosa Island)	EN	D
Pinus wangii Hu & W. C. Cheng	China, SE Yunnan (Xichou, Malipo)	EN	B1+2bd
Pseudotsuga japonica (Shirasawa) Beissn.	Japan, W Honshu, Shikoku, Kyushu	VU	D2
Pseudotsuga macrocarpa (Vasey) Mayr	S California	LRnt	
Pseudotsuga sinensis Dode var. *brevifolia* (W. C. Cheng & L. K. Fu) Farjon & Silba	China, Guangxi, Guizhou (Lipuo, Anlong)	VU	B1+2c

Pinus nelsonii, Tamaulipas, Mexico.

20

Pseudotsuga sinensis var. *gaussenii* (Flous) Silba	China, N and NW Zhejiang, SE Anhui, Sichuan, Jingxi (Dexing), Fujian?	VU	B1+2c
Pseudotsuga sinensis Dode var. *sinensis* (incl. *P. forrestii* Craib, *P. wilsoniana* Hayata, *P. xichangensis* C. T. Kuan & L. J. Zhou)	China; Taiwan (EN, A1c)	VU	A1d
Tsuga caroliniana Engelm.	U.S.A., Appalachian Mts.	LRnt	
Tsuga forrestii Downie	China, NW Yunnan, SW Sichuan, Guizhou (Fanjinshen)	VU	A1d
Tsuga mertensiana (Bong.) Carrière ssp. *grandicona* Farjon	U.S.A., S Oregon?, California (Siskiyou Mts., Sierra Nevada)	LRcd	
Tsuga mertensiana ssp. *mertensiana* var. *jeffreyi* (A. Henry) C. K. Schneid.	U.S.A., N Washington; Canada, B.C. (Vancouver Island)	DD	

PODOCARPACEAE

Acmopyle pancheri (Brongn. & Gris) Pilg.	New Caledonia	LRnt	
Acmopyle sahniana J. Buchholz & N. E. Gray	Fiji Islands (Viti Levu, Mt. Evans Forest Park)	CR	D
Afrocarpus mannii (Hook. f.) C. N. Page	Gulf of Guinea Is., Sâo Tomé	VU	D2
Afrocarpus usambarensis (Pilg.) C. N. Page	Burundi, Rwanda, Tanzania (Mbulu & Lushoto Districts); Zaire	DD	
Dacrycarpus kinabaluensis (Wasscher) de Laub.	Malaysia, Sabah (Mt. Kinabalu)	LRcd	
Dacrycarpus steupii (Wasscher) de Laub.	Kalimantan (Balikpapan) (EW), Sulawesi (Latimodjong Mts.) (CR), New Guinea (LR)	LRnt	
Dacrydium comosum Corner	Malaysia, Malaya	EN	B1+2c
Dacrydium cornwalliana de Laub.	New Guinea	DD	
Dacrydium ericioides de Laub.	Malaysia, Sarawak (Merurong Plateau)	VU	D2
Dacrydium gibbsiae Stapf	Malaysia, Sabah (Mt. Kinabalu)	LRcd	
Dacrydium gracile de Laub.	Malaysia, Sabah (Mt. Kinabalu)	VU	D2
Dacrydium guillauminii J. Buchholz	New Caledonia (Lac en Huit, Rivière des Lacs)	CR	B1+2c, C1
Dacrydium lycopodioides Brongn. & Gris	New Caledonia (SE part)	LRcd	
Dacrydium magnum de Laub.	Moluccas (Obi & Sudest Is.)	LRnt	
Dacrydium nausoriense de Laub.	Fiji Islands (Viti Levu)	EN	A1cd, B1+2ce, C1
Dacrydium spathoides de Laub.	Irian Jaya (central)	DD	
Falcatifolium angustum de Laub.	Malaysia, Sarawak (two locations on coast)	VU	D2
Halocarpus kirkii (F. Muell. ex Parl.) Quinn	New Zealand, North Island (betw. Hokiana and Manukau Harbor)	VU	A1a+2b
Lagarostrobus franklinii (Hook. f.) Quinn	Tasmania (S & W coast)	LRcd	
Lepidothamnus fonkii Phil.	Chile (Los Lagos, Aisen, Magallanes); Argentina (Andes)	VU	B1+2c
Microstrobos fitzgeraldii (F. Muell.) J. Garden & L. A. S. Johnson	Australia, N.S.W. (Blue Mountains)	EN	C2a
Nageia maxima (de Laub.) de Laub.	Malaysia, Sarawak	VU	D2
Nageia nagi (Thunb.) Kuntze	S China; Taiwan; Japan, Shikoku, Kyushu, Ryukyu Is.	DD	
Parasitaxus ustus (Vieill.) de Laub.	New Caledonia	LRnt	
Podocarpus acuminatus de Laub.	Brazil (Amazonas, Serra da Neblina); Venezuela (Amazonas, Sierra de la Neblina, Bolivar, Chimantá, SW Amuri-tepui)	DD	
Podocarpus affinis Seem.	Fiji Is. (Vitu Levu, Namosi, Voma Peak)	VU	A1c+2c

Podocarpus angustifolius Griseb.	Cuba (Las Villas, Pinar del Rio)	EN	B1+2c
Podocarpus annamiensis N. E. Gray	China, Guangdong (Hainan Island); E Myanmar; Vietnam	DD	
Podocarpus aristulatus Parl.	Cuba; Haiti (Massif de la Selle) (EN); Dominican Rep. (Cordillera Central) (EN)	VU	B2ac
Podocarpus atjehensis (Wasscher) de Laub.	N Sumatra (Gajo Lands); Irian Jaya (Wissel Lakes)	DD	
Podocarpus borneensis de Laub.	Borneo (incl. Karimata Island)	DD	
Podocarpus brevifolius (Stapf) Foxw.	Malaysia, Sabah (Mount Kinabalu)	VU	D2
Podocarpus costalis C. Presl	S Taiwan, Orchid Island; Philippines (N Luzon?, islands in the Luzon Strait)	EN	A1c
Podocarpus decumbens N. E. Gray	New Caledonia	VU	D2
Podocarpus deflexus Ridl.	Malaya; N Sumatra (Gajo Lands)	DD	
Podocarpus dispermus C. T. White	NE Queensland (Atherton Tableland)	DD	
Podocarpus fasciculus de Laub.	Taiwan (EN); Japan, Ryukyu Is.	LRnt	
Podocarpus gibbsiae N. E. Gray	Malaysia, Sabah (Mt. Kinabalu)	VU	D2
Podocarpus globulus de Laub.	Malaysia, Sabah, Sarawak; N Kalimantan	DD	
Podocarpus guatemalensis Standl.	Mexico; Guatemala (EN); Honduras (VU); El Salvador; Belize; Costa Rica (CR); Colombia; Venezuela	DD	
Podocarpus hispaniolensis de Laub.	Dominican Rep. (Cordillera Central)	EN	B1+2e
Podocarpus laubenfelsii Tiong	Borneo	DD	
Podocarpus lophatus de Laub.	Philippines, Luzon (Mt. Tapulao)	VU	D2
Podocarpus matudae Lundell	Mexico, Vera Cruz, Puebla, Chiapas; Guatemala (Huehuetenango)	DD	
Podocarpus micropedunculatus de Laub.	Malaysia, NW Sabah, N Sarawak	DD	
Podocarpus monteverdeensis de Laub.	Costa Rica (Cordillera de Tilarán, Monteverde Res.)	LRcd	
Podocarpus nakaii Hayata	Taiwan (Taichung, Nanton)	EN	A1ad, C2a
Podocarpus nubigenus Lindl.	S Argentina; S Chile	LRnt	
Podocarpus pallidus N. E. Gray	Polynesia, E Tongan Is.	DD	
Podocarpus parlatorei Pilg.	Argentina; Bolivia; Peru	DD	
Podocarpus pendulifolius J. Buchholz & N. E. Gray	Venezuela	DD	
Podocarpus polyspermus de Laub.	New Caledonia	VU	B1+2b
Podocarpus roraimae Pilg.	Venezuela (Mt. Roraima and mts. betw. Venezuela and Guyana)	DD	
Podocarpus salignus D. Don	S Chile	VU	A1d+2b
Podocarpus smithii de Laub.	Australia, Queensland (Mt. Lewis)	LRcd	
Podocarpus spathoides de Laub.	Malaysia (Mt. Ophir); N Moluccas (Morotai); P.N.G. (Rossel Island); Solomon Is.	DD	
Podocarpus subtropicalis de Laub.	China, Yunnan, Sichuan (Emei Shan)	DD	
Podocarpus transiens (Pilg.) de Laub.	Brazil (Bahia, Minas Gerais)	DD	
Podocarpus urbanii Pilg.	Jamaica (Blue Mts.)	LRnt	

Prumnopitys andina (Poepp. ex Endl.) de Laub.	Chile (Regions VII-X) (VU); Argentina (Andes)	VU	A1cd, C2a
Prumnopitys exigua de Laub.	Bolivia	DD	
Prumnopitys harmsiana (Pilg.) de Laub.	Bolivia (VU); Colombia; Peru; Venezuela	LRnt	
Prumnopitys ladei (F. M. Bailey) de Laub.	NE Queensland (Mt. Sturgeon)	LRcd	
Prumnopitys standleyi (J. Buchholz & N. E. Gray) de Laub.	Costa Rica (Volcan de Poas, Cerro las Vueltas)	DD	
Retrophyllum minor (Carrière) C. N. Page	SE New Caledonia	EN	C1+2a
Retrophyllum piresii (Silba) C. N. Page	Brazil, Rondonia (Serra Pacas Novos)	DD	
Retrophyllum rospigliosii (Pilg.) C. N. Page	Venezuela; E Colombia (EN?); Central Peru (on mountains) (EN?)	LRnt	
Saxegothaea conspicua Lindl.	S Argentina; S Chile	LRnt	

SCIADOPITYACEAE

Sciadopitys verticillata (Thunb.) Siebold & Zucc.	Japan, S Honshu, Shikoku, Kyushu	VU	A1c+2c

TAXACEAE

Amentotaxus argotaenia (Hance) Pilg.	China, Jiangsu, Zhejiang?, Fujian, Jiangxi, Guangdong, Hunan, Guangxi, Guizhou, Hubei, Sichuan, Gansu, E Xizang Zizhiqu	VU	A1c
Amentotaxus argotaenia var. *brevifolia* K. M. Lan & F. H. Zhang	China, Guizhou	VU	A1c
Amentotaxus assamica D. K. Ferguson	India, Arunachal Pradesh	VU	A1c
Amentotaxus formosana H. L. Li	Taiwan (southeast)	CR	C2b
Amentotaxus poilanei (Ferré & Rouane) D. K. Ferguson	Vietnam	VU	A1c

Retrophyllum minor, New Caledonia.

Saxegothaea conspicua, Southern Chile.

23

Amentotaxis yunnanensis H. L. Li	China, Yunnan (Wengshanzhou), Guizhou (Xingyi); Vietnam (Ha Tuyen province)	EN	A1c
Austrotaxus spicata R. H. Compton	New Caledonia	LRnt	
Pseudotaxus chienii (W. C. Cheng) W. C. Cheng	China, Guangdong (Ruyian), Guangxi, Hunan, Zhejiang, Jiangxi	EN	A1c
Taxus brevifolia Nutt.	NW North America, Pacific Coast region, Rocky Mountain region	LRnt	
Taxus floridana Nutt. ex Chapm.	Florida (along the Apalachicola River)	CR	B1+2c
Taxus globosa Schltdl.	Guatemala; Mexico	LRnt	
Taxus fuana Nan Li & R. R. Mill	China, SW Xizang-Zizhiqu	VU	D2
Taxus wallichiana Zucc.	Hindu Kush, Himalaya, SW China	DD	
Torreya californica Torr.	California (Coast Ranges, Sierra Nevada)	LRcd	
Torreya grandis Fortune ex Lindl. var. *fargesii* (Franch.) Silba	China, W Hubei, NE Sichuan (and Emei Shan), S Shaanxi, Jiangxi?	VU	A1c
Torreya jackii Chun	China, Fujian (Taining, Puchen), Zhejiang	EN	A1c
Torreya taxifolia Arn.	U.S.A., NW Florida, SW Georgia	CR	A1c
Torreya yunnanensis W. C. Cheng & L. K. Fu	China, NW Yunnan	DD	

TAXODIACEAE (Cupressaceae *s.l.*)

Athrotaxis cupressoides D. Don	Tasmania	VU	A1ac
Athrotaxis x *laxifolia* Hook.	Tasmania	VU	D1
Athrotaxis selaginoides D. Don	Tasmania	VU	A1ac
Cryptomeria japonica (Thunb. ex L. f.) D. Don	Japan, Honshu, Shikoku, Kyushu	LRnt	
Cunninghamia konishii Hayata	Taiwan (N-central); China, Fujian; Laos, Houa Phan; Vietnam (Mt. Bu Huong)	VU	A1c
Metasequoia glyptostroboides Hu & W. C. Cheng	China, Sichuan (Shizhu), Hubei, (Lichuan), Hunan (Longshan, Sangzhi)	CR	A1c, C2a
Sequoia sempervirens (D. Don) Endl.	U.S.A., Pacific Coast region from SW Oregon (Curry Co.), to California (Monterey Co.)	LRcd	

Sciadopitys verticillata, in cultivation at the Royal Botanic Garden, Edinburgh, Scotland.

Sequoiadendron giganteum, in cultivation at the Royal Botanic Garden, Edinburgh, Scotland.

Sequoiadendron giganteum (Lindl.) J. Buchholz	California (Calaveras, Tuolumne, Mariposa, Madera, Fresno and Tulare Co.)	VU	A1cd
Taiwania cryptomerioides Hayata	Taiwan (Mt. Morrison) (EN); China, NW Yunnan (VU); N Myanmar (EN)	VU	A1d
Taxodium mucronatum Ten.	U.S.A., S Texas; Mexico; Guatemala	DD	

Total number of taxa of conservation concern   **355**

Total number of taxa threatened with extinction (CR, EN, VU)   **200**

Total number of taxa considered critically endangered (CR)   20
Total number of taxa considered endangered (EN)   50
Total number of taxa considered vulnerable (VU)   130

Given the known total of c. 800 conifer taxa (c. 630 species, see Farjon, 1998), this means that 45% appear to be of conservation concern, and at least 25% are threatened with extinction. This figure is likely to increase with further investigation, especially in the tropics. One species, *Thuja sutchuenensis* (still cultivated in China), is recorded as being Extinct in the Wild (EW).

Pseudolarix amabilis, in cultivation at the Royal Botanic Garden, Edinburgh, Scotland.

As was stated in our introduction to this list, the status of all conifer taxa is not known; there are several Data Deficient (DD) taxa which are still felt to be of conservation concern. In addition, a number of species categorised as E (Endangered) or V (Vulnerable) according to pre-1994 IUCN Red List Categories (Farjon *et al.* 1993) were, for lack of data, unable to be re-evaluated using the new categories and criteria (IUCN, 1994). Rather than listing them as 'Data Deficient' (DD) in the main list, we judged it more useful to list them separately here. These taxa are in urgent need of re-evaluation as many may possibly be VU (Vulnerable) or even EN (Endangered) under the new criteria; it is particularly evident that there are many tropical podocarps which may be under severe threat. The following taxa were counted in the above summary as being 'of conservation concern', but will not be considered as 'threatened with extinction' unless they can be assessed as CR, EN, or VU with the new criteria.

Taxon	Distribution
CUPRESSACEAE	
Juniperus taxifolia Hook. & Arn.	Japan, Ryuku Is., Bonin Is.
PINACEAE	
Pinus bungeana Zucc. ex Endl.	China, N Sichuan, S Gansu, Hubei (Badong Xian), Shaanxi, Shanxi, Henan, NE Hebei
Pinus canariensis C. Smith	Canary Islands
Pseudolarix amabilis (J. Nelson) Rehder	China, lower Chang Jiang [Yangtse] valley, Hunan, N. Jiangxi, N. Zhejiang, N Fujian
Tsuga chinensis (Franch.) E. Pritz. var. *oblongisquamata* W. C. Cheng & L. K. Fu	China, Sichuan, W Hunei, Gansu (Zhouqu)
Tsuga chinensis var. *robusta* W. C. Cheng & L. K. Fu	China, Sichuan (Yalong Valley), Hubei
PODOCARPACEAE	
Dacrydium leptophyllum (Wasscher) de Laub.	Irian Jaya (Mt. Goliath)
Nageia fleuryi (Hickel) de Laub.	Vietnam; Kampuchea; China, Guangdong (Gaoyao, Longmen,Zengcheng), Guangxi (Hepu), Yunnan (Mengzi, Pingbian)
Nageia formosensis (Dummer) C. N. Page	Taiwan (south)
Podocarpus capuronii de Laub.	Madagascar (Mt. Ambatomenaloha)
Podocarpus costaricensis de Laub.	Costa Rica (San Marcos de Irazu); Panama
Podocarpus drouynianus F. Muell.	SW Australia (Warren District)
Podocarpus humbertii de Laub.	Madagascar
Podocarpus lambertii Klotzsch ex Endl.	Argentina (EN); Brazil (near São Paulo)
Podocarpus madagascariensis Baker var. *procerus* de Laub.	Madagascar (Fort Dauphin)
Podocarpus rostratus L. Laurent	Madagascar
Podocarpus rotundus de Laub.	E Kalimantan (Mt. Beratus); Philippines, Luzon (Mt. Banajao, Lucban)
Podocarpus purdieanus Hook.	Jamaica (Mt. Diablo)
Podocarpus rusbyi J. Buchholz & N. E. Gray	Bolivia (Mapiri, Cocopunco)
Podocarpus salomoniensis Wasscher	Solomon Is. (San Cristobal Island)
Podocarpus sellowii Klotzsch ex Endl.	Brazil (near São Paulo)
Podocarpus trinitensis J. Buchholz & N. E. Gray	Trinidad/Tobago (summit of El Tucuche)
TAXODIACEAE (Cupressaceae *s.l.*)	
Glyptostrobus pensilis (Staunton) K. Koch	SE China, Fujian, Jiangxi, Guangdong (incl. Hainan Island), Guangxi, SE Yunnan, Sichuan; N Vietnam (EW)

Chapter 2
Conservation Issues

Conservation incentives

There are many good reasons, economical, ecological, and ethical, to give high priority to the conservation of conifer species and to the natural vegetation in which they occur.

Versatile market. The great diversity of timber and the multitude of uses, from paper to sophisticated furniture, that conifers provide stems directly from the diversity of species. Today, exploitation emphasises massive extraction for bulk purposes in many forests. Better management aiming at sustainable use of these resources, together with recycling of paper and critical consumerism, should lead to a more versatile market for conifer timber at higher values. Societies will recognise that a tree yielding a piece of wood that took centuries to grow should only be put to very high quality and durable kinds of use.

Genetic diversity. Genetic diversity of wild-growing conifers is essential as a gene pool to draw upon in plantation forestry and horticulture. Such diversity is dependent on the maintenance of large and dispersed populations under natural selection processes.

Medicinal prospects. For many species, especially those in the tropics, chemical properties are scarcely known. The likelihood of finding yet other useful compounds (besides taxol in yews) is great in this evolutionarily ancient and diverse group of plants that are so different from angiosperms. Preservation of conifer genetic diversity in wild populations is again a prerequisite in order to realise this potential.

Ecosystem stability. In the wild, conifers are often the dominant tree species in mountain areas, where many species have an important soil-stabilising role in the ecosystem. Long-term surface stabilisation is only achieved by indigenous conifer species, which are unequalled in their ability to regenerate under the adverse climatic and edaphic conditions to which they are specifically adapted. Under these conditions, replacement by alien tree species is hardly ever successful and results eventually in severe soil degradation or loss.

Amenity planting. Ecological adaptation to adverse climatic and edaphic conditions unsuitable for most angiosperms make conifers potential candidates for amenity plantings, along streets and in public parks. Many species have hardly or not at all been investigated for this purpose. Conservation as well as ecological research of wild populations of especially rare 'relict' species which have often clung to unusual sites is essential.

Habitat conservation. Many coniferous woodlands and forests, especially those with diverse species and vegetation structure, are habitats for other organisms of great biodiversity value. Of special importance in this respect are conifer-dominated temperate rainforests around the Pacific Rim which often harbour large and long-lived conifer trees. These trees are frequently found to be so-called keystone species in their respective ecosystems. Removal of such species can easily lead to collapse of the whole ecosystem structure, from macrobiota to microbiota. Their conservation importance therefore greatly exceeds their intrinsic value.

Indicator species. In the case of relictual conifers, the surviving species can often be indicators of entire ancient ecosystems. These are very likely to harbour other relictual biota worth conserving. In New Caledonia, for instance, the genera *Austrotaxus*, *Dacrydium*, and *Neocallitropsis* are often associated with ancient fern genera forming a distinct type of vegetation. These communities are of great scientific research value.

Ecotourism and scientific research. Forests, and among them natural coniferous forests, are attractive for quiet types of outdoor recreation. Many conifer species occur in very scenic environments such as wild coastlines, steep ocean islands, and high mountains that offer outstanding recreational opportunities. Educational and research activities blend well with this type of tourism. Local communities, when properly involved in management policies and practice, can benefit from this largely sustainable type of forest use. It is well established that large-scale forest exploitation such as clearcutting spoils the tourist potential even for adjacent untouched forest: the two types of use apparently do not mix. Long-term investment in tourism is increasingly recognised as an economically as well as ecologically sound alternative.

Conservation priorities

The goal of IUCN Red Lists is to evaluate and monitor the global status of species, regardless of national or other political boundaries. While there are numerous cases of species declining or even becoming extinct in certain areas, these species often occur elsewhere. In this Action Plan, decline is only taken into account if it is significant in relation to the whole known range of the species. Many countries now compile or have already compiled national Red Lists of plants and attention should be drawn to these more local conservation concerns in these publications. The list proposed in this Action Plan represents a global overview, which is, in itself, a form of prioritisation in that only taxa whose total occurrence is significantly declining, has declined, or whose status is data deficient are listed. Yet, even with these criteria, the list is still a very long one, and it could be argued that some further set of criteria might have to be applied to set further global priorities. The question is: how to prioritise?

The authors can see two approaches. One is to short-list the number of taxa to those which, for various reasons, are thought to be the most important conifers to receive urgent conservation action. The other is an area-based approach: from the list, 'hot spots' could be identified where conservation efforts would give protection to a substantial number of species simultaneously. Obviously all *in situ* conservation is ultimately area-based; therefore, the more short-listed species which could be found to occur in 'hot spots' the better.

1. Short-listing

It is important to distinguish between criteria used to assess the category of threat, as explicitly stated in the Guidelines given by SSC (IUCN 1994), and those suggested below for further prioritisation. Factors such as rarity, endemism, decline, slow regeneration, and growth all impinge on a taxon's chances of survival under human pressure and were already used to estimate the category of threat. We have assessed all conifer taxa using a data form for tree species on which many of these factors are indicated. This form was developed by the WCMC/SSC Conservation and Sustainable Use of Trees Project. Therefore, the authors believe that the **category of threat** itself is a first criterion to be used for short-listing but it is not the only criterion for prioritisation.

Phylogenetic distinction (as a reflection of genetic distinctness) is another important criterion with which to short-list species. The application of this criterion assigns higher conservation value to a monotypic genus (i.e. a genus with a single known species) than to a species belonging to a genus with many other species. Likewise, distinct species are given higher priority than varieties. That this criterion, apart from its scientific basis, has some pragmatic value becomes clear when one realises that taxonomists do not always agree on species delimitations, especially among closely related species. Controversy is unlikely regarding the phylogenetically more distinct taxa.

Ecological importance is another criterion that can be used to prioritise taxa on the list for conservation action. Conifer species can play a major role in an ecosystem ('keystone species'), supporting many other unrelated organisms especially when forming (co-) dominants in slow growing forests.

Genetic diversity is an important criterion as well. Species known to be unusually rich in regional genetic diversity, often expressed in high levels of morphological variation or varied ecological adaptation, are of conservation importance. A special case could be made for such species where genetic depletion is suspected due to known rates of decline, ranking them higher on the list of priorities.

Prioritisation then follows a formula by which values are assigned to each factor. This formula is as follows:

category of threat x (phylogenetic distinction + ecological importance + genetic diversity)

categories of threat: CR = 4, EN = 3, VU = 2, LR = 1.

Phylogenetic distinction: monotypic family = 5, monotypic genus = 4, species, subspecies or variety of small genus (2-5 spp.) or single representative of a section within a genus = 3, species of a large genus (>6 spp.) = 2, subspecies or variety of a large genus = 1.

Ecological importance: keystone species of a biotic community = 3, co-dominant species in a distinct vegetation type = 2, species is a minor constituent of the vegetation, or a pioneer in early successional phases only = 1.

Genetic diversity: significant genetic diversity known or suspected within populations = 2, no evidence of genetic diversity = 1.

Threshold levels are determined from the resulting numerical values of the taxa. The range of possible values is between 3-40. Further calculation showed that there is a large cluster of values between 4-15. It seems reasonable to place the threshold for short-listed taxa at a value of 16. **This treatment short-lists a total of 43 species falling in 27 genera** (Table 2.1).

Additionally, there are five other species that warrant consideration for short-listing. Although they have not been evaluated using the most recent categories (IUCN, 1994), they all were listed as Endangered (E) in Farjon *et al.* (1993), using the old categories. This as well as their high score in the remaining three variables in the short-listing formula merits their inclusion in a list of candidate species for short-listing (Table 2.2).

2. Hot spots

Analysis of the Global Red List of Conifers presented in this Action Plan reveals a number of areas (countries, states, mountain ranges, or islands) within which there is a high concentration of threatened conifer taxa. Just how many taxa an area must have and how large it can be to be listed as a 'hot spot' for conifers remains somewhat arbitrary. Obviously, islands provide natural boundaries for conifers which political borders do not. The average size of conifers' ranges can be taken as a rough measure, but areas proclaimed 'hot spots' had to be defined along political borders for practical reasons. We define a 'hot spot' as an area within a definable boundary that contains a minimum of eight conifer taxa that are of conservation concern (2% of the Global Red List of Conifers). Species that are not of conservation concern but

Table 2.1. Threatened species short-listed by using the above criteria.

Species	Distribution
Abies beshanzuensis	Zhejiang, CHINA
Abies fanjingshanensis	Guizhou, CHINA
Abies nebrodensis	Sicily, ITALY
Abies yuanbaoshanensis	Guangxi, CHINA
Abies ziyuanensis	Guangxi, Hunan, CHINA
Acmopyle sahniana	Viti Levu, FIJI
Amentotaxus formosana	Taiwan
Araucaria nemorosa	New Caledonia
Araucaria rulei	New Caledonia
Chamaecyparis formosensis	Taiwan
Chamaecyparis lawsoniana	California, Oregon, USA
Chamaecyparis obtusa var. *formosana*	Taiwan
Cunninghamia konishii	Taiwan
Cupressus chengiana var. *jiangeensis*	Sichuan, CHINA
Cupressus dupreziana	Algeria
Cupressus guadalupensis var. *guadalupensis*	Guadalupe Island, MEXICO
Dacrydium guillauminii	New Caledonia
Fitzroya cupressoides	S Chile, Argentina
Juniperus barbadensis	St. Lucia
Juniperus bermudiana	Bermudas
Juniperus gracilior var. *ekmanii*	Haiti
Libocedrus chevalieri	New Caledonia
Metasequoia glyptostroboides	Sichuan, Hubei, Hunan, CHINA
Microstrobos fitzgeraldii	New South Wales, AUSTRALIA
Nothotsuga longibracteata	China
Picea martinezii	Nuevo Leôn, MEXICO
Pilgerodendron uviferum	S Chile, Argentina
Pinus culminicola	Coahuila, Nuevo Leôn, MEXICO
Pinus maximartinezii	Zacatecas, MEXICO
Pinus rzedowskii	Michoacán, MEXICO
Pinus squamata	Yunnan, CHINA
Podocarpus gibbsiae	Mt. Kinabalu, Sabah, MALAYSIA
Pseudotaxus chienii	China
Retrophyllum minor	New Caledonia
Sciadopitys verticillata	Japan
Sequoiadendron giganteum	California, USA
Taiwania cryptomerioides	Taiwan; Yunnan, CHINA; Myanmar
Taxus floridana	N Florida, USA
Torreya jackii	Fujian, Zhejiang, CHINA
Torreya taxifolia	Florida-Georgia, USA
Widdringtonia cedarbergensis	Cape Province, SOUTH AFRICA
Widdringtonia whytei	Malawi
Wollemia nobilis	New South Wales, AUSTRALIA

Table 2.2. Candidate species for short-listing.

Species	Distribution
Dacrydium leptophyllum	Irian Jaya, INDONESIA
Glyptostrobus pensilis	SE China, Vietnam
Pinus bungeana	China
Podocarpus rostratus	Madagascar
Pseudolarix amabilis	E China

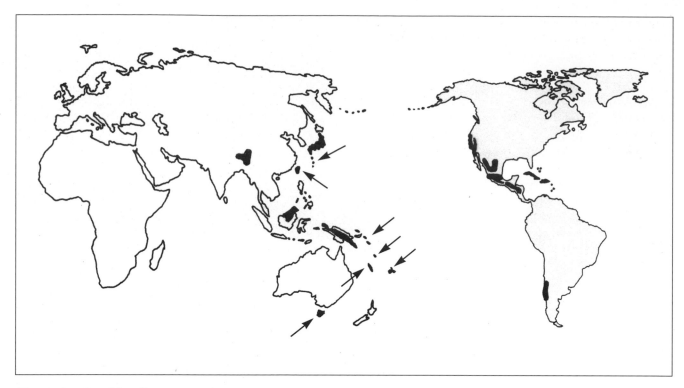

Fig 2.1. Conifer 'hotspots' are areas with high diversity *and* high numbers of threatened species.

which exist in the same area are not immediately taken into account. However, diversity of these species often parallels that of species of conservation concern; positive conservation action will eventually benefit both. For this reason we have given the overall diversity some additional weight where appropriate.

On this basis, the following areas (see Figure 2.1) are considered to be 'hot spots' for conifers:

CAL — In this region there are two areas with more than eight taxa of conservation concern: **Northern California**, which encompasses the coastal ranges from Monterey north to southern Oregon, merging in the north with the Sierra Nevada and the Cascades ranges; and **Southern California**, which includes the coastal ranges from Monterey south, the

Burnt conifer-broadleaved rainforest in coastal Chile, west of Osomo.

southern half of the Sierra Nevada, and mountains in northern Baja California, as well as Cedros and Guadalupe Islands and smaller islands off the Pacific coast. The latter area is not only larger than the former, but also has more than twice as many taxa of concern: 20 as opposed to 9.

MEX — Mexico and Central America divide into three hot spots, each with a similar number of taxa of conservation concern (14, 12 and 15 respectively). **Northern Mexico**, i.e. the Sierra Madres Oriental and Occidental and their foothills in the interior; **Central Mexico**, i.e. the Eje Volcanico Transversal, the Mesa Central, and the mountains east and west along the ocean coasts, ending with the Sierra Madre del Sur; and **Mesoamerica**, i.e. Oaxaca, Chiapas, and the Central American states as far as Costa Rica.

FLO — In this region, only the **islands in the Caribbean** have a combined total of 15 taxa of conservation concern, most of which are on Hispaniola and Cuba. None of the islands is in itself a hot spot for conifers.

SAM — In South America, **temperate southern Chile and adjacent Patagonian Argentina** form a hot spot with 11 taxa, or just over 3% of the global taxa of conservation concern; two of these are short-listed above.

SIN — In this vast region, two areas are hot spots. By far the richest in threatened taxa is the mountainous region of **SW Sichuan, NW Yunnan, SE Xizang Zizhiqu, and border areas of Myanmar and Arunachal Pradesh**, with nearly 40 conifer taxa of conservation concern. This area extends naturally into the eastern Himalayas, where several further listed taxa are found. The second hot spot is the island of **Taiwan** with 14 listed taxa.

JAP - While no continental area of this region has sufficient taxa of concern to be considered a hot spot, several parts of Japan do. We listed 10 taxa on **Honshu** and 11 taxa on **Shikoku, Kyushu, and the Ryukyu Islands.**

MAL — In the Malesian floristic region, the island of **Borneo** stands out with 20 taxa of conservation concern. Most of these are in the north and north-west (Sabah, Sarawak), while a few are in the central part of the island. **New Guinea** just qualifies with eight taxa of conservation concern, but as some species' status is unknown, the total may be higher.

AUS — Although at present only seven taxa are considered to be of conservation concern on the island of **Tasmania,** both its overall diversity of conifers and the worrying situation with deforestation and forest transformation into 'production forest' merit its designation as a hot spot for conifers.

PAC — In the Southwest Pacific, **New Caledonia** is one of the most obvious conifer hot spots in the world with 29 taxa of conservation concern on an island the size of Wales. It is, therefore, fully justified that this island be given priority in the drafting of a regional status report and Action Plan; this report is included in Chapter 3. In addition, we have thought it appropriate to include the smaller oceanic island groups in the Southwest Pacific (**Fiji, Vanuatu, and Solomon Islands**) as forming collectively a further hot spot on account of their total diversity and isolation.

Recommendations for conservation action

There are two principal strategies that can be implemented to slow the decline or to prevent the loss of species diversity; these are generally distinguished as *in situ* and *ex situ* conservation and are often used to complement each other. The leading principle in species conservation is that viable and sustained populations need to perpetuate themselves in a natural or at least semi-natural environment. The most powerful argument for this is that what is ultimately important in nature conservation is the ecosystem, of which species are integral parts. This is achieved only by *in situ* strategies, which all amount to measures taken within or around the natural range of the species to curb or mitigate negative effects and to stimulate positive effects on the populations. This kind of conservation is naturally area-oriented. Indeed, one of its most effective and widely-used strategies is the establishment and management of protected areas or reserves to conserve specific ecosystems or species. On the other hand, *ex situ* strategies are measures usually taken outside the natural range of the species in order to safeguard it against extinction

Burnt conifers (*Pigerodendron uviferum*) in Chiloé, Chile.

M. Gardner

caused by negative human action or influence. Propagation (breeding) in botanic gardens, nurseries, or forest plots can be effective *ex situ* strategies, but legislation pertaining to trade, such as the Convention on International Trade in Endangered Species of Wild Fauna and Flora (CITES), belong in this category as well. Usually there is agreement that *ex situ* strategies are complementary to *in situ* strategies; the former may in extreme cases become 'last ditch' rescue operations to prevent total extinction.

Guidelines for *in situ* strategies

It is of utmost importance to protect populations of species in their natural habitat which represent the greatest possible genetic diversity. In the absence of direct knowledge of this diversity, circumstantial evidence such as morphological and ecological variation should be considered. Protected areas should include as much of this variation as is possible; for instance, it means that on mountains at least the entire altitudinal gradient of a species should be included.

An ecosystem approach is essential, which means that knowledge about autecology, synecology, and dynamic processes, e.g. in relation to natural disturbances affecting the species of concern, should be known or studied if unknown. The regeneration cycle of many conifer species involves temporally and spatially distinct 'cohorts' forming a mosaic pattern of stages in forest succession in the landscape. Having reserves of sufficient size to encompass all stages several-fold is the only guarantee that the ecosystem is capable of perpetuating itself. In many cases where species exist within protected areas, this pattern has been disturbed, sometimes with the best objectives in mind. For example, in the 'groves' of *Sequoiadendron giganteum* overprotection against forest fires has benefited competitors rather than the protected species. In other cases, protection has only arrived when populations were depleted to such an extent that only residual and often senescent individuals remain, such as with *Widdringtonia cedarbergensis* and *Cupressus dupreziana*.

Habitat restoration is essential in all cases where such changes are known to be man-made and the situation seems reversible. This can take a variety of forms, ranging from relatively simple measures, such as the elimination of feral goats on oceanic islands, to much more complex schemes involving reforestation on eroded soils. Human activities, where tolerated, must not interfere with the restoration process and will often have to be banned altogether until the ecosystem has regained its former robustness and resilience to disturbance.

Involvement of local people is always essential, whether it involves conservation-minded groups such as those concerned with the 'Redwoods' in California or rural communities who derive some economic benefits from forests or rare conifer species, such as *Pinus maximartinezii* in Mexico (see species account p.101 and regional account for Nueva Galicia, Mexico p.55). Without the collaboration of these people, conservation will in many cases remain unsupported or even boycotted, while with their support, success is often guaranteed, even against economic pressures from outside. In this context, the Conifer Specialist Group urges and encourages the compilation and publication of regional Action Plans as well as specific case studies and recommendations for single taxa. Examples of both of these are included in this Action Plan and can be used as guidelines to be followed and improved upon. Regional Action Plans should

Intact boggy conifer forest with *Fitzroya cupressoides* (trees) and *Lepidothamnus fonkii* (low shrubs) in southern Chile.

especially be written for 'hot spot' areas or parts thereof as identified in this Action Plan (Figure 2.1); several of these are included in this Action Plan. Single taxa reports for species which 'appeal' to the public (e.g. very long-lived or majestic conifers), or which are economically very valuable, are recommended. Such 'appeal' can be world-wide or local and examples of both are given in this Action Plan.

Strategies for *ex situ* conservation

In this Action Plan we include within *ex situ* conservation any actions taken to conserve a species outside its natural habitat. Therefore, in addition to the planting of threatened conifers in botanic gardens and preservation in seed banks, we also discuss trade legislation (e.g. CITES) and the raising of consumer awareness.

The world-wide pressure on old growth conifer forest for timber exploitation must be considerably eased if not removed. Harvesting timber via plantation forestry enterprises should eventually take its place if we are serious about *in situ* conservation of conifers on a sufficient scale to protect species and their genetic diversity. That this is economically feasible is demonstrated by the extraordinary success of exploitation of *Pinus radiata* outside its limited natural range. However, where such exploitation using introduced species replaces natural forest, conservation is often not served. In addition, these species or varieties, often selected for fast growth and vigour, may become invasive weeds that replace invaluable native vegetation and species. Careful land use planning, now often lacking, is essential for providing alternatives to exploitation of natural forests. It must also be acknowledged that many very slow-growing conifers cannot be economically cultivated. Timber extraction from natural stands can only be sustainable at a rate which does not exceed their growth. For several species, such as *Fitzroya cupressoides*, this remains impossible within human time scales. *Fitzroya cupressoides* has therefore been legally banned from exploitation both through national and international (CITES) legislation.

In relation to this and analogous to what has been achieved for certain animals, consumer awareness should be stimulated. Several major retail companies are already exploring alternatives, such as greenwood certification, in answer to such awareness regarding wood products from tropical rainforest; similar results may be possible for wood from threatened conifers. The World Wide Fund for Nature (WWF) has a well-established forest certification program that is involved in these issues. The public appeal of the 'Redwoods' in the USA shows the feasibility of such approaches, which should be extended to other suitable conifer species.

Legislation, both national and international, should be directed at the protection of both forests and the individual species and should be complementary. One of the most important examples of conservation legislation is CITES, a species-based international trade convention. It has been signed and ratified by a sufficient number of states to be effective for global trade. Some tree species involved in the timber trade are now included on its lists of taxa for which international 'trade' (= movement) is either:

1) allowed only under exceptional circumstances and thus effectively prohibited (Appendix I) or

2) regulated and monitored through issuance of export permits (Appendix II).

A few conifers are either listed or proposed, the most recent situation (as of 1999) is presented in Table 2.3. Assessment of the feasibility to list other threatened taxa (which must be internationally traded) is urgently needed.

There is a draft proposal for listing *Chamaecyparis lawsoniana* (in consideration for Appendix II). But, while some other species are of reported concern (e.g. *Dacrydium guillauminii, Neocallitropsis pancheri, Parasitaxus ustus, Sequoia sempervirens, Widdringtonia whytei*), no others have been proposed formally. For such proposals to be considered formally, there must be considerable international trade (or potential of trade) of whole plants or parts thereof which is detrimental to the survival of the species, or could become so when not regulated. Trees have only recently entered the CITES scene and much has still to be learned about the possibilities and effectiveness of regulation or banning of their international trade. In 1994, a Timber Working Group was established by the CITES Parties to examine many of these issues.

Ex situ conservation in a stricter sense involves the preservation of living individual plants or their propagules (i.e. seeds in conifers) outside their natural range and habitat. Botanic gardens, arboreta, forest plantations, and nurseries are all suitable establishments for *ex situ* conservation, provided that they contain "scientifically ordered and maintained collections of plants, usually documented and labelled, and open to the public for the purposes of recreation, education and research" (BGCS 1989). It is generally agreed that this strategy should be complementary to *in situ* conservation and is best seen as either an insurance policy or, in extreme cases of risk of extinction, as a 'last ditch' effort to rescue a species from extinction. A very substantial heritage, especially present in the industrialised countries resulting from past collecting, planting, and maintenance, effectively provides the currency of an insurance policy. The important task of documenting and curating this stock should be seen as a substantial international contribution to the *ex situ* conservation strategy for conifers, a cause worthy of continued financial support. Unlike many older trees held in these collections, more recent acquisitions are increasingly from wild-collected, well-documented provenances and have therefore a higher conservation value. On the other hand, in many cases, only single individuals are as yet in cultivation, and holdings of several gardens may in effect represent just a single genotype (Page 1998). Current moves are being made in many countries to establish *ex situ* collections. Besides the long established western botanic gardens, new developments are taking place in e.g. Chile, China, Mexico, New Zealand, Tasmania, and Taiwan. Creating an inventory of these gardens, which are or might become important for conifer conservation, is a high priority as a follow-up task of this Action Plan. A selection of such gardens, each of which holds many threatened conifers, among which are a good number of CR or EN taxa, is presented in Table 2.4.

A few other gardens hold fair numbers of Critically Endangered or Endangered conifers, such as the Sir Harold Hillier Garden and Arboretum, Ampfield, England, UK (16 taxa) and the Botanic Garden of Adelaide, Australia (12 taxa). What springs immediately into view from these data is that often the same species are held (in several cases with the same provenance). It is also apparent that many CR and EN taxa are absent in botanic gardens, especially species of Podocarpaceae (not a single species of *Podocarpus* listed as CR or EN appears in the database, although we believe *P. drouynianus* to be cultivated in Australia). Also, several famous gardens rich in conifers of the northern hemisphere (e.g. the Arnold Arboretum of Harvard University, USA and the National Pinetum at Bedgebury, England, UK) hold rather few of the highly endangered species. Active collection and communication on present-day taxonomic research in conifers is crucial: many collections date from years back when the emphasis was different and conservation status of trees either unknown or not a serious concern.

In addition, more specific *ex situ* conservation programmes targeting species in the higher categories of risk should be initiated and conducted in collaboration with governmental forestry and/or conservation institutes of the countries involved and botanic gardens both domestically and abroad. The overall aim should be propagation under more favourable conditions and the maintenance of a diverse gene pool with which to restock original sites once environmental conditions have resumed to be favourable to reforestation with the threatened species. In the interim, such schemes, in which ideally several institutes should collaborate, provide opportunities for scientific research which will benefit the programme of restoration. The Conifer Conservation Programme of the Royal Botanic Garden, Edinburgh, proves

Table 2.3. Conifer species listed in the two Appendices of CITES to date.

Appendix I	Appendix II
Abies guatemalensis	*Araucaria araucana* (other)
Araucaria araucana (population of Chile)	*Taxus wallichiana*
Fitzroya cupressoides	
Pilgerodendron uviferum	
Podocarpus parlatorei	

Table 2.4. Botanic gardens which are known to hold 20 or more (15 or more for southern hemisphere gardens) endangered conifer taxa. Source: BGCI-DATA (report February 1997), the database of Botanic Gardens Conservation International, Descanso House, 199 Kew Road, Richmond, Surrey TW9 3BW, UK.

Pinetum Blijdenstein, Hilversum (University of Amsterdam), The Netherlands

Abies nebrodensis	(CR, short-listed, provenance: wild source via Berlin-Dahlem)
Acmopyle sahniana	(CR, short-listed, provenance: wild source)
Amentotaxus formosana	(CR, short-listed, provenance: wild source)
Araucaria nemorosa	(CR, short-listed, provenance: wild source)
Callitris sulcata	(EN, provenance: wild source)
Chamaecyparis formosensis	(EN, short-listed, provenance: wild source)
Cunninghamia konishii	(VU, short-listed, provenance: wild source)
Cupressus atlantica	(EN, provenance: wild source)
Cupressus dupreziana	(CR, short-listed, provenance: wild source)
Cupressus goveniana var. *abramsiana*	(EN, provenance: wild source)
Fitzroya cupressoides	(EN, short-listed, provenance: wild source)
Glyptostrobus pensilis	(short-list candidate, provenance: wild source)
Juniperus bermudiana	(CR, short-listed, provenance: wild source)
Juniperus brevifolia	(EN, provenance: wild source)
Juniperus cedrus	(EN, provenance: wild source)
Metasequoia glyptostroboides	(CR, short-listed, provenance: wild source)
Microstrobos fitzgeraldii	(EN, short-listed, provenance: wild source)
Picea aurantiaca	(EN, provenance: not of known wild source)
Picea chihuahuana	(EN, provenance: wild source)
Picea engelmannii ssp. *mexicana*	(EN, provenance: wild source)
Picea farreri	(EN, provenance: seed from cultivated tree in Exbury Garden)
Picea koyamae	(EN, provenance: wild source)
Picea likiangensis var. *montigena*	(EN, provenance: wild source)
Picea neoveitchii	(EN, provenance: wild source)
Pinus bungeana	(short-list candidate, provenance: not of known wild source)
Pinus culminicola	(EN, short-listed, provenance: wild source)
Pinus maximartinezii	(EN, short-listed, provenance: wild source)
Pinus torreyana	(EN, provenance: wild source)
Pseudolarix amabilis	(short-list candidate, provenance: not of known wild source)
Torreya taxifolia	(CR, short-listed, provenance: wild source)
Widdringtonia cedarbergensis	(EN, short-listed, provenance: wild source)

Royal Botanic Garden, Edinburgh (with 4 gardens in Scotland), UK

Abies nebrodensis	(CR, short-listed, provenance: not recorded)
Amentotaxus formosana	(CR, short-listed, provenance: wild source)
Araucaria rulei	(EN, short-listed, provenance: wild source)
Araucaria scopulorum	(EN, provenance: propagated from a wild source in cultivation)
Araucaria luxurians	(EN, provenance: wild source)
Chamaecyparis formosensis	(EN, short-listed, provenance: wild source)
Cupressus atlantica	(EN, provenance: wild source)
Cupressus goveniana var. *abramsiana*	(EN, provenance: wild source)
Dacrydium guillauminii	(CR, short-listed, provenance: wild source)
Fitzroya cupressoides	(EN, short-listed, provenance: wild source)
Glyptostrobus pensilis	(short-list candidate, provenance: wild source)
Juniperus cedrus	(EN, provenance: wild source)
Metasequoia glyptostroboides	(CR, short-listed, provenance: wild source)
Microstrobos fitzgeraldii	(EN, short-listed, provenance: not of known wild source)
Picea engelmannii ssp. *mexicana*	(EN, provenance: wild source)
Picea koyamae	(EN, provenance: wild source)
Picea likiangensis var. *montigena*	(EN, provenance: not recorded)
Picea martinezii	(CR, short-listed, provenance: wild source)
Pinus bungeana	(short-list candidate, provenance: wild source)
Pseudolarix amabilis	(short-list candidate, provenance: not of known wild source)
Taxus floridana	(CR, short-listed, provenance: wild source)
Torreya taxifolia	(CR, short-listed, provenance: wild source)
Widdringtonia cedarbergensis	(EN, short-listed, provenance: wild source)

Royal Botanic Gardens, Kew (gardens at Kew and Wakehurst Place), England, UK

Abies nebrodensis	(CR, short-listed, provenance: wild source)
Acmopyle sahniana	(CR, short-listed, provenance: wild source)
Araucaria nemorosa	(CR, short-listed, provenance: wild source)
Chamaecyparis formosensis	(EN, short-listed, provenance: not of known wild source)
Cupressus atlantica	(EN, provenance: not of known wild source)
Cupressus dupreziana	(CR, short-listed, provenance: wild source)
Cupressus goveniana var. *abramsiana*	(EN, provenance: wild source)
Fitzroya cupressoides	(EN, short-listed, provenance: wild source)
Juniperus bermudiana	(CR, short-listed, provenance: wild source)
Juniperus cedrus	(EN, provenance: wild source)
Metasequoia glyptostroboides	(CR, short-listed, provenance: wild source)
Picea chihuahuana	(EN, provenance: wild source)
Picea engelmannii ssp. *mexicana*	(EN, provenance: wild source)
Picea farreri	(EN, provenance: wild source via cutting from tree at Exbury Garden)
Picea koyamae	(EN, provenance: wild source)
Picea likiangensis var. *montigena*	(EN, provenance: not of known wild source)
Picea martinezii	(CR, short-listed, provenance: wild source)
Pinus bungeana	(short-list candidate, provenance: wild source)
Pinus torreyana	(EN, provenance: wild source)
Pseudolarix amabilis	(short-list candidate, provenance: not of known wild source)
Widdringtonia cedarbergensis	(EN, short-listed, provenance: wild source)
Wollemia nobilis	(CR, short-listed, provenance: wild source)

Royal Botanic Gardens, Sydney, Australia

Acmopyle sahniana	(CR, short-listed, provenance: wild source)
Araucaria luxurians	(EN, provenance: wild source)
Araucaria nemorosa	(CR, short-listed, provenance: wild source)
Chamaecyparis formosensis	(EN, short-listed, provenance: wild source)
Cupressus goveniana var. *abramsiana*	(EN, provenance: wild source)
Dacrydium guillauminii	(CR, short-listed, provenance: wild source)
Fitzroya cupressoides	(EN, short-listed, provenance: wild source)
Glyptostrobus pensilis	(short-list candidate, provenance: not of known wild source)
Juniperus taxifolia	(provenance: not of known wild source)
Metasequoia glyptostroboides	(CR, short-listed, provenance: wild source)
Microstrobos fitzgeraldii	(EN, short-listed, provenance: wild source)
Picea engelmannii ssp. *mexicana*	(EN, provenance: not of known wild source)
Pinus bungeana	(short-list candidate, provenance: not of known wild source)
Pinus massoniana var. *hainanensis*	(EN, provenance: not of known wild source)
Pseudolarix amabilis	(short-list candidate, provenance: not of known wild source)
Wollemia nobilis	(CR, short-listed, provenance: wild source)

that most conifers are ideal subjects with which to establish *ex situ* plantations (Page 1990b; Gardner and Thomas 1996).

There is a need to initiate and develop such programmes in other countries as well. Examples include Scandinavia with its more northerly climate and excellent network of suitable arboreta, France, Italy, and California, USA (especially for conifers of Mediterranean climates). In all these countries collaboration schemes with private landowners as well as countries of origin appear to be as possible as they proved to be in Britain and should be urgently encouraged. Similarly, some countries, such as the USA and China, both with a very large diversity of conifers as well as topography and climate, are potentially capable of conducting such programmes within their national borders. In effect China has established similar schemes for several endangered tree species, among which are a few conifers such as *Cathaya argyrophylla* and

Abies beshanzuensis. In the Southern Hemisphere, Australia with its wide range of climate conditions offers both the infrastructure and expertise to set up an *ex situ* programme for conifers of the southern continents and islands. In Tasmania, the Royal Botanic Garden at Hobart has attempted to establish a Conservation Centre focusing on the conifers of that island.

These specific programmes differ from more 'traditional' collecting and maintenance in botanic gardens and arboreta in that they seek to sample genetic diversity of a species and maintain purity of *ex situ* 'breeding populations' by preventing cross pollination between provenances, usually achieved by physical distance (out-planting). In this, their management bears elements both of botanic garden and forestry experience and will benefit from the involvement of both disciplines. It is very important to stress that only 'pure', nonhybridised seed from *ex situ* grown conifers can be considered to be of any value to the aim of species conservation. Such guarantees can usually not be given for seed gathered from trees in the commonly mixed collections of botanic gardens and arboreta; consequently the only method of propagation left open to these is by vegetative means, which naturally narrows the available gene pool.

The seed of conifers varies according to species in the time that elapses before it begins to germinate. Many conifer seeds can now be stored under controlled conditions in seed banks; the Royal Botanic Gardens, Kew are developing a large establishment in the UK with emphasis on species from arid to semi-arid regions of the world. Among these will be several threatened species of conifers, providing potential stock with a broad and 'pure' gene pool available for re-introduction programmes in the future. Coupled with the project will be training programmes especially targeted at agriculturists and foresters from the home countries of the seeds.

Ancient Pencil pines (*Athrotaxis cupressoides*) in a national park in Tasmania, Australia.

Integration of *in situ* and *ex situ* strategies

'Repatriation' is the ultimate goal of *ex situ* conservation programmes as described previously. To be at all effective, adequate protection and, where necessary, restoration of re-introduction sites must be in place prior to 'repatriation' of endangered (or locally extinct) conifers.

Research into the causes of decline, the ecology and biology (especially reproductive biology), and role in the ecosystem of the target species must be conducted. Simultaneously, experimentation with propagation techniques and monitoring of the *ex situ* sites will yield knowledge that is useful in the re-introduction phase. Both scientific programmes offer opportunities for education and training, especially for nationals of the countries where the endangered conifers originally occur and will need to be protected into the future.

Material from *ex situ* stock can be used *in situ* in three ways:

1) Reinforcement of still extant, but too small (sub-)populations to enhance the possibility of regeneration and recruitment.

2) Reintroduction to sites where a population has become extinct, and

3) Introduction to new sites (suitable habitats) where the taxon is not known to have occurred in historical time.

In all three strategies, the genetic integrity of the material supplied from *ex situ* stock is of the utmost importance. Restrictions to what material can be used are greatest with reinforcement schemes; in fact in most cases no other material than that derived from the still extant remnant population should be used (Henry 1997). The other schemes allow for a wider choice, but care should be taken to prevent hybridisation between stock from geographically widely separated origins, not only while in an *ex situ* situation, but also after (re-)introduction to the natural habitat.

The role of botanic gardens in conservation of conifers

Conifers are highly amenable subjects to introduce into cultivation, and once introduced and established, have a long life expectancy and a long reproductive age. They can be maintained in cultivation at very low cost per tree. Despite these significant assets, which make conifers quite ideal subjects for *ex situ* conservation and which would be the envy of any animal breeding programme, the cultivation of conifers by botanic gardens for conservation purposes (i.e. integration with *in situ* programmes) remains largely in its infancy. Very few species can yet be regarded as significantly protected through this route.

Strides have been made, mainly in the last decade, particularly in Australia, Denmark and Scotland, to recognise the principles of integrated *ex situ* conservation and to begin to implement them. However, these efforts are mostly due to

A. Farjon

the drive of a few dedicated individuals with usually inadequate funds at their disposal. Much more work is needed, with the full support of funds and staff made available, if botanic gardens desire to play a significant role in conifer conservation. Two stages can be recognised in the process of establishing this potentially useful conservation strategy.

The first stage

The first stage is achieving **any** successful introduction of a rare and threatened conifer taxon (species, subspecies, or variety) into cultivation. This is perhaps the least difficult stage, but then it must be stated at once that the mere holding of one or a few individual plants by a botanic garden does not constitute *ex situ* conservation. Questions of provenance, genetic diversity (purity of), sexual versus vegetative reproduction need to be addressed. Long-term management, often difficult in botanic gardens with shifting programmes and priorities, needs to be guaranteed. Plantings of more than a few individuals from different provenances need to be kept sheltered from cross-pollinating neighbours of the same or related species, if their seeds (when viable at all) are to be useful for re-introduction programmes. Like the odd rare animal in the zoo, one rare conifer in a collection, however good for the image of the botanic garden, is not conservation, although it may superficially appear to be.

However, certain benefits can still emanate from the cultivation of limited numbers of individuals of a species planted among others. The main one is the promotion of conservation awareness and the contribution botanic gardens can make. The second benefit is the experience obtained by both horticulture and science with the conditions and requirements for successful propagation and cultivation under *ex situ* conservation programmes. We think, however, that much more recorded trial-and-error experimenting should take place for these plantings to be beneficial to conservation.

The second stage

This stage begins with the commitment of a botanic garden to conifer conservation and its onward development under dedicated conditions, structured around a coherent policy and a long-term strategic plan.

This involves the active acquisition of germplasm material of a limited number of taxa, with an attempt to identify and introduce into cultivation as great a range of genetic variation as seems feasible. Known wild-origin material is essential. Older cultivated stock should only be considered when, if identified, it can be shown to represent genotypes no longer available from populations in the wild. This material can be of value especially in programmes aiming at reinforcement of genetically depleted wild populations, but should be used only if the old stock material can be shown to have come from the same locality. For new acquisitions, once in cultivation, experimental research into their genetic identity and horticultural conditions related to genetic diversity and its perpetuation is essential. The material needs to be continually bulked up into sister replicated 'populations' each containing the full spectrum of genetic diversity originally sampled. From these, out-plantings of sample 'populations' need to be established in 'safe-haven' sites, each as an insurance against loss of either the initial propagees or whole planted sites. There is also an absolute requirement that the whole process be subject to continuous documentation and recording in order to identify the progress of clones from their point of origin in the wild through their progress in cultivation. Effective clonal isolation of cultivated 'populations' each representing discrete wild populations is essential; over and above this, isolation from any cross-pollination by congeneric species must be guaranteed (Page 1994).

The large amount of separated space required prohibits the successful implementation of such a programme even for a single species within the premises of a single botanic garden. Only taxonomically highly distinct species (usually monotypic) can be expected to retain their genetic purity within the inherent diversity of a botanic garden. Consequently, it is necessary to venture outside the walls of the botanic garden and to involve many other individuals and organisations in the acquisition of planting space. The extremely long-term aspects involved are a major barrier to funding bodies, who typically want to see results within a few years at the longest. Often, very few results can be expected of such a programme this side of a period of 50 years, as several rare conifers do not produce seeds any sooner. Yet, once planted and established, most conifers soon become sufficiently self-maintaining to ensure that they are of minimal burden to management. Also, it should be pointed out that such programmes, if truly integrated, are to supplement *in situ* conservation action and need only to be undertaken when the latter seems incapable of achieving its aims alone. The efforts required are substantial, so it must be obvious that support of this kind is essential before it is undertaken.

Establishment from the outset of such *ex situ* work as joint ventures, with the accredited ownership of the germplasm material linked closely to the rights of the country of origin under the Biodiversity Convention, will be fundamental in future successful application of conifer *ex situ* programmes.

Summary of action recommendations

The two main recommendations (I and II) in the following Summary list are seen as the most urgent projects to be undertaken, the remainder follow logically from such initiatives. The Conifer Specialist Group (its members are listed in Appendix 1) is too small, and its members have too many other commitments, to be able to carry all this out under the present circumstances. Others have to take up the challenge, especially professionals from both governmental and non-governmental organisations in the regions concerned dealing with conservation. Members of the CSG can and will help and advise. In due time it is hoped their ranks will swell and, together with the people of the countries still rich in conifer diversity, the CSG may be able to curb the downward trend. As made abundantly clear in this report, there is no time left to wait: action is needed now.

Summary of Action Recommendations

Throughout this Action Plan, recommendations have been made that can bring effective conservation of threatened conifers nearer. In order to focus attention on these, we summarise them below. They are further elaborated upon in each regional account.

Conservation actions for conifers follow two basic strategic categories:

I. **Conserve existing diversity.** The overall goal of species conservation is to maintain genetic variation and diversity within a taxon. This strategy invites numerous approaches each falling within, or integrating, *in situ* or *ex situ* conservation. Information on existing and potential threats, ecology, autecology, synecology, and present population and threat status on individual species, integrated with the social dynamics of resource use and conservation, forms the foundation for this strategy.

II. **Reduce pressure on conifers as a resource.** This requires educating managers and resource consumers about sustainable harvest and use. With the few wild stands of coniferous forest remaining today and the rate of destruction constantly increasing, this strategy might best be applied by transferring the use of wild forest for timber resources to well-managed plantation forestry enterprises. Development of "greenwood" programs such as that supported by WWF and consumer education about them complement this.

Although this Action Plan does not provide specific local actions to be taken, aside from the examples of regional Action Plans and species-specific data sheets, numerous types of actions have been discussed briefly. These strategies for action are developed a little more here. It is our hope that individuals and local conservation organisations or institutions will adapt these action recommendations to local and species-specific situations and needs.

I. **Conserve existing diversity.**

A. **Strategies for prioritised taxa**. Develop individual strategies for the conifer taxa prioritised in this Action Plan and for all others listed as Critically Endangered or Endangered. Due to their likely relictual nature and distinct genetic composition, endemic taxa, which likely enjoyed a much wider distribution during the Mesozoic and Tertiary periods, should be first priority in conservation.

B. **Funding.** Establish funding sources for basic research (assessment) and, most importantly, implementation of conservation actions. As much as possible gain support for local researchers and institutions and/or international collaboration. Implementation should be supported by long-term funding.

C. **Reduce threats**. Identify principle causes of threat at the local level for individual species, develop monitoring techniques, and work towards their removal. Establish reserve areas around prioritised taxa or habitat to include a maximum of ecological variation as a measure of genetic diversity. Establish national and regional political support to ensure enforcement of conservation measures, particularly of protected areas.

D. **Conserve genetic variation.** Concern must be given for the effects of genetic depletion on species survival, or to what extent such depletion has occurred in individual cases. This is an important area of research. In the absence of direct knowledge of the genetics of a population, circumstantial evidence such as morphological and ecological variation should be considered.

E. **Protected areas**. Establish protected areas for populations that include as much genetic variation as possible.

F. **Public access**. Integrate long-term biological conservation objectives with those of public access, amenity, and ecotourism. Conservation measures must take into account the local social, economic, and political dynamics of resource use. This includes timber and non-timber uses, land use, and access to natural resources when planning protected areas. They must be considered in policy decisions from the local to the international level.

G. **Basic biological research.** Develop research and assessment programs (on range, population numbers and dynamics, ecology, reproductive biology, life history, genetic structure) for these threatened taxa. This information should provide the foundation for conservation and management decisions.

H. **Information transfer.** Design channels for information flow (and translation into accessible form) from researchers into the hands of policy makers and resource or protected area managers.

I. **Amenity planting.** Explore the use of conifers in amenity planting. Conifers can often grow in climatic and edaphic conditions unsuitable for angiosperms. Conifer species may be appropriate for recolonising degraded areas in habitat restoration. Native species should be used wherever possible.

J. Ex situ. Long-term multilevel (local to international) programmes should focus on target priorities of the countries to which threatened species are native. Promote interchange of germplasm material between accredited conservation programmes. Identify botanic gardens world-wide with potential and expertise to safeguard ex situ material and to guarantee its genetic purity for later reintroduction programmes.

II. Reduce pressure on conifers as a resource.

A. Sustainable timber management. Encourage collaboration between international forestry agencies and local tree utilisation programmes with an aim to reduce pressure on wild populations of useful species. Sustainable management of timber and non-timber resources should be promoted and established. Before the exploitation of non-timber resources, such as the chemical taxol from the yew, decimates a population, maintain low harvest levels and pay careful attention to population regeneration.

B. Education. Educate conifer resource users and consumers about sustainable harvest goals.

C. Diversify the timber market. Promote wood from faster growing and more realistically renewable conifer species. Instil an appreciation by consumers of the irreplaceable nature of the very slow growing species, so that the public will demand alternatives.

D. Legislation and Certification. Explore usefulness of CITES listing for conifer conservation as well as forest certification programs like those supported by WWF.

References

Baillie, J. 1996. Analysis. In: IUCN. *1996 IUCN Red List of Threatened Animals*. IUCN The World Conservation Union, Gland, Switzerland.

Beck, C. B. (ed.) 1988. *Origin and Evolution of gymnosperms*. Columbia University Press, New York.

BGCS 1989. *The Botanic Garden Conservation Strategy*. Botanical Gardens Conservation Secretariat. WWF and IUCN, Gland, Switzerland.

Challinor, D. & D. B. Wingate 1971. The struggle for survival of the Bermuda cedar. *Biol. Conserv.* 3(3): 220-222.

Enright, N. J. and R. S. Hill (eds.) 1995. *Ecology of the Southern Conifers*. Melbourne University Press, Melbourne.

Farjon, A. 1998. *World Checklist and Bibliography of Conifers*. Royal Botanic Gardens, Kew.

Farjon, A., C. N. Page and N. Schellevis 1993. A preliminary world list of threatened conifer taxa. *Biodiv. Conserv.* 2: 304-326.

Gardner, M. F. and P. Thomas 1996. The Conifer Conservation Programme. *The New Plantsman* 3 (1): 5-22.

Henry, J.-P. 1997. Integrating *in situ* and *ex situ* conservation. *Plant Talk* 8: 23-25.

IUCN. 1994. *IUCN Red List Categories*, IUCN, Gland, Switzerland.

IUCN. 1996. *1996 IUCN Red List of Threatened Animals*. IUCN - The World Conservation Union, Gland, Switzerland.

Johnson, D. (ed.) and the IUCN/SSC Palm Specialist Group. 1996. *Palms: Their Conservation and Sustained Utilization. Status Survey and Conservation Action Plan*. IUCN, Gland, Switzerland and Cambridge, UK.

Oldfield, S., C. Lusty and A. MacKinven 1998. *The World List of Threatened Trees*. World Conservation Press, Cambridge, UK.

Page, C. N. 1990a. The families and genera of conifers. Pp. 278-361 in Kubitsky, K. (ed.). *The Families and Genera of Vascular Plants*. Vol. 1. Springerverlag, Berlin & Heidelerberg.

Page, C. N. 1990b. The role of Edinburgh Botanic Garden in the international conservation of conifers. *International Dendrology Society Yearbook 1989*: 112-115.

Page, C. N. 1994. The *ex situ* conservation of temperate rainforest conifer tree species: a British-based programme. *Biodiv. Conserv.* 3: 191-199.

Page, C. N. 1998. The *ex situ* conservation of conifers, its limitations and potential role. *International Dendrology Society Yearbook 1997*: 47-50.

Pauw, C. A. & H. P. Linder 1997. Tropical African cedars (Widdringtonia, Cupressaceae): systematics, ecology and conservation status. *Bot. J. Linn. Soc.* 123 (4): 297-319.

Walter, K. S. and H. J. Gillett (eds.) 1998. *1997 IUCN Red List of Threatened Plants*. Compiled by the World Conservation Monitoring Centre. IUCN - The World Conservation Union, Gland, Switzerland and Cambridge, UK.

Chapter 3
Regional Accounts

Introduction

The accounts in the third and fourth chapters of the Action Plan have been intended to focus on the 'hot spots' and the short-listed taxa mentioned in chapter two. A preferred requirement has been that they be researched and written by members of the Conifer Specialist Group working in and, if possible, native to the regions concerned, presenting the problems as perceived from within individual areas. Involvement at regional levels is all-important to obtain a broad base of support for this Action Plan. For these reasons, the compilers (Farjon and Page) have asked members preferably to prepare reports of the regions designated as 'hot spots' and of the species short-listed. However, we have not in any way wanted to indicate that conifer conservation outside the 'hot spots' or of species not on the short-list is not important. Although the reports highlight issues at the local level, they likely are applicable to challenges faced elsewhere.

Much of the effort put into this Action Plan by the compilers has gone into the stimulation and coaching of these regional inputs. The professional input of all those who responded positively has made the third and fourth chapters of the Action Plan possible. It is acknowledged that while basic requirements as to content had to be met, approaches and styles of presentation among regions and authors would differ. We have judged that it is appropriate to retain these differences, rather than heavily edit the reports. In many countries there is a predominantly national emphasis on the use and conservation of national resources. Inevitably, these biases are reflected to the extent that in some accounts the species discussed are not of global conservation concern. We have decided to incorporate the reports in their entirety.

More problematic has been the difficulty of obtaining accounts for all the 'hot spots' and all the short-listed species. In several cases (e.g. Borneo and New Guinea) this is at least partly due to the as yet fragmentary knowledge of the status of many of the conifers that occur there. Years of additional basic groundwork is needed. In other areas, political overtones may have proved restrictive. And lastly, but perhaps most importantly, the Conifer Specialist Group was only established in 1987 and recruitment of sufficient qualified members to start gathering information took a further year or more. This has given us barely 10 years, with a membership that has grown only slowly to 37 members, to produce the Red List as well as the Action Plan for conifers. On account of the virtually world-wide range of conifers and their conservation problems, this is too short a timeframe to accomplish it all. The dilemma is that to wait longer for the group to grow and do more, would put the conifers at risk even more since much of the recommended action needs to be taken now. Reports of the following major areas are not yet available: Borneo, Chile, China, Japan, Mexico, New Guinea, and Taiwan. For several of the short-listed species too, even though we know enough to assign a category of threat, detailed information needed for a report with sound recommendations is still wanting. Thus, the majority of short-listed species are not yet dealt with here. We urgently need to find members capable and willing to undertake these reports. We therefore, while acknowledging that the gaps need to be filled, urge that proposals of the Action Plan begin to be implemented from the earliest possible opportunity.

Regional Action Plan

Conifers of New Caledonia

Alistair Watt
Otway Ridge Arboretum, Victoria, Australia

Description of the area

The French Pacific territory of New Caledonia justly deserves its reputation in the botanical world for its rich and varied flora. In the instance of the conifers, particularly those of southern hemisphere (Gondwanan) origins, we see this richness well-reflected. Although of small size on a world scale (~19,000km^2), the island has no fewer than 43 species of conifers, of which all are endemic, in 14 genera, of which three are endemic (Laubenfels 1972). To put this distinctive flora in perspective, we should consider that the whole world total number of conifer species is only around 630, and that in New Caledonia we are considering a land area similar to that of the state of Massachusetts in the USA (21,500km^2) or the country of Wales in the UK (21,000km^2). Thus, no other comparable territory remotely approaches this degree of conifer diversity. It is one of the major conifer 'hot spots' recognised in this Conifer Action Plan.

It is natural to assume that with so many species in such a small area, some of them will have limited abundance and distribution. For example, *Dacrydium guillauminii*, found only in a very restricted area of the Rivière des Lacs basin, is undoubtedly one of the rarest conifers in the world. The unique parasitic podocarp *Parasitaxus ustus* is certainly one of the most unusual. To add to the value of this particular island biota, it is important to consider the origins of the conifer families. It is becoming increasingly clear that the New Caledonian conifer flora reflects its relictual character, the ancient forests of Gondwana with, for example, clear connections with the Tasmanian flora of around 40 million years ago, where climatic conditions were totally different from those of today.

Many of the 43 species of New Caledonian conifers are rare and endangered or threatened. The greatest threat is undoubtedly that of human-generated wildfires, followed by the effects of mining activities in certain areas. Often the latter indirectly increases the former: mining means roads, roads mean access, people cause fires. Different species may be subject to different threats, or a combination of threats, however the majority of these can be significantly reduced. The purpose of this report will be to summarise the conservation status of the conifers of New Caledonia, including existing threats to species populations, and to make suggestions for immediate action to overcome these problems.

Conifer distribution in New Caledonia

Despite the small land area of New Caledonia, there exists a very wide range of plant community habitats, which is reflected in conifer species distribution throughout the territory. New Caledonia includes 'high' islands of continental origin, volcanic emergents and coral islets. Plant communities extend from the littoral environment, through open heathland and sclerophyll dry forest to high altitude montane rainforest. Most savannas occurring on the Grande Terre are man-made secondary vegetation (Morat *et al.* 1981). Communities are influenced by climatic factors, e.g. rainfall varying between 800mm and 8000mm per annum. Occasionally, temperatures may reach frost conditions on summits such as Mt. Humboldt. In addition, there is an enormous variation in soil substrates, from the vast extent of the sterile and mineralised ultramafics of the southern massifs, the rich mica schists of the Mt. Panié massif to the calcareous limestones of offshore islands. The New Caledonian conifer flora, therefore, has speciated to occupy niches in these various situations. This is well illustrated in the Araucariaceae, with 13 species occupying a range from sea level to an altitude of 1400m, and in Libocedrus, with three species from 150m to 1600m altitude. Jaffré (1995) has well summarised the distribution of all New Caledonian species.

The conservation situation in New Caledonia

New Caledonia is essentially composed of a main island, Grande Terre, approximately 450km long by 50km wide, with extending offshore islands, and a line of volcanic islands, the Loyalty Islands, to the east at about 100km distance. Although New Caledonia is an overseas territory of France, the principal responsibility for conservation issues is on a self-rule basis and is determined separately in each of the three provinces of New Caledonia. The territory is politically and administratively divided in Province Sud, Province Nord, and the Loyalty Islands. All this could be further complicated by any changes in the island's political status. Each province applies distinct and differing systems of land management. The Province Sud, based around Nouméa, the capital, has a small but active Service de l'Environnement. The Province Nord undertakes conservation management through the forestry services, which have a special section devoted to conservation, based in Koumac. The Loyalty Islands do not appear to have an agency or a policy.

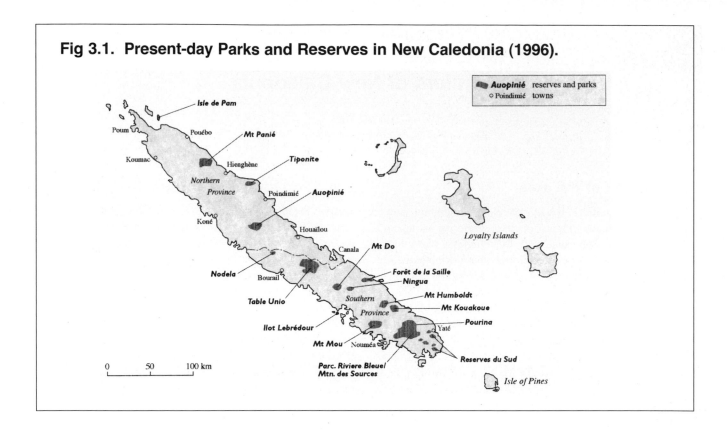

Fig 3.1. Present-day Parks and Reserves in New Caledonia (1996).

Province Sud

This administrative region possesses a significant number of land areas gazetted for some degree of protected status. The major reserves are the Parc Territorial de la Rivière Bleue and the adjoining Rèserve naturelle integrale de la Montagne des Sources. These two areas, close to Nouméa, can be equated, in their levels of protection, to the status of a National Park in Australia or the USA - specifically in the degree of unalienable protection and management level afforded. The Montagne des Sources is essentially closed for public use as a protected water catchment area (i.e. no tourism), whereas the Rivière Bleue park with tourist facilities, access drives, and walks etc., is a more typical 'park'. The latter is also patrolled by rangers on a daily schedule. Fortunately, these two parks contain highly significant sites for conifer conservation in a range of habitats. Therefore, adequate administrative protection is in place for conifer species including *Acmopyle pancheri, Agathis ovata, Araucaria bernieri, A. muelleri, Callitris neocaledonica, Libocedrus austrocaledonica, Neocallitropsis pancheri, Podocarpus decumbens,* and *P. gnidioides*. Conservation status for these parks is excellent; however, we can clearly identify that there is a significant risk from wildfire that continues to threaten certain areas. Much has been done to maintain a fire-fighting force in place, including the use of a helicopter, to extinguish fires that threaten the Montagne des Sources as this area also serves as the source of drinking water for the capital. As a result, no major fires have occurred there in 30 years (J. M. Veillon, pers. comm.). Similar vigilance is needed for other areas within these parks, especially in relation to tourist camping activities.

In addition to the above two major reserves, there are a dozen or so sites listed as flora (or fauna) reserves (Jaffré *et al.* 1998). These are intended to give a degree of protection for the conservation of specific plant or animal communities or species. These reserves, although inherently highly significant, do not necessarily afford the quality of adequate long-term protection. Mining activities could still proceed in some instances, and damage from excessive visitor numbers could occur in some relatively unchecked sites. The most sensitive site in this category is undoubtedly the flora reserve at the Chûtes de la Madeleine (Madeleine Falls) on the Rivière des Lacs to the south of Nouméa. This small reserve of 400ha contains among seven species three conifer 'treasures': *Dacrydium guillauminii* (CR), *Neocallitropsis pancheri* (VU) and *Retrophyllum minor* (EN). For the first species it is virtually the only existing site; for the last, none of the most important populations are within a reserve (Jaffré, pers. comm.). At present this site is very much exposed to damage from excessive visitor numbers in a too small area. However, this could be managed with better practices applied to control visitor movement through the reserve. Also included in this special reserve category and significant for their conifer populations are:

- Mt. Do, with e.g. *Araucaria biramulata, A. laubenfelsii;*
- Mt. Humboldt, with e.g. *Araucaria humboldtensis, Libocedrus chevalieri, Podocarpus gnidioides;*
- Mt. Kouakoué, a new reserve with possibly the most diverse range of New Caledonian conifers in a virtually unspoiled area of c. 7000ha;
- Mt. Mou, with e.g. *Acmopyle pancheri, Dacrydium lycopodioides.*

42

Neocallitropsis pancheri, Plaine des Lacs, New Caledonia.

Outside these reserves are extensive areas of significant maquis shrub lands and various forest types. Most of those situated on the relevant 'mineralised' zones are held under mining leases, private land, or forestry extraction zones. In these areas, protection is very much on an ad hoc basis and inadequate; e.g. one of the most significant sites for *Parasitaxus ustus* known on Mt. Dzumac was in 1995 on the verge of destruction by the 'illegal' extraction of forest soil for use in pot plant production. The Service de l'Environnement of Province Sud has now taken steps to prevent this from happening again (Jaffré, pers. comm.). Especially for this difficult to find unique conifer, a thorough inventory and mapping programme is much needed.

Retrophyllum minor in a river on the Plaine des Lacs, New Caledonia.

Province Nord

It is convenient, for simplicity, to divide the northern province into eastern and western sections. The east, or wet side of the island has several areas gazetted for flora (or fauna) reserve status. The most significant of these for conifers is that of the Mt. Panié massif, which affords protection to a range of rare conifers including *Agathis montana, A. schmidii, Austrotaxus spicata*, and *Parasitaxus ustus*. The greatest threat to these east coast wet forest reserves would be logging under future decision-making. The isolated stand of *Libocedrus yateensis* recently found near Hienghène (Roche Ouaième) is not protected at present.

On the west coast of the Province Nord, problems for conifer conservation are more critical. Along the chain of mountains are many 'island' massifs of ultramafic rock such as Koniambo, Paéoua, and Kapeto. These can have a significant conifer population e.g. *Araucaria montana* on Mt. Koniambo. The recent and interesting discovery on Mt. Paéoua (Jaffré *et al.* 1987) of relict populations of *Libocedrus austrocaledonica, Neocallitropsis pancheri*, and *Parasitaxus ustus* indicates that much botanical investigation remains to be done in the Northern province. The site on Mt. Paéoua is an example of an extremely important site for conifers lacking any legal protection. They occur inside areas designated for mining leases, although the low grade ore does not at present justify extraction. Fires are the principal menace to these stands at present. There is naturally a discrepancy between both provinces when it comes to protected sites due to the fact that the north is more sparsely populated than the south, so that population pressures on the environment are generally less severe; moreover, the present system of reserves antedates the setting up of conservation agencies in both provinces.

Loyalty Islands

Much of the forested area of the Loyalty Islands is held as native, private land, hence there do not appear to be conservation management practices applied. At present, this is not a significant problem for consideration here, as the only conifer species, *Araucaria columnaris*, is relatively abundant. However, should land clearing or excessive logging occur, it would be necessary to impose some kind of reserve status for the most significant *Araucaria* forest areas.

Wildfire in the environment

Although there is a great deal of discussion in New Caledonia regarding dangers from mining exploitation, this is not at present the major problem. The principal threat is wildfire. An uncontrolled fire on the Montagne des Sources, however unlikely this may seem to some given present vigilance, could eliminate the majority of the island's individuals of *Neocallitropsis pancheri*. Even in recent years, this species has been badly affected by fires in the area of the Plaine des Lacs. Similarly, a fire along the upper Rivière Bleue would devastate *Libocedrus yateensis*. On the western flank of Mt. Mou one can observe the fire scars which have reached up to 1200m altitude where *Dacrydium lycopodi-*

oides occurs. In the dry spring season such fires can even have a devastating effect on 'wet' rainforest.

Fires which could cause this type of damage should not be underestimated. They can be started accidentally from campfires, or deliberately, for instance by those who want to reduce the 'brush' for livestock grazing or want easier access, such as hunters. Many parts of the world have similar problems, e.g. Central America, Brazil, Eastern Africa, California, and South-eastern Australia. This will be dealt with below under 'recommendations'. The absence of an adequate legally imposed fire control regime is the biggest threat to the unique New Caledonian flora, both conifers and non-conifers.

Conservation status of individual threatened species in New Caledonia

ARAUCARIACEAE

Agathis corbassonii de Laub.
Widespread, but not common, in the northern half of the Grande Terre, but threatened by over exploitation from logging locally and perhaps increasingly in the future without further protective regulation. Vulnerable under criteria B1 + 2c.

Agathis lanceolata (Lindl. ex Sebert and Pancher) Warb.
Originally very common in the south; much reduced (particularly large specimens) through over exploitation. Protected in several reserves and in Rivière Bleue and Montagne des Sources. Protection of genetic diversity is important. Lower Risk, conservation dependent.

Agathis montana de Laub.
Confined to Mt. Panié massif of NW New Caledonia, protected in Mt. Panié reserve but illegal logging might pose a problem in the near future. Lower Risk, conservation dependent.

Agathis moorei (Lindl.) Mast.
Widespread throughout the main island (Grande Terre), but a substantial decline has occurred through over exploitation in recent years, whereby there is also a risk of genetic depletion. Vulnerable under criteria B1 +2c.

Agathis ovata (C. Moore ex Veillard) Warb.
Widespread in Province Sud on ultramafic maquis sites; protected in Rivière Bleue and Mt. des Sources park and reserve.

The rich vegetation with several endemic conifers on the Plaine des Lacs, New Caledonia.

Wildfires are a threat in some areas. Lower Risk, conservation dependent.

Araucaria bernieri J. Buchholz
Widespread in Province Sud on ultramafic sites, dispersed in small populations in wet forests. Protected in Rivière Bleue park and Mt. des Sources reserve and other reserves. Lower Risk, conservation dependent.

Araucaria biramulata J. Buchholz
Dispersed along the central mountain chain on rocky slopes in Province Sud. Protected in Rivière Bleue park and Mt. Do and Pic du Pin reserves. Lower Risk, conservation dependent.

Araucaria humboldtensis J. Buchholz
In isolated populations on mountain ridges and slopes above 800m in Province Sud; protected in several mountain reserves. Lower Risk, conservation dependent.

Araucaria laubenfelsii Corbasson
Dispersed but not common in the ultramafic massifs of Province Sud; protected on Mt. Do, Mt. Mou and elsewhere. Lower Risk, conservation dependent.

Araucaria luxurians (Brongn. and Gris) de Laub.
Confined to a few coastal sites on ultramafic rocks near human habitation areas, where there is a continuing decline and erosion of the sites in part due to mining activities. Populations less than five and no protection in a reserve. Fires are a secondary hazard. Endangered under criteria B1 + 2c.

Araucaria muelleri (Carrière) Brongn. and Gris
Southern mountain ridges on ultramafics, in isolated and small populations. This species is protected in Mt. des Sources, in the Rivière Bleue Park, and in other reserves, but grows slow and is susceptible to the fire hazard in several places. Lower Risk, conservation dependent.

Araucaria nemorosa de Laub.
A single small population on the coast near human habitation at Port Boisé on tribal (private) land, where it is both being cut and threatened by fires. There were plans to establish in 1997 a small reserve for part of the population on the eastern side of the bay of Port Boisé. Critically Endangered under criteria B1 + 2c.

Araucaria rulei F. Muell.
Dispersed on ultramafic rocks and soils in the NW of Grande Terre in small populations. There is a decline of 20% or more in most populations due to expansion of mining operations in the area (nickel) while regeneration is poor and growth very slow. It is not protected in a reserve at all. Endangered under criterion C1.

Araucaria schmidii de Laub.
Occurs in a few high altitude sites on Mt. Panié massif; pro-

tected in Mt. Panié reserve under active management. Its restricted occurrence qualifies it as Vulnerable under criterion D2 despite its present protection in a reserve.

Araucaria scopulorum de Laub.
Restricted to two to three small populations in coastal sites on the eastern coast of Province Nord, in the vicinity of human habitation where it is susceptible to fire. It is outside any reserve. Endangered under criteria B1 + 2c.

Araucaria subulata Vieill.
Dispersed in the ultramafic massifs of southern New Caledonia, where it is protected in the Mt. des Sources and Rivière Bleue reserve and park. Outside these reserves there is a risk from (illegal) logging locally. Lower Risk, conservation dependent.

CUPRESSACEAE

Callitris neocaledonica Dummer
Limited to the higher altitudes in localised populations on the southern massifs; protected in Mt. des Sources and Mt. Humboldt reserves, but fire is a hazard. Lower Risk, conservation dependent.

Callitris sulcata (Parl.) Schltr.
Limited to three river drainages/valleys near Nouméa, where it is not common. Timber extraction is reported from the Comboui valley. Fires are an additional threat, while regeneration is often poor. Protection in ad hoc river bank reserves is inadequate. Endangered under criteria B1 + 2c.

Libocedrus austrocaledonica Brogn. and Gris
On a few higher mountains in Province Sud where it is dispersed in humid forests. It is protected in Mt. des Sources reserve and Rivière Bleue park, but the population on Mt. Paéoua is potentially threatened by wildfires and appears not to regenerate well. Lower Risk, conservation dependent.

Libocedrus chevalieri J. Buchholz
Isolated populations on the summits of Mts. Humboldt and Kouakoué only, where it is protected in reserves. It is restricted to high altitude maquis which is highly susceptible to fire; due to the limited size of the populations it is therefore at considerable risk. Endangered under criteria B1 + 2de.

Libocedrus yateensis Guillaumin
Restricted to a few kilometres along two rivers in southern New Caledonia and a single record from the central part of Grande Terre at Roche Ouaieme. Protected in Rivière Bleue park (Rivière Bleue de Yaté) but not in the Ouinné location. Vulnerable under criteria B1+3d, C2a.

Neocallitropsis pancheri (Carrière) de Laub.
Nearly confined to less than 10 small populations, in total not exceeding an area of occupation greater than 150ha, on ultra-mafics in Province Sud, one recently discovered in Province Nord, most are in protected areas but also in environment with a high fire risk. In the past exploited for oil extraction. Listed by Jaffré *et al.* (1998) as LRcd, but this species fulfils the criteria A1c, B1 + 2b under Vulnerable, which therefore prevails.

PODOCARPACEAE

Acmopyle pancheri (Brongn. and Gris) Pilg.
Widespread in the humid, shady forests of the Grande Terre. Locally threatened by changes in land use after logging and by mining, but protected especially in the southern parks and reserves. More protected areas are needed in the north. Lower Risk, near threatened.

Dacrydium guillauminii J. Buchholz
Extremely restricted in two or three small populations on the Plaine des Lacs; inadequately protected in the Chûtes de la Madeleine reserve. Strictly rheophitic and susceptible to fire, tourism, and possibly pollution from (future) upstream mining operations. Critically Endangered under criteria B1 + 2c, C1.

Dacrydium lycopodioides Brongn. and Gris
Restricted populations on the higher parts of the southern massifs on ultramafic rocks. Regeneration is good, it is protected in Mt. Humboldt, Mt. Mou, and Mt. Ningua reserves. Lower Risk, conservation dependent.

[Plants that were recently found by A. Watt at the Chûtes de la Madeleine appeared to be intermediate in vegetative characters and habitat between *D. araucarioides* and *D. guillauminii*; if turning out to be a new taxon (*D."suprinii"*) very few specimens are known and it could be endangered. Good taxonomic research, including molecular work, is recommended before this is taken up.]

Parasitaxus ustus (Vieill.) de Laub.
Widely dispersed but small populations, dependent on host (*Falcatifolium taxoides*); its total range and occurrence are probably as yet incompletely known. Despite concern about the safety of some populations, the species is not threatened at present. It is protected by law in New Caledonia. Lower Risk, near threatened.

Podocarpus decumbens N. E. Gray
Restricted to three known sites in the southern ultramafic massifs of Province Sud; protected in Rivière Bleue and Mt. des Sources park and reserve, in wet forest. It qualifies for Vulnerable under criterion D2 despite its occurrence within nature reserves.

Retrophyllum minor (Carrière) C. N. Page
Restricted to river banks and lake shores (rheophytic) on the Plaine des Lacs. Protected, but inadequately, in the Chûtes de la Madeleine reserve. Threatened by fires in the dry season. Endangered under criteria C1 + 2a.

The beauty spot 'Chûtes de la Madeleine' on the Plaine des Lacs, New Caledonia, is a 'hot spot' for endemic and extremely rare

TAXACEAE

Austrotaxus spicata R. H. Compton
Dispersed small populations on acidic substrates in wet forest in mountains of Province Nord. Protected in Table Union and Mt. Panié reserves. Taxol-related exploitation, in case the chemical were demonstrated to occur, might become a risk. Lower Risk, near threatened.

Recommendations for conservation action

Conservation of whole plant communities and ecosystems is considered the most effective strategy, especially since most New Caledonian conifers are only components of a diverse vegetation. Legal and managerial protection needs to be made effective on the ground in order to ensure success. This involves allocation of resources, both funds and manpower, to properly manage and protect the nature reserves, which, if of sufficient number and extent to cover all plant communities, will then automatically ensure conifer species conservation.

1. Wildfire control measures

It is impossible to ignore the overwhelming problem and threat that human-caused wildfire poses to both the habitat and individual species of conifers in New Caledonia. This threat is particularly severe on the ultramafic massifs where the terrain, the critical dry season, and the inflammable nature of the vegetation make control of such fires almost impossible. It is clearly necessary for the relevant New Caledonian authorities to take all actions possible to discourage any deliberate fire threat. This could involve imposition of fines heavy enough to discourage offenders, and even jail sentences. In some cases the problem may arise from the traditional use of fire as a land clearing 'tool', which unfortunately becomes a serious threat to remaining intact plant communities. On the other hand, there is anecdotal evidence that the military plays a not insignificant role in causing unintentional serious bush fires. In this latter case we have an organisation where existing lines of responsibility and discipline can be immediately exploited to eliminate the problem. Clearly in this section of New Caledonian society, it would

be anticipated that an anti-wildfire education programme would have an immediate effect.

These efforts could be combined with proclamations of 'Total Fire Ban' days, as practised in Victoria, Australia, where such critical high wind/high temperature/dry vegetation conditions can combine to give potentially disastrous situations. Access to certain areas, e.g. the Chûtes de la Madeleine and the Montagne des Sources, may have to be prohibited on such days. Legally-imposed penalties could be combined with an education programme, e.g. on television and in newspapers, as to why fires should not be lit. This will be expensive and possibly difficult in application, but there is no alternative. One would have to consider the value to conservation and in the long run to the considerable ecotourism potential of the island. Relevant New Caledonian authorities could communicate with, for example, the forestry authorities of Victoria, Australia, to obtain up-to-date policies and methods. This problem of wildfire prevention must be tackled immediately and resolutely. Fortunately, the Province Sud has commenced to develop a programme of education which deserves every encouragement and support. It is also imperative that a much more proactive attitude be adopted to extinguishing and controlling fires already alight. The military establishment in New Caledonia could play a more active and useful role as they obviously have both the material resources and the personnel to curb this menace to biodiversity.

2. Management of the nature reserves

At present, only the Province Sud, through the Service de l'Environnement, has any kind of adequate management system, with the Rivière Bleue Park rapidly improving. Unfortunately, the specific flora reserves are usually not adequately protected. Although gazetted for conservation reasons, i.e. for particular species or communities, management is lacking for proper control of visitors to these reserves. For conifers this has become particularly obvious at the Chûtes de la Madeleine. A balance between conifer conservation and tourism could be achieved if the tourism and scientific values of the reserves were quantified and necessary funds applied for proper management, ranger supervision, walkways, designated campsites, waste disposal etc. Over the years an increase in tourism 'away from the beaches' has been apparent. Not all of this is ecotourism, but the part that is will be increasingly dependent on sound reserve management.

The new catch-phrase is indeed 'ecotourism', and it has significant potentials, particularly in stimulating protection of natural forests for passive recreation. In this instance, we have a section of the tourist market, often possessing a high discretionary spending ability, whose main object as a traveller is to experience, and learn from, the natural environment of the country being visited. These tourists will, for example, make a specific visit (and spend money on accommodation, guides, car hire etc. in doing so) to a particular reserve or park that is of interest to them. This segment of the tourist market is rapidly growing: ecotourism will be the

The touristic developments near the 'Chûtes de la Madeleine' are an immediate threat to the survival of one of the rarest conifers.

key to increasing visitor numbers to New Caledonia and particularly to getting them beyond Nouméa. Therefore, ecotourism must and will impart a clear monetary value to the reserves and parks of the island: an economic asset that will in turn justify and necessitate that a proper management regime be implemented.

3. Recommendations for new reserves and expansion of existing reserves

More reserves must be created, and these must be inalienable and safeguarded against future exploitation. In some cases, access could be greatly improved to produce a significant tourist destination, e.g. Plaine des Lacs, Mts. Dzumac-Upper Ouinné River, Mt. Paéoua. Access to a botanical reserve, e.g. to Mt. Do or Mt. Koniambo, would encourage tourists to seek accommodation in towns such as Boulupari or Koné. The reserves would of course not only fill requirements for further conservation of specific conifer populations but also for communities containing other fabulous New Caledonian flora.

However, these recommendations are made from the point of view of further protecting conifer species. Obviously, final decisions on new or enlarged reserves will be made upon assessment of the entire known biota of the island as a whole.

1. Plaine des Lacs
Incorporating the whole basin of the Rivière des Lacs. This would include populations of *Dacrydium guillauminii*, *Neocallitropsis pancheri*, and other rare conifers.

2. Mt. Dzumac-Upper Ouinné River
This would include the major sites of the rare *Parasitaxus ustus* and the road-accessible humid forests with *Acmopyle pancheri* among other species. An upgraded road to this area would be a great asset to tourism, as there is very little general two-wheel-drive vehicular access to the mountain zones in the southern massifs.

3. Mt. Kouakoué
The summit area of this inaccessible massif contains the greatest concentration of New Caledonian conifers. It could be designated as a specific conifer study reference reserve. Action is well underway by the Service de l'Environnement (Province Sud) to achieve this goal, and in 1995, as a first step, a special reserve for flora and fauna was established in the summit area.

4. Plateau Dogny-Table Union
This area could easily be developed for a tourist 'territorial park' and would include good sites for conservation of *Austrotaxus spicata* in particular. The local hotel owner indicated his enthusiastic support for this suggestion, and he is already co-operating to that end with the Province Sud.

5. Mt. Paéoua
It is extraordinary that there are no reserves to protect any of the 'island' massifs of the north-west coast. Mt. Paéoua with its highly interesting conifer flora is obviously at the top of the list of priorities. The assembly of relict conifer species in

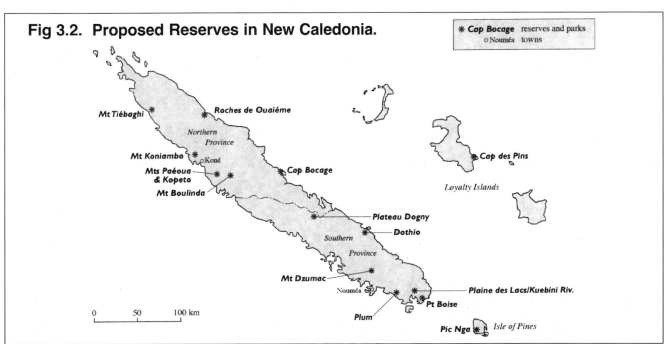

Fig 3.2. Proposed Reserves in New Caledonia.

* Cap Bocage   reserves and parks
o Nouméa   towns

Mt Tiébaghi
Roches de Ouaiéme
Northern Province
Mt Koniambo
o Koné
Mts Paéoua & Kopeto
Cap Bocage
Mt Boulinda
Cap des Pins
Loyalty Islands
Plateau Dogny
Dothio
Southern Province
Mt Dzumac
Nouméa
Plaine des Lacs/Kuebini Riv.
Pt Boise
Plum
Pic Nga
Isle of Pines

0   50   100 km

such a restricted, isolated area is quite outstanding. Perhaps the part of Mt. Koniambo with the *Araucaria montana* population could be added. These massifs have significant value for mineral extraction, which makes it all the more pressing to conserve some areas to reach a balanced decision about the management of this mountain range. The area has outstanding scenery with superb views from some of these mountain summits, which would be a tourist asset for Province Nord if carefully developed.

6. Port Boisé

A reserve is necessary to protect the only known stand of *Araucaria nemorosa*. The stand is on tribal lands so negotiations would be necessary with landowners. Planning was underway to establish a special reserve for flora and fauna on the eastern side of the bay in 1997.

7. Upper Kuebini River basin

This area contains recently discovered populations of *Neocallitropsis pancheri* and also *Agathis ovata* in what appears to be a primary forest not ravaged by fires. The existing small botanical reserve should be expanded so that this area could reflect an original section of vegetation not altered by human impact. In this instance, a reserve closed to the public would be necessary to ensure protection against wildfire. Both this reserve and the expanded Plaine des Lacs reserve (1) could be developed in conjunction with planning for the proposed nearby Goro mine - thus combining conservation, tourism, and mining development economic strategies in an integrated plan of land management.

8. Boulinda Massif

A reserve is required to protect a representative and significant population of *Araucaria rulei* e.g. Boulinda Massif and/or Tiébaghi. Preferably, this reserve should be accessible for tourism potential and could add welcome destination value to the whole of the NW Karé-Koumac area.

9. East coast, Roches de Ouaième

A reserve would be required to protect the summit area of this interesting, isolated mountain with *Araucaria* spp. and other species.

10. East coast, Dothio

A reserve would be required here to protect *Araucaria scopulorum*.

11. Loyalty Islands

Gazetted reserve to protect representative habitat for *Araucaria columnaris*. There is potential for tourism to be developed in connection with a designated reserve.

12. Ile des Pins (Isle of Pines)

A reserve is required centred on Pic N'ga. Besides the common *Araucaria columnaris*, there are sites with *Podocarpus* sp. on the southern slopes. The collections of MacKee cited by de Laubenfels (1972) as *P. sylvestris* appear to be an unknown species. Such a reserve would also protect vital water supplies, while there certainly is potential for tourism, which would be attracted by its advertisement e.g. on a map and pictures. This area is tribal, i.e. private land, and a reserve needs to be negotiated, but the added tourist destination value could be an incentive.

Dacrydium araucarioides is fairly widespread on Grande Terre, New Caledonia, and not threatened with extinction.

Ex situ conservation of endangered species

In some specific instances, a real direct threat exists to warrant the insurance of propagating and 'holding' endangered species at other locations. Much progress in this field has been made by both Alistair Watt of the Otway Ridge Arboretum in Victoria and the Melbourne Botanic Gardens, Victoria. This work needs to continue, but its efforts must be re-directed into action in New Caledonia. A horticultural training programme for personnel from the Département de l'Environnement could be easily and inexpensively undertaken from Australia if funds were available. The following species are suggested to be priorities for this programme:

Callitris sulcata
Dacrydium guillauminii
Libocedrus chevalieri
Libocedrus yateensis
Neocallitropsis pancheri
Podocarpus decumbens
Retrophyllum minor

A range of infraspecific genetic variation must be covered by this programme. The Conifer Specialist Group supports the proposal of M. Marcel Boulet (Département de l'Environnement, Nouméa) to establish a reference arboretum at the Rivière Bleue Park in conjunction with this programme and as an addition to *in situ* protection management. Eventually, re-planting species on particular sites from where they have been eliminated, for example by fire, could be an objective.

Although not considered threatened in a higher category, *Parasitaxus ustus* is of interest because of its peculiar parasitic relationship with another conifer, *Falcatifolium taxoides* (both Podocarpaceae) and its complicated and little understood mechanisms of regeneration. Developmental studies undertaken by Conifer Specialist Group member Dr. Philippe Woltz at the University of Marseille (France) will help to further understanding of this conifer. It is also hoped that a special project can be undertaken at the Royal Botanic Garden, Tasmania, in conjunction with the University of

Tasmania, to investigate seed viability and the germination factors involved with this species. Initial funding has been made available and liaison with New Caledonian authorities will be made in the near future.

Enhanced legal protection for threatened species
The following species of conifers endemic in New Caledonia merit consideration for special legal protection as endangered plants, both in provincial legislation and international convention: *Dacrydium guillauminii, Neocallitropsis pancheri, Parasitaxus ustus*, and perhaps, if taxol-related compounds are confirmed in it, *Austrotaxus spicata*. The only species legally protected under New Caledonian law at present is *Parasitaxus ustus*.

Acknowledgements

All opinions and conclusions are those of the author. However, much help and factual information were provided by colleagues in New Caledonia, particularly: M. Marcel Boulet and M. Bernard Suprin of the Département de l'Environnement, Province Sud; Dr. Tanguy Jaffré (member of the CSG), ORSTOM, Nouméa; Prof. René Pineau, French University of the South Pacific, Nouméa; M. Christian Papineau, Service des Forêts, Province Nord; Dr. Robèrt Nasi, ex-Director of Cirad-Forêt, Nouméa.

References

Jaffré, T, J.-M. Veillon and J.-F. Cherrier 1987. Sur la présence de deux Cupressacées, *Neocallitropsis pancheri* (Carrière) Laubenfels et *Libocedrus austrocaledonica* Brongn. et Gris dans le massif du Paéoua et localités nouvelles de gymnospermes en Nouvelle Calédonie. *Bull. Mus. Nation. Hist. Nat., sect. B, Adansonia* 9 (3): 273-288.

Jaffré, T. 1995. *Distribution and Ecology of the Conifers of New Caledonia*. In: Enright, N. J. and Hill, R. S. (eds.). *Ecology of the Southern Conifers*. Melbourne University Press, Melbourne.

Jaffré, T., P. Bouchet and J.-M. Veillon (1998). Threatened plants of New Caledonia. Is the system of protected areas adequate? *Biodiv. Conserv* . 7 (1): 109-135.

Laubenfels, D. J. 1972. Gymnospermes. *Flore de la Nouvelle-Calédonie et Dépendances*. Vol. 4. Muséum National d'Histoire Naturelle, Paris.

Morat, P., T. Jaffré, J.-M. Veillon and H. S. Mackee 1981. Les formations végétales, Pl. 15. *Atlas de la Nouvelle-Caledonie*. ORSTOM, Paris.

Regional Action Plan

Conifers of the Himalayas and their Endangered Genetic Resources

Prem D. Dogra[1]
Forest Research Institute (ICFRE)
Dehra Dun, India

Description of the area

The Himalayas are one of the highest and longest mountain chains of the world. They stretch from latitude 24°N to 38°N and longitude 68°E to 100°E, and extend from Kashmir in the north to the bend of river Tsangpo and Assam in the east, ending in offshoots of the Garo, Khasia, and Jaintia hills and the Naga and Lushai hills. This mountain-belt, extending over 2250km in length and 250 to 450km in width, isolates the Indian-subcontinent from Tibet and China. The Himalayas arose from the lifting and folding of the bed of the ancient Tethys Sea during the late Cretaceous and early Tertiary. The rocks, the soils, and the climates vary considerably in different regions and within very narrow geographic areas in the Himalayas. The mountain slope gradients are steep and along their ascent the climate change is great and abrupt. The east to west longitudinal/latitudinal climatic gradient is also great especially in extremes in rainfall. The summer-rains formed from the moisture bearing south-western monsoon winds, trapped by the Himalayas from the Indian and Pacific Oceans, come earliest and fall the heaviest in the Eastern Himalayas and weaken from east to west. They also diminish in a south-north direction along the length of the Himalayas and in some innermost valleys, summer rains are partially or totally absent. Farjon (1990), after an analysis of world wide distribution ranges of genera and species of Pinaceae, identified 9 coniferous floristic regions in which the Sino-Himalayan region (see map p. 8, Farjon l.c.) is evaluated to be the richest in diversity of taxa in Pinaceae.

Taxonomic distribution of conifer genera

The conifer tree genera forming extensive forests in the Himalayas are the same as those found in such forests over much of the northern hemisphere. Only two genera, *Podocarpus* and *Nageia,* with a main distribution in the southern hemisphere, (one species each in India: *P. neriifolius* and *N. wallichiana*) are indigenous to the eastern Himalayas as well as South India, the Andamans and Nicobar Islands, and to some countries to the east. *Nageia wallichiana* is the only conifer native to the Indian Peninsula. The conifer tree genera distributed along the length of the Himalayas represent five of the total of seven to eight conifer families. The Pinaceae has six and the Cupressaceae two genera represented; the remaining families, i.e. Podocarpaceae, Taxaceae, and Cephalotaxaceae, have one genus each. In the Himalayas, the eastern region has a greater number of genera and species than the western region. The area covered by a few genera in the west, however, is far more extensive than the area covered by many genera in the east. Extensive forests of environmental and commercial value are composed of species in four genera: *Pinus, Cedrus, Abies*, and *Picea*. Not as extensive as these, the forests of *Tsuga, Cupressus, Juniperus,* and *Larix* are also of value but cover far lesser areas. *Taxus, Podocarpus,* and *Cupressus torulosa* populations distributed along the entire length of the Himalayas do not cover large areas and grow only as scattered trees in mixed forests or in small-stand patches or groves. Some rare genera like *Cephalotaxus* and *Amentotaxus* are regionally endemic and restricted to small local areas.

Distribution of conifer species.

The data on conifer tree species of the Himalayas are arranged below into five groups, on the basis of distribution-types and the extent of area they cover. The size and continuity or discontinuity of the distribution range (*inter alia*) affects the level and distribution of genetic variation within species of Himalayan conifers. Where populations decline, the genetic loss is greatest from gene pools of species distributed in restricted ranges and in disjunct populations. This grouping helps to identify such species. In wild forest trees, conservation at the species level is a first important stage to achieve, but beyond this, at the intraspecific level of variant populations (provenances) conservation will ultimately provide much greater value to the forests. The variants which need to be preserved the most are adaptive variants. Work done so far on intraspecific variation and its spatial distribution in Himalayan conifers is insignificant and even ecological surveys of species are incomplete. Use of biochemical genetic markers in such studies can furnish the needed results more quickly. These are necessary to understand the genetic structure of the species and populations because it tells what

[1] *Guest Scientist, Indian National Science Academy, New Dehli 110002. Financial help from the Academy and facilities provided by FRI (ICFRE), Dehra Dun, for this work, are gratefully acknowledged.

to conserve and how to design management-interventions for such conservation. This account on present day Himalayan conifer forests is based on field observations made during the years 1954-1965 and 1969-1996 (Dogra 1964, 1972, 1981, 1985, 1986a, b, 1989, unpubl. field books) and on published information provided by others (mainly Dallimore and Jackson, rev. Harrison 1966; Critchfield and Little 1966; Liu 1971; Grierson and Long 1983; Mehra 1988; Sahni 1990; Farjon 1990, 1993, 1994). Unless stated otherwise, the species altitudinal ranges, based on the collections of the F.R.I. herbarium at Dehradun, are from Sahni (1990).

Overview: Distribution of conifer species in the Himalayas

I. Widely distributed in large regions, covering considerable areas

1. Widely distributed along nearly the entire length of the Himalayas:

Taxus wallichiana (Zucc.) Pilg.: 2300-3400m.

Pinus wallichiana A .B. Jacks.: 1200-3800m (Dogra 1986b), intraspecific variation high, 7 Himalayan populations defined (Dogra 1972, 1981).

Pinus roxburghii Sarg.: 450-2300m, intraspecific variation present (Champion 1925, Dogra 1986b, Mehra 1988).

Abies spectabilis (D.Don) Spach: 2750-3900m, intraspecific variation high (Dogra 1986b) wild interspecific hybrid population crosses with *A. pindrow* (Mehra 1988), morphological variants may be present (Farjon 1990).

Juniperus indica Bertol. (syn.: *J. wallichiana* Hook. f. ex Brandis 1906): 2800-4600.

Juniperus squamata Buch.-Ham. ex D. Don: 2400-4300m.

2. Distributed in large regions in western Himalayas:

Picea smithiana (Wall.) Boiss.: 2150-3300m.

Abies pindrow (Royle ex D. Don) Royle: 2150-3300m, intraspecific variation high (Dogra 1986b), wild interspecific hybrid population crosses with *A. spectabilis*, intermediate variants may be present (Farjon 1990).

Cedrus deodara (Roxb.) G. Don: 2300-3350m, intraspecific variation high. (Troup 1921, Gamble 1922, Gorrie 1953, Dogra 1986b).

Cupressus torulosa D. Don: 1800-2800m.

Juniperus communis L.: 1700-4300m.

Juniperus semiglobosa Regel (syn. *J. macropoda* auct., non Boiss., *J. polycarpos* auct., non K. Koch): 2400-4300m.

3. Distributed in large regions in Eastern Himalayas:

Abies densa Griff. (sometimes considered to be a variety or a synonym of *A. spectabilis*): 2450-4000m (Farjon 1990), occurring from eastern Nepal into Arunachal Pradesh.

Pinus kesiya Royle ex Gordon: 800-2000m, intraspecific variation high within and between populations (Gibson and Barnes 1984).

Tsuga dumosa (D.Don) Eichler: 2400-3000m.

Larix griffithiana Carrière: 2400-3650m, variety recognised (Farjon 1990).

Juniperus recurva Buch-Ham ex D. Don: 2700-4600m.

Podocarpus neriifolius D. Don: plains-900m, highly variable, many varieties may be recognised (Dallimore and Jackson 1966).

Nageia wallichiana (C. Presl) de Laub.: 900-1500m.

II. Narrowly distributed within limited regions, covering small areas

1. Restricted to scattered, small disjunct areas in a narrow region of western Himalayas and nearby Pakistan and eastern Afghanistan mountains:

Pinus gerardiana Wall.: 1800-3000m, restricted and local to very small populations in inner dry valleys of north-western Himalayas, from Kinnaur and Pangi in Himachal Pradesh to Kashmir, Pakistan, Chitral to northern Baluchistan and eastern Afghanistan (Dogra 1964). Disjunct populations are further differentiated within a small area (Kinnaur, Pangi in Himachal Pradesh) isolated from each other by very high mountains. Tree to tree variation is present within populations (Brandis 1906; Dogra 1964, 1986a,b; Mehra 1988).

2. Narrow distribution with small areas in Eastern Himalayas and/or adjacent mountains:

Cephalotaxus mannii Hook. f.: 1370-2590m, Khasia, Jaintia, Naga and Upper Burma hills (Sahni 1990).

Cephalotaxus griffithii Hook. f.: 1520-1820m, Mishmi Hills, Upper Assam Kameng District, Arunachal Pradesh, Naga, Manipur and Mishmi Hills (Sahni 1990).

Picea spinulosa (Griff.) A. Henry: 2400-3600m, in southern Xizang Zizhiqu (Tibet) 2900-3600m, distributed in a narrow region of eastern Himalayas from the upper drainage of the Tista River in Sikkim in west to the head-waters of the Manas River, Bhutan in east, in small areas.

III. Rare endemic species within a small region and covering a small area

1. Rare, endemic, restricted to a small region in eastern Himalayas:

Pinus bhutanica Grierson *et al.*: 1750-2440m, restricted to eastern Bhutan, Punakha, Mongar, and Tashiang districts (Grierson et al. 1980), Tenga Valley in Arunachal Pradesh 1700-2000m (Sahni 1990), but entire distribution as yet unknown.

Larix potaninii var. *himalaica* (W. C. Cheng and L. K. Fu) Farjon and Silba (syn. *L. himalaica*): 2400-4000m, endemic to Central Nepal and southern Xizang Zizhiqu (Tibet), in mixed forests, sometimes dominant (Hara *et al.* 1978; Sahni 1990).

Cupressus cashmeriana Carrière: 2550-3000m, probably endemic to central Bhutan, Pho Chu Valley north-east of Punakha and western slopes of Pele La, in moist mixed forests (Grierson and Long 1983, as *C. corneyana* Carrière, but see Farjon 1994). The exact range of this species is unknown, most trees from which collections were made since Griffith (under *C. pendula* Griff., non Thunb.) are planted near habitations or temples.

IV. Very rare endemic in a local area occurring as scattered trees or populations

1. Very rare, endemic, restricted to a very small area in Eastern Himalayas:

Amentotaxus assamica D. K. Ferguson: 1800m, collected by J. L. Lister from the Daffla Hills, 1874; by Kingdon-Ward from Delei Valley, Chibon, 1928 (Ferguson 1985) and recently by Haridasan (1988), from Delei Valley, Mithumma-Mailing. The species is endemic within the Lohit District, Arunachal Pradesh. The three discoveries of the species were made at intervals of about 50 years each, proving it very rare and of high conservation concern (Sahni 1990).

V. Restricted or scattered populations in Eastern Himalayas of species from adjacent natural distribution ranges in neighbouring countries beyond the Himalayas

Species found to be rare in eastern Himalayas (mostly in Arunachal Pradesh and/or eastern Bhutan), but which have large natural distributions in neighbouring countries (mainly south-eastern Xizang Zizhiqu (Tibet), Yunnan, and in Myanmar) such as:

Pinus merkusii Jungh. and de Vriese: distributed naturally and mainly in Myanmar and Thailand, and in other eastern countries. It has been collected from the Lohit district of Arunachal Pradesh (Sahni 1990).

Pinus armandii Franch.: widely distributed in mountains of west and south-west China. It is reported from the Lohit District in Arunachal Pradesh.

Abies delavayi Franch. is native in China from western and south-western Sichuan to north-western Yunnan and south-eastern Xizang Zizhiqu (Tibet). The species is reported from three localities, i.e. Peri La, above Twang, and Se La (Sahni 1990) in the Kameng District, Arunachal Pradesh.

Picea brachytyla (Franch.) Pritz. occurs over an extensive area in south-west China. This species is reported in the eastern Himalayas from eastern Bhutan, Bhumtang District, in Gyetsa Valley, Ura and Ura La (Grierson and Long 1983) and from Arunachal Pradesh, Kameng District, Mago, growing mixed or in pure patches (Sahni 1990), this is probably var. *complanata* (Masters) Cheng ex Rehder (Farjon 1990).

The area covered by each of these species in the eastern Himalayas, though comparatively small, is not well-known.

The data presented here show that conifer species distributed in the Himalayas in the western region are different from those of the eastern region, but some species listed in Group I occur in both regions distributed along nearly the whole length of the Himalayas. These latter species form pure or mixed-species forests and many have continuous distribution ranges. Only towards the eastern Himalayan region some species like *Pinus wallichiana* (see Critchfield and Little 1966) show disjunct areas. *Cedrus deodara* has more scattered populations in the western part of its range. The various species grow in specific narrow or broad altitudinal belts situated one above the other. Species grow in pure or mixed forests in continuous or discontinuous distributions. This is characteristic of conifer forest belts of the eastern as well as the western Himalayas. The altitudinal range of most species is narrow except in *Pinus wallichiana* where it is very wide: 1200-3800m (Dogra 1986a). The rare endemic species of the eastern Himalayas are restricted to narrow altitudinal bands where they occupy well-defined habitats. The species arrangements on southern and northern mountain aspects differ. The natural ranges of conifers overlap extremely diverse geographical regions. These can vary sharply in climates and sites, especially in inner dry and outer monsoon zones in mountains and in the extreme eastern and western Himalayan regions. Most of the species, therefore, show high intraspecific genetic variation within and between populations (Dogra 1964, 1972, 1981, 1986a,b, 1989). The Himalayan high montane region is therefore rich in conifer species and also in their intraspecific (genetic variation) diversity. Populations of species of *Cedrus, Pinus, Abies,* and *Picea* show continuous (clinal) variability as a result of adaptation to climatic gradations on the one hand and to disjunct variability between separate populations on the other. It is this genetic diversity within the species that is threatened in these regions.

Threats to conifer diversity

Threats to conifer diversity occur at the species and within the species (at population and individual) levels. They arise from ineffective protection from damage by logging, new road construction, forest floor disturbance by nomad livestock; collection of firewood, edible seeds and medicinal plant material; shifting cultivation, clearance for agriculture, expanding urban and village areas; increased incidence of insect, pathogen, and parasite (e.g. *Arceuthobium* on *Pinus*) attacks; and unchecked man-made or naturally-caused forest fires. For *Cedrus deodara*, easily accessible stands (near roads, rivers) are residual stands from which the best trees have been harvested to the limit and good trees with large heights and girths are extinct. Tree mutilation is severe in:

1) *Pinus roxburghii* due to excessive numbers of oleoresin tap-blazes per tree, lopping for vegetable props and firewood by farmers, logging, and fire damage;

2) *Pinus gerardiana* due to heavy yearly branch lopping for cone and edible seed collection;

3) *Taxus wallichiana* due to medicinal bark and leaf collection.

Unchecked summer fires in low altitude dry sub-tropical *Pinus roxburghii* forests show an increased frequency and intensity. *Pinus kesiya* suffers heavy damage from shifting cultivation and heavy logging. Human and livestock overpopulation in the Himalayas and their uncontrolled activities lie at the root of the most severe threats to trees and their forest floors. Deforestation has created large cleared areas or open degraded forests where soil erosion is high and regeneration and survival of new trees difficult. Natural regeneration and tree establishment in timberline fir and spruce forests, which are very sensitive to environmental change, are poor and in several places absent. This has lead to a general decline of high quality conifer forests.

Most of the widespread conifer species (Group I) in the Himalayas have genetically different trees, populations, taxonomic forms, and varieties within a species (Dogra 1986b, Mehra 1988). A substantial number of conifer species have smaller populations in disjunct areas, such as *Taxus wallichiana* and *Cupressus torulosa* (group I), and *Pinus gerardiana* and *Picea spinulosa* (group II). Smaller than these are populations of all the rare and very rare endemic species (groups III and IV). The populations of these species seem to have undergone a significant reduction in genetic variation over several generations and the present rate of depletion in these, if unchecked, will lead to their extinction. Erosion of genetic variation within the conifer species has made them less adaptable to the fast pace of environmental changes presently occurring in the Himalayas. Slow growth, disturbed environment, insufficient moisture, heavy top soil erosion, disturbed reproductive biology, erratic seed-set, seed sterility, poor natural regeneration, heavy mortality, poor disease resistance, and low tree establishment have become prevalent, making wild conifer forest tree replacement difficult.

The deforestation of conifers of the western Himalayas, begun in 1890 with large railroad expansion, took a toll of *Cedrus deodara* populations for supply of railway sleepers and construction timber (Westoby 1989). Extensive removal of previously untouched high-elevation deodar, blue pine, spruce, and fir for timber and for fruit-packing cases was made possible only after 1947 with the opening up of high mountain roads. The steep rise in timber prices encouraged heavy logging, including timber-line extraction, with new techniques. Sudden removal of high-altitude forests and their degradation caused swift snow melts, flooding, and heavy soil erosion. Tree removal from large tracts in lower and higher regions continued unabated throughout the Indian post-independence period until the Forest (Conservation) Act of 1980.

The situation in deforestation and its effects on survival or decline of conifers is best seen in the two most important and highly-priced commercial timber species *Cedrus deodara* and *Pinus wallichiana*. Geographically variable, these and other conifer species have been observed by the author for the past 38 years (see Dogra, 1964, 1972, 1981, 1985, 1986a,b, 1989) in the inner and outer Himalayas in Jammu and Kashmir, Himachal Pradesh, and Uttar Pradesh states. The removal of *Cedrus deodara* has taken place continuously from very early times. The estimate of tree removal in deodar during this period of observation is roughly 30-40 % in easily accessible areas in these states, and that of *Pinus wallichiana* is 25-50% in Jammu and Kashmir. Many of the best stands of these have been clear-felled in some regions. Most of the heavy felling took place before the promulgation of the Forest (Conservation) Act 1980 of the Government of India (see Bagga 1989). Successful conservation of naturally regenerating whole stands especially of unfelled wild trees is still needed to preserve the natural genetic resources of timber species, as well as of rare threatened species.

Current conservation measures and needs for the future

The legal measures in effect at present are:

The "Indian Forest Act 1927 (Act XVI of 1927)" and the "National Forest Policy" enunciated by the Government of India in the Ministry of Food and Agriculture (Resolution No. 13-1/52-F.3) under which State Governments have power to reserve forests through announcement in the official gazette, to declare forest land area as "Protected Forests", and to protect any government forest land not included in a forest reserve. The "Forest (Conservation) Act 1980" extends to the whole of India the conservation of forests to check deforestation. It restricts de-reservation and use of forest land for non-forest purposes and states that the permission of the Government of India is needed before any forest land can be cleared of trees which have grown naturally on that land (Bagga 1989).

[Recommendations:
The author thus rightly outlines the fundamental importance of support for four main issues:

1. Arresting the spiral of conditions causing continued forest degradation;

2. Rebuilding and positively enhancing conditions under which natural tree regeneration can again occur;

3. Focusing attention not just on conservation of isolated species, but on their genetic variation which adapts them to the continuously varying aspects of the topography;

4. Involving the support of local people in conservation and management plans;

Because the current Conifer Specialist Group membership in South Asia is limited to the author of this report, we wish to acknowledge gaps in the information available for the Himalayan region. The Conifer Specialist Group hopes to be extended in the region and to be able to include more information in future reports including: an assessment of the effectiveness or ineffectiveness of these laws; identification of the present forest reserves in view of logging and encroachment; an outline of legal as well as conservation measures needed on top of these to curb deforestation, with emphasis on (areas of) rare or restricted species mentioned above. In order to be able to make recommendations for the entire Himalayan region, international collaboration, as far as politically feasible, e.g. between India, Nepal, Sikkim, and Bhutan is recommended. - the compilers]

References

Bagga., R. (ed. and revised) 1989. *Beotras Law of Forests - Central and States*, 5th Edition. The Law Book Company (P) Ltd. Allahabad 211001, India.

Brandis, D. 1906. *Indian Trees*. Constable and Co. Ltd. London.

Critchfield, W. B. and E. L. Little, Jr. 1966. Geographic distribution of the pines of the World. *USDA Forest Service, Washington DC Misc. Publ.* 990: 1-97.

Dallimore, W. and A. D. Jackson (4th ed. revised by G. S. Harrison) 1966. *A Handbook of Coniferae and Ginkgoaceae*. Edward Arnold, London.

Dogra, P. D. 1964. Gymnosperms of India II. Chilgoza Pine (*Pinus gerardiana* Wall). *Bull. Nat. Bot. Gard. Lucknow* 109: 1-47.

Dogra, P. D. 1972. Intrinsic qualities of growth and adaptation potential of *Pinus wallichiana*. In: R. T. Bingham, T. S. Hoff and G. I. Macdonald (eds.). Biology of rust resistance in forest trees. *USDA Forest Service, Washington DC Misc. Publ.* 1121: 163- 178.

Dogra, P. D. 1981. Variability in biology of flowering in blue pine provenances of Northwest Himalaya in relation to reproductive barriers and gene flow. In: S. L. Krugman and M. Katsuta (eds.). *Proc. Symp. Flowering Physiology, IUFRO, WP Reprod. Processes.* 17 IUFRO World Congress Japan, Forest Tree Breeding Assoc. Tokyo: 8-11.

Dogra, P. D. 1985. Conifers of India and their wild gene resources in relation to tree breeding. *Indian Forest.* 111: 935-955.

Dogra, P. D. 1986a. Species diversity and gene conservation in Indian tree species in relation to forestry. *Indian Forest.* 112: 596- 607.

Dogra, P. D. 1986b. Conifers of India and their wild gene resources in relation to forestry and Himalayan environment. In: P. K. K. Nair (ed.). *Glimpses in Plant Research* VIII: 129-194. Today and Tomorrow Printers and Publishers, New Delhi.

Dogra, P. D. 1989. Intraspecific variation and gene conservation in Indian tree species in relation to forestry. In: M. L. Trivedi, B. S. Gill and S. S. Saini (eds.). *Plant Research In India:* 265-278. Today and Tommorrow Printers and Publishers, New Delhi.

Farjon, A. 1990. Pinaceae. Drawings and descriptions of the genera *Abies, Cedrus, Pseudolarix, Keteleeria, Nothotsuga, Tsuga, Cathaya, Pseudotsuga, Larix* and *Picea. Regnum Vegetabile* Vol. 121. Koeltz Scientific Books, Königstein, Germany.

Farjon, A. 1993. The taxonomy of multiseed junipers (*Juniperus* sect. *Sabina*) in Southwest Asia and East Africa. (Taxonomic notes on Cupressaceae I). *Edinburgh J. Bot.* 49 (3): 251-283.

Farjon, A. 1994. 253: *Cupressus cashmeriana* - Cupressaceae. *Kew Mag.* 11 (4): 156-166.

Ferguson, D. F. 1985. A new species of *Amentotaxus* (Taxaceae) from north eastern India. *Kew Bull.* 40 (1): 115-119.

Gamble, J. S. 1922. *A Manual of Indian Timbers*. Sampson Low, Marston and Co. Ltd. London, UK.

Gorrie, R. M. 1953. The Sutlej deodar, its ecology and timber production. *Indian Forest. Rec. (Silv. Ser.)* 17: 1-140.

Grierson, A. J. C. and D. C. Long 1983. *Flora of Bhutan* Vol. 1, Part 1. Royal Botanic Garden, Edinburgh.

Grierson, A. J. C., D. C. Long and C. N. Page 1980. Notes relating to the flora of Bhutan: III. *Pinus bhutanica* : a new 5-needle pine from Bhutan and India. *Notes Roy. Bot. Gard. Edinburgh* 38: 297-310.

Hara, H., W. T. Stearn and L. H. J. Williams 1978. *An Enumeration of the Flowering Plants of Nepal*, Vol. 1. Trustees of the British Museum (Natural History), London.

Haridasan, K. 1988. *Amentotaxus* (Taxaceae) a rare gymnosperm from Arunachal Pradesh. *Indian Forest.* 114 (12): 868-870.

Liu, T. S. 1971. *A Monograph of the Genus Abies*. Nat. Taiwan Univ., Taipeh, Taiwan.

Mehra, P. N. 1988. *Indian Conifers, Gnetophytes and Phylogeny of Gymnosperms*. Dept. of Botany, Punjab Univ., Chandigarh, India. Printed: Pramodh P. Kapur, Ray Bahadur Industrial Co. C-61, Mayapuri Industrial Area Phase II. New Delhi.

Sahni, K. C. 1990. *Gymnosperms of India and Adjacent Countries*. Bishen Singh Mahendra Pal Singh, Dehra Dun, India.

Troup, R. S. 1921. *Silviculture of Indian Trees*. Vol. III. Oxford University Press, Oxford.

Westoby, J. 1989. *Introduction to World Forestry*. Basil Blackwell Inc. New York.

Regional Action Plan

Conifers threatened in Nueva Galicia, Mexico

Jorge A. Pérez de la Rosa
Departamento de Botanico
Universidad de Guadalajara, Mexico

Description of the area

The ancient territory of Virreinato de la Nueva Galicia is located in a region now encompassed within the states of Jalisco, Colima, and Aguascalientes with some portions in Nayarit, Durango, Zacatecas, Guanajuanto, and Michoacán. The area covers approximately 125,000km^2. In this zone, five principal mountain ranges converge: the southern extreme of the Sierra Madre Occidental, the western part of the Eje Volcánico Transversal, the northern edge of the Sierra Madre del Sur, the south-western section of the Altiplanicie Mexicana and the northern reach of the Cuenca del Balsas. Due to the heterogeneous topography of the region there is a broad variation in climate and microclimate, from the true tropics with temperatures of 25-27°C to the highest mountains with altitudes greater than 3000m where frost is frequent in winter. Precipitation generally falls between May and October, with an annual variation from 750-1000mm and with extremes between 500-1500mm. The north-eastern part of this region is the driest part while the peaks of the highest mountains near the coast are most humid (Rzedowski and McVaugh 1966).

The conifers of Nueva Galicia

According to Carvajal and McVaugh (1992), there are 36 conifer taxa in this region divided into the following families:

Cupressaceae - 3 genera, 9 species, 1 variety
Three species of the genus *Juniperus* are sparsely represented in the area of Nueva Galicia. However, two of them (*J. monticola* and *J. erythrocarpa*) have a greater distribution in other states of Mexico; only *J. jaliscana* is seriously threatened due to its endemic nature.

Pinaceae - 2 genera, 19 species, 5 varieties
Seven species are threatened; their status is discussed below.

Podocarpaceae - 1 genus, 1 species
The one representative of this family in Nueva Galicia is *Podocarpus reichei*. While it is not abundant in this area, it enjoys a broader national distribution. Nevertheless, a thorough taxonomic study should be conducted on this species along with a study to determine the distribution of the family in Mexico.

Threatened conifers

Cupressaceae

Juniperus jaliscana Martínez [EN, B1+2c]. Until a few years ago this species was considered an endemic species in Jalisco, when Zanoni and Adams (1979) reported finding this small conifer in the state of Durango; it is now known only in these two localities. *Juniperus jaliscana* enjoys one of the most humid habitats in Nueva Galicia; therefore, fires are not frequent in this zone. The locality in Jalisco (Sierra de Cuale, Talpa de Allende municipality) is difficult to access. These two factors contribute to the adequate conservation of this species. This plant is a large shrub or small tree, branched nearly from the ground, up to 5-6m in height. It grows in association with a variety of species of oaks (*Quercus* spp.) and pines (*Pinus* spp.), and though it is frequent in this zone, it is never dominant. While the trunks are frequently used for fences and rafters in construction, good regeneration from the stumps has been observed. There is little cattle ranching in this region and no grazing on the leaves of *Juniperus*. Furthermore, this is a mountainous zone that is not adequate for agricultural use.

Recommendation: As access is difficult in the highlands where *Juniperus jaliscana* grows and until now its habitat has not been disturbed, it seems that its disappearance is not imminent. Nevertheless, forest authorities should protect this species by preventing the use of the land in this region for intensive agriculture or grazing since with continued expansion of land use this is otherwise likely to occur.

Pinaceae

The Pinaceae is the best represented family of conifers in Mexico, particularly in Nueva Galicia, both in species diversity and number of individuals. However, some are scarce and threatened with extinction.

Abies guatemalensis var. ***jaliscana*** Martínez [VU, A1d]. The species, principally distributed in Central America, reaches heights of up to 45m and forms small forest stands in high humid mountains near the coast. All of the known localities for this variety are close together, lying within the municipalities of Talpa de Allende and San Sebastián del Oeste in the state of Jalisco. The area covered by this species in known populations is not greater than 5km². Even though the steep slopes make access to this habitat difficult, these populations and their habitats are threatened by clandestine felling and occasional forest fires.

Recommendation: These remaining populations should be protected by forest laws forbidding clandestine felling; inhabitants in the surrounding communities should be encouraged and involved in preventing and controlling forest fires that threaten these stands.

Pinus ayacahuite Ehrenb. ex Schltdl. [LRnt]. Nueva Galicia lies within the northern limit of this species' distribution in Mexico. It has only been found in two small areas in the municipalities of Talpa de Allende, Jalisco and Los Reyes, Michoacán, separated from each other by more than 200km. In both areas *P. ayacahuite* is seriously threatened by clandestine felling. These two localities must be protected principally because these populations can provide information on the ancestral distribution of the species and its taxonomic and evolutionary ties with *P. strobiformis* Engelm. whose distribution lies further north. It should be mentioned that in Nueva Galicia *P. ayacahuite* produces the largest cones of any population of this species, up to 60cm in length and sometimes longer.

Recommendation: This species should be protected from excessive logging and forest fires. Following the disappearance of the species from broad areas of its natural distribution, reintroduction is suggested in productive plantations from selected seeds from the region.

Pinus hartwegii Lindl. This species can be found at altitudes greater than 4000m, making it one of the highest growing pines in the world. It is very common on the peaks of the high volcanoes of Mexico and Central America, including those of Nueva Galicia, such as El Volcán de Fuego and El Nevado de Colima, where it forms monospecific forests at the upper limits of tree line. Its presence in these areas, as well as in other areas of the country, is threatened by the attack of a debarking insect, *Dendroctonus mexicanus* Hopk. (Perry 1991).

Recommendation: The distribution of *P. hartwegii* is diminishing all over Mexico. In Nueva Galicia it is found on the highest peaks where the impact of *Dendroctonus mexicanus* is increasing. It is urgent that an integrated study be made of this forest type and measures be proposed for its recuperation, such as the biological control of insect pests.

Pinus jaliscana Pérez de la Rosa [LRnt]. Of all pine species described for Mexico following the work of Maximino Martínez in 1948, this is one of the few belonging to the subgenus *Pinus* (*fide* Little and Critchfield 1969). Until now it has only been reported in semi-tropical forests in the west of Jalisco, and can be considered endemic to the western slopes of the coastal mountains in this state. *P. jaliscana* is a species of high stature and has great timber potential, as much for its

rapid growth as for its natural pruning tendency, which leaves much of the trunk clear of branches in maturity. Such characteristics make the species popular in the local timber industry and have resulted in a restriction of the species to less accessible areas. The regeneration method used by foresters in this part of Mexico is to leave seed trees after harvest. However, forest fires are very frequent in the habitat of *P. jaliscana*, and seedlings are easily eliminated.

Recommendation: Due to its level of endemism, *P. jaliscana* was assessed as threatened by Perry (1991). [*It has been assessed as LRnt under current IUCN criteria mainly because large tracts of forest in the area remain relatively intact as access is limited; however it may approach the status of VU.* - the compilers]. The control of wildfires is imperative for the protection of this species. There are various sawmills in the region, and the cutting of this species has been conducted for many years without reforestation activities. To help conserve this species it is thus suggested that logging in pristine forests should be arrested and commercial plantations with *P. jaliscana* should be established in selected deforested zones.

Pinus martinezii E. Larsen [not listed on the Global Red List of Conifers, but locally vulnerable]. For some researchers (Farjon and Styles 1997, Carvajal and McVaugh 1992, Cuevas *et al.* 1988) this species is a southern form of *P. durangensis* Martínez. Independent of its taxonomy, the entire population of *P. martinezii* is restricted to three small areas in Jalisco and Michoacán and can be considered in danger of total extinction in two of these. Biologist Lidia Guiridi (pers. comm.) found wood samples collected from one locality near Morelia, Michoacán, revealing tracheids of approximately 2cm which is unusual in Mexican species.

Recommendation: As with the majority of tree species in Mexico, excessive cutting is the principle threat to *P. martinezii*. The solution to this problem is to prevent cutting of any of these trees for a period of 30 years or more; in addition, plantations of this taxon should be created within its natural range.

Pinus maximartinezii Rzed. [EN, B1+2bc]. This is one of the most distinct species of Mexican pine belonging to the group of white pines with edible seeds, and whose seeds reach record dimensions of up to 2cm in length. It is also the species of *Pinus* with the greatest number of cotyledonary leaves (up to 24). Due to the persistence for many years of the primary leaves and its blue-grey colour, this is a species with great potential as an ornamental tree. However, its natural distribution is restricted to the high and medium parts of Sierra de Morones in the south of Zacatecas state in the northern part of Nueva Galicia. Due to the exploitation of the seeds for sale in local markets, its natural regeneration is very low and occasional fires can cause serious injury to the forest. For this reason this species can be considered at risk of extinction.

Pinus maximartinezii in Zacatecas, Mexico.

Cone and rare seedling of *Pinus maximartinezii*.

Recommendation: One of the most viable measures for protecting *P. maximartinezii* would be to cultivate this species in plantations on terrain that it previously occupied. The local people must be involved in this activity with a sense of ownership and responsibility for the successful recuperation of this valuable forest resource. See also under Species accounts for a more detailed account (p. 101) of this remarkable pine and its threats and conservation proposals.

Pinus rzedowskii Madrigal and M. Caball. [EN, D]. This endemic species is found in some very restricted, habitat limited areas in calcareous soils in karst limestone on the high part of the Coalcomán mountains of Michoacán in the extreme south of Nueva Galicia. This pine is the most difficult to place in a classification of (Mexican) pines following the scheme of Little and Critchfield (1969). It shows characteristics of both the subgenera *Pinus* and *Strobus*. Its scarcity and evolutionary value makes it a good candidate for effective protection measures. Detailed studies of this species will help elaborate an explanation of the presence and evolution of the genus in Mexico (Farjon 1996).

Recommendation: Due to the evolutionary importance of the species and the restriction in its distribution, the most effective protection measure would be to create reserves for all three populations in the highest part of the Sierra de Coalcomán out of harm from human activity. Vigilance against forest fires in and around these populations is of the highest priority. *Ex situ* conservation by means of small forestry plantations using (and keeping separate!) seed, especially from the two smallest populations is recommended. [*Additional introduction from all three populations into botanic garden collections would provide a further* ex situ *safeguard.* - the compilers].

Summary of recommendations

Nueva Galicia is one of the regions of Mexico most rich in conifer species. The growing human population in this region has had a negative impact on the natural resources and in particular on the conifer forests. Given this fact, it is urgent to implement conservation measures for their recuperation, protection, and development such as:

1. Enact a new forest law that permits the establishment of commercial forests in deforested areas and those in danger of erosion. Make use of high technology that recuperates the highest yield of the harvest for appropriate use, i.e. saw timber, chips for pulp, etc.

2. Strictly enforce forestry laws through the intervention of trained personnel, such as forest rangers.

3. Urgently carry out studies to determine the present status of each conifer taxon of Mexico covering the distribution, reproductive biology, health, human impact, etc. of each species.

4. In the case of species with very limited distribution, reserves should be created that prevent any form of exploitation. The consideration and support of local people should be integrated into conservation and management plans.

Pinus rzedowskii In Michoacán, Mexico.

Cones and foliage of *Pinus rzedowskii* .

References

Carvajal, S. and R. McVaugh 1992. *Pinus*. In: R. McVaugh, *Flora Novo-Galiciana* 17:32-100. The University of Michigan Herbarium, Ann Arbor.

Cuevas, G., R. Nuñez L. and M. Nuñez 1988. *Taxonomía de los pinos de la Sierra de Manantlán, Jalisco*. Tesis, Facultad de Agricultura, Universidad de Guadalajara.

Farjon, A. 1996. Biodiversity of *Pinus* (Pinaceae) in Mexico: speciation and palaeo-endemism. *Bot. J. Linn. Soc. London* 121 (4): 365-384.

Farjon, A. and B. T. Styles 1997. *Pinus* (Pinaceae). *Flora Neotropica* Monograph 75. The New York Botanical Garden, New York.

Little, E. L., Jr. and W. B. Critchfield 1969. Subdivisions of the genus Pinus. *U.S. Forest Serv. Misc. Publ.* 1144. Washington, DC.

Martínez, M. 1948. *Los Pinos Mexicanos*. De. 2. Botas. México.

Martínez, M. 1953. *Las Pináceas Mexicanas*. Secretarìa de Agricultura y Ganaderia. Subsecretaría de Recursos Forestales y Caza. México.

Perry, J. P., Jr. 1991. *The Pines of Mexico and Central America*. Timber Press, Portland, Oregon, USA.

Rzedowski, J. and R. McVaugh 1966. La Vegetación de Nueva Galicia. *Contrib. Univ. Mich. Herb.* 9 (1): 1-123.

Zanoni, T. A. and R. P. Adams 1979. The genus *Juniperus* (Cupressaceae) in Mexico and Guatemala: synonymy, key and distribution of the taxa. *Bol. Soc. Bot. México* 35: 55-78.

Regional Action Plan

Caribbean Conifers: Current Status

Thomas A. Zanoni
New York Botanical Garden, New York, USA

Description of the area

Floristically, the Caribbean Islands have been traditionally divided into three areas, each comprised of a number of islands. The Greater Antilles includes the Cayman Islands, Cuba, Jamaica, Hispaniola (Haiti and the Dominican Republic), Puerto Rico, and the British and the U.S. Virgin Islands. These include the largest land masses in the region, varying from below sea-level to very high elevation, c. 3075m. The Bahama Islands are comprised of many small islands with low elevations, mainly near sea-level. The Lesser Antilles encompass islands from Saint-Martin to Grenada, including the Leeward and Windward Islands and the Netherlands Antilles. There are many more islands here, but they comprise a smaller area than the Greater Antilles, with elevations ranging from sea-level to c. 1500m. Trinidad and Tobago and the other islands off the coast of Venezuela are considered to have a more South American floristic affinity.

The flora of the Caribbean shows diverse origins (Howard 1973) but has components that tie into the southernmost United States, Central America, and South America resulting from the complex geological history of the origin of the islands. For example, geologists consider that Hispaniola was formed from several parts that collided millions of years ago and have remained together ever since.

Conifers

The coniferous component of the flora is rather low in species numbers, but quite remarkable in its differentiation, probably as a result of the isolation caused by mountainous barriers and separation by seas. A few species occur on several, distant islands. Most do not cover extensive areas of land, but two species of pine (*Pinus*) cover a considerable area of the larger islands: *Pinus occidentalis* in Hispaniola, *P. caribaea* in Cuba (as var. *caribaea*) and on the Bahamas (as var. *bahamensis*) (Barrett and Golfari 1962, Critchfield and Little 1966, Farjon and Styles 1997). *Podocarpus coriaceus* is rather remarkable in its distribution; it is found from western Puerto Rico through the Lesser Antilles, but does not occur in large populations anywhere.

Threats

Most of the taxa cover small areas on one or a few islands. Major factors affecting the survival of these trees (one taxon, *Juniperus gracilior* var. *urbaniana*, is only known as a small shrub) are changes in vegetation cover due to deforestation,

natural or man-caused fires (then often related to clearing for agriculture), and harvesting of trees for wood. In most instances, the loss is not directly related to the need to clear land for human habitation, except perhaps in the low-elevation pine forests. Propagation is fairly simple in *Juniperus* and *Pinus*; both genera have been used commercially and locally for lumber. These taxa have been used in reforestation in the islands to some extent, although it is more common to bring in exotic species because seeds of these are more readily available commercially or from governmental and non-governmental sources. The single native species of *Podocarpus*, probably because it has rarely been used for timber, seems to have received the least attention in relation to propagation from wild-collected seed and is rarely propagated in nurseries.

The taxa of conifers, their distribution, and current status are reviewed in the list below. All conifers are listed, including those not considered threatened on a world-wide basis under IUCN criteria. The status given is that for the species as a whole, not for a specific island or region.

Caribbean Conifers: by genus and island

Podocarpus

Currently, 7 species are recognised to occur in the Caribbean. (Staszkiewicz 1988 seems to recognise too many taxa, particularly in the Cuban plants; the text here follows Buchholz and Gray 1948, de Laubenfels 1984,1985). All species are known to occur as scattered trees, rarely becoming the principal component in a forest.

Cuba

Podocarpus ekmanii Urb. Endemic, eastern Cuba, higher montane, high rainfall. [This taxon has been considered a taxonomic synonym of the next species, see Farjon 1998]

Podocarpus angustifolius Griseb. [EN, B1 + 2c]. This tree is "very rare" (Bisse 1981). Western Cuba, montane, high rainfall.

Podocarpus aristulatus Parl. [VU, B2ac]. Eastern Cuba, lower montane forests, high rainfall.

Hispaniola

Podocarpus hispaniolensis de Laub. [EN, B1+2e]. Recently described from Hispaniola by de Laubenfels (1984), but collected long before its recognition as a distinct taxon. Found below the lower limits of elevation of *P. aristulatus*, mainly in the eastern Cordillera Central on Hispaniola, occurring at levels where coffee plantations and minor farming are still feasible, resulting in some loss of habitat by deforestation.

Podocarpus aristulatus Parl. [VU, B2ac]. In montane high rainfall forests of the Cordillera Septentrional, Cordillera Central, Sierra de Neiba, Sierra de Baoruco and Massif de la Selle. This is *P. buchii* Urb. of earlier reports.

Jamaica:

Podocarpus purdieanus Hook. [Data Deficient, but listed as of conservation concern according to old IUCN categories]. Mountains of central and eastern Jamaica (particularly on Mt. Diablo) at middle elevations, 800-1200m.

Podocarpus urbanii Pilg. [LRnt]. Blue Mountains of Jamaica, high montane forests, at 1500-2300m., high rainfall.

Puerto Rico and Lesser Antilles:

Podocarpus coriaceus Rich. and A. Rich. In montane forests of high rainfall: eastern and western Puerto Rico; Guadeloupe, Montserrat, St. Kitts, Martinique, Dominica, (and Trinidad and Tobago).

Juniperus

All taxa are known to occur in scattered (small) populations now, and a few are very limited in their distributions (Adams 1983, 1989, 1995; Adams *et al.* 1987; Florin 1933; Zanoni and Mejía 1986).

Cuba:

Juniperus barbadensis **var.** ***lucayana*** (Britton) R. P. Adams [VU, B1+2c]. Scattered through Cuba: Prov. Holguin, Guantánamo and Isla de la Juventud (Isla de Pinos); scarce, needing protection (Bisse 1981).

Juniperus saxicola Britton and P. Wilson [VU, D2]. Only known from the slopes of Pico Turquino, Granma, and Sierra Maestra in several localities, eastern Cuba; very scarce (Bisse 1981). The trees with acicular leaves are considered by Adams (1995) to be neotenic forms of the normally scale-leaved species of the genus. There were reports of the use of this species in Cuba for pencil production near the beginning of the present century, but the intensity of harvesting for that purpose is not known.

Hispaniola:

Juniperus barbadensis **L.** **var.** ***lucayana*** (Britton) R. P. Adams [VU, B1+2c]. May still occur in Haiti near St. Michel de l'Atalaye, Massif du Nord. Florin (1933) reported it in Massif du Nord and Central Plateau near St. Michel de l'Atalaye, Haiti; also in Bahamas and Jamaica. Adams (1995) reported that a search for this variety in Haiti was unsuccessful and that it is presumed to be extinct on Hispaniola.

Juniperus gracilior var. ***ekmanii*** (Florin) R. P. Adams [CR, D]. In the Massif de la Selle, Haiti, at c. 2100m. These trees, occurring in a very small area between Morne La Visite and Mare Rouge (part or all of the area now in Parc National La Visite), were reported by the local people as once having been

more common and also logged. Zanoni and Mejía (1986) showed a photograph of a stump of a dead tree that was over 2m in diameter. Very few individuals remain. A small population above Puerto Escondido, Duvergé, Dominican Republic in the Sierra de Baoruco (the eastern portion of the Haitian Massif de la Selle) is referable to this variety. Taxonomic research is recommended to verify its exact identity.

Juniperus gracilior **Pilg.** **var.** ***gracilior*** [EN, B1+2c]. Eastern Cordillera Central, and formerly in the Sierra Martin Garcia, Dominican Republic. Once it seemed to be common enough for it to be used for fence posts and lumber (for furniture, at artisan level), but not to an extensive degree, since it was only known from a small region. During the early 1980s the Dominican Republic forest service had propagated some from seed collected in the wild but planted them out without any particular reforestation plan. Small pockets of this variety are now in or very near the Parque Nacional Bermudez.

Juniperus gracilior var. ***urbaniana*** (Pilg.) R. P. Adams [EN, B1+2c]. Only known from very few individuals occurring near the summit of Pic La Selle, Massif de la Selle, Haiti, elev. c. 2550m.

Jamaica:

Juniperus barbadensis **L.** **var.** ***lucayana*** (Britton) R. P. Adams [VU, B1 + 2c]. Near Clydesdale, St Andrew Parish, elev. 1100-1200m. Apparently not common.

Bahamas:

Juniperus barbadensis **L.** **var.** ***lucayana*** (Britton) R. P. Adams [VU, B1 + 2c]. On Andros, Bahama and Great Abaco Islands, low elevation.

Lesser Antilles:

Juniperus barbadensis **L.** **var.** ***barbadensis*** [CR, D]. Apparently the original material is from Barbados, but the variety is not known on that island for a very long time (over 200 years). Recently verified in St. Lucia (Adams *et al.* 1987); this is the only extant population, which consists of a few trees on a mountain top (Petit Piton). Thus it can be considered extremely rare.

Pinus

The species of Pinus (Carabia 1941, Critchfield and Little 1966, Darrow and Zanoni 1990, Farjon and Styles 1997, Florin 1933) tend to be covering rather broader areas than most other conifers, and have fared better in survival, probably because most of them are pioneer trees that invade areas after disturbance. Most have potential for reforestation within the region.

Cuba:

Pinus tropicalis Morelet. Pinar del Río and Isla de la Juventud (Isla de Pinos). Endemic, widely distributed on sandy soils.

Pinus cubensis Griseb. (syn.: *P. maestrensis* Bisse). Sierra Maestra and northern part of eastern Cuba.

Pinus caribaea Morelet var. *caribaea* [VU, A1c+2]. Pinar del Río and Isla de la Juventud (Isla de Pinos), widespread, also commonly in cultivation in plantations.

Hispaniola:
Pinus occidentalis Sw. [LRnt]. NW Haiti, Massif du Nord, Massif de la Hotte, Massif de la Selle; Dominican Rep., Ile Gonave (formerly), Cordillera Central, Sierra de Neiba, and Sierra de Baoruco. This species has been commercially and non-commercially harvested, particularly in this century (Darrow and Zanoni 1990). It has a very broad distribution that has suffered some reduction, particularly at lower elevations, due to harvesting and fire. Perhaps of greatest interest is the very broad altitudinal range from near sea level to c. 3085m (highest point on the island and the Caribbean Islands). Nothing is known about the adaptations to the range of environmental conditions and the potential value of the species for plantation forestry or reforestation in Hispaniola or elsewhere.

Bahama Islands:
Pinus caribaea Morelet var. *bahamensis* (Griseb.) W. H. Barrett and Golfari. On the Bahamas and Turks-Caicos Islands, at low elevation. Fairly common on most islands.

Conservation needs and recommendations

Little has been done for the simple conservation of most of the conifers in this region. It is by geographic coincidence that some populations of the taxa now occur within the limits of scientific reserves or national parks. This often provides the only protection.

A concerted effort should be made to assure that habitats of the single populations of certain taxa, such as *Juniperus barbadensis* var. *barbadensis*, *J. gracilior* var *ekmanii*, *J. gracilior* var. *urbanii*, *J. saxicola* are protected from destruction. This must include protection from harvesting and from fire, because junipers in general are readily damaged or killed by fire. The junipers are often adapted altitudinally, and any attempt to protect them by propagation artificially or from seed would require growing the new plants in conditions close to the temperatures and rainfall found in their natural habitat. The effects of inappropriate conditions for high-altitude taxa grown at low altitude include the perpetuation of juvenile or abnormal foliage and no flowering and seed production.

The rather broadly distributed pines have a somewhat natural safeguard against overall loss because of their existence in very large numbers over large areas. Perhaps, in this genus in the Caribbean the greater concern would be in the maintenance of genetic diversity on the basis of broad ecological factors such as altitude and substrate (e.g. determining whether there are populations that do not occur in limestone areas, which are the most frequent substrates in the islands). A plan to guard populations in different habitats would be suitable. Also, since very little is known of the bio-logical characteristics of the pines (and of junipers and podocarps), basic investigations should be undertaken of naturally occurring trees, e.g. reproductive cycle-flowering, pollination, fertilisation, seed formation, seed germination, when are seeds ready for dispersal/harvest, seedling establishment and survival, and survival of established young and older trees under natural conditions and also man-caused fires and mycorrhizal requirements.

The podocarps may present some of the more unusual problems in conservation. Most of these species occur in the middle to higher elevations in higher rainfall regions, especially as compared to the junipers and pines, which tend toward drier habitats. The junipers and podocarps may require additional observation on seed dispersal mechanisms, involving usually unknown animal vectors.

In situ conservation is desirable; however, it will be apparent that *ex situ* conservation may be a necessary adjunct for the most geographically/ecologically-isolated taxa. This will require the maintenance of the new individuals in environmentally similar conditions to those of the countryside. One of the greatest concerns here is the planning and assurance that today's efforts at species conservation will be upheld by future governments in the long term, and in the short term, by successive wildlife management agencies. This concerns particularly the long-term studies relating to the pines that have a current and future economic potential. Changes in technicians and administrations have resulted in disincentives to long-term studies when there has been no assurance of follow up or even survival of plants in protected localities. In the past, the mere presence of national forest or scientific reserve lands has not guaranteed survival of plants or animals.

Particular needs on the islands include: 1) assignment of active conservation work to an organisation capable of the scientific investigations, including a minimal staff to do field status studies and to collect materials for study and for propagation, and capable of traditional propagation techniques (initially seeds and cuttings); 2) field stations for propagation of the plants, ideally at several elevations; 3) long-term designation of areas where new plants may be placed out in the wild or even in plantations or gardens for survival over decades. It is obvious that the scientific research teams will have to secure permission and agreements to co-operate with forest and park departments of the nations to attain these goals. Little has been done on the inter-institutional level to do this in most of the countries. Co-operative efforts to increase use of the local pines will require national reforestation efforts to use locally collected seed of native species rather than to continue current practices by using exotic species from distant seed suppliers. Much of this has yet to be achieved in most areas of the Caribbean.

References

Adams, R. P. 1983. The junipers (*Juniperus*, Cupressaceae) of Hispaniola: Comparisons with other Caribbean species and among collections from Hispaniola. *Moscosoa* 2: 77-89.

Adams, R. P. 1989. *Biogeography and Evolution of the Junipers of the West Indies*. Sand Hill Crane Press: Gainesville, Florida.

Adams, R. P. 1995. Revisionary study of Caribbean species of *Juniperus* (Cupressaceae). *Phytologia* 78 (2): 134-150.

Adams, R. P., C. E. Jarvis, V. Slane and T. A. Zanoni. 1987. Typicfication of *Juniperus barbadensis* L. and *J. bermudiana* L. and the rediscovery of *J. barbadensis* from St. Lucia, BWI. *Taxon* 36 (2): 441-445.

Barrett, W. H. G. and L. Golfari. 1962. Descripción de dos nuevas variedades del "pino del Caribe" (*Pinus caribaea* Morelet). *Caribbean Forester* 23: 59-71.

Bisse, J. 1981. *Arboles de Cuba*. Editorial Científico-Técnica: La Habana, Cuba.

Buchholz, J. T. and N. E. Gray. 1948. A taxonomic revision of *Podocarpus*. IV. The American species of section *Eupodocarpus*, sub-sections C and D. *J. Arnold Arbor.* 29: 123-151, pls. I-VIII.

Carabia, J. P. 1941. Contribuciones al estudio de la flora cubana. *Caribbean Forester* 2 (2): 83-99.

Critchfield, W. B. and E. L. Little, Jr. 1966. Geographic distibution of the pines of the world. U.S. Department of Agriculture, *Forest Service Misc. Publ.* 991.: i-vi, 1-97.

Darrow, W. K. and T. A. Zanoni. 1990. Hispaniolan pine (*Pinus occidentalis* Swartz): a little known subtropical pine of economic potential. *Commonw. Forest.* Rev. 69 (2): 133-146; 69 (3): 259-271.

Farjon, A. 1998. *World Checklist and Bibliography of Conifers*. The Royal Botanic Gardens, Kew.

Farjon, A. and B. T. Styles 1997. *Pinus* (Pinaceae). *(Flora Neotropica* Monograph 75). The New York Botanical Garden., New York.

Florin, R. 1933. Die von E. I. Ekman in Westindien gesammelten Koniferen. *Arkiv för Botanik* 25A (5): 1-22.

Howard, R. A. 1973. The vegetation of the Antilles, pp. 1-38 in A. Graham (ed.). *Vegetation and vegetational history of northern Latin America*. Elsevier Scientific Publishing Co., New York.

Laubenfels, D. J. de 1984. Un nuevo *Podocarpus* (Podocarpaceae) de la Española. *Moscosoa* 3: 149-150.

Laubenfels, D. J. de 1985. A taxonomic revision of the genus *Podocarpus*. *Blumea* 30: 251-278.

Staszkiewicz, J. 1988. A taxonomic revision of the genus *Podocarpus* from the Greater and Lesser Antilles. *Fragm. Fr. Geobot.* 33 (1-2): 71-106.

Zanoni, T. A. and M. M. Mejía P. 1986. Notas sobre la flora de la isla Española. II. *Moscosoa* 4: 105-132.

Regional Action Plan

Conifers of Tasmania

Mick J. Brown and Robert S. Hill
Forestry Tasmania and University of Tasmania
Hobart, Tasmania, Australia

Description of the area

Tasmania is an island of 6.84 million ha with a cool temperate maritime climate and is situated at 40-43°S. The island is mountainous and forested with strong east-west ecological gradients driven by climate, geology, and geomorphology. Tenure is split between private (39%) and public land. Forty percent of public land is in reserves, about 27% of which is IUCN category I-IV Protected Area (For definition of IUCN Protected Areas Categories, see Appendix 3). A further 20% is State forest, which is available for wood production (Brown 1996, R.F.A. 1997). Conifers are found in most Tasmanian ecosystems, but are of comparatively minor extent in the Tasmanian landscape when compared with the sclerophyll flora. However, they are highly significant for evolutionary, aesthetic, and conservation reasons.

Ecological diversity

Tasmania has a more diverse cool temperate conifer flora than the rest of Australia combined, with 11 species (including a putative hybrid), eight of which are endemic to the island (*Callitris oblonga*, *C. rhomboidea*, and *Podocarpus lawrencei* are not). These species fall within two families, Cupressaceae (*Athrotaxis cupressoides*, *A. x laxifolia*, *A. selaginoides*, *Callitris oblonga*, *C. rhomboidea*, *Diselma archeri*) and Podocarpaceae (*Lagarostrobos franklinii*, *Microcachrys tetragona*, *Microstrobos niphophilus*, *Phyllocladus aspleniifolius*, *Podocarpus lawrencei* (formerly *P. alpinus*)).

The conifers are found mainly in the forests and on the mountains. Forests in Tasmania are of three broad types (Brown 1996) - temperate rainforest, dominated largely by *Nothofagus* together with *Atherosperma*, *Eucryphia*, and conifers (Jarman and Brown 1983); wet eucalypt forest (Kirkpatrick *et al*. 1988); and dry sclerophyll forest, (Duncan and Brown 1985) which are dominated by *Eucalyptus* although *Allocasuarina* may be locally dominant. Each of these broad forest types has more than 30% of their extent in Protected Areas. More than 80% of the distribution range of the montane conifers in Tasmania and on the Australian mainland is within IUCN category I-IV Protected Areas.

The ecology of the conifers was recently summarised by Gibson *et al*. (1995) and Bowman and Harris (1995) and the following information is taken from those sources unless otherwise referenced. *Microcachrys tetragona* and *Microstrobos niphophilus* are restricted to alpine and sub-alpine habitats in Tasmania, generally growing above the eucalypt tree-line. The former species is a prostrate shrub that occurs commonly on alpine plateaux, while the latter can grow up to 2m in height and forms dense shrubs in wind-sheltered areas. *Diselma archeri* is also largely confined to montane regions, but also occurs in some high-altitude rainforests dominated by *Athrotaxis* spp. and *Nothofagus gunnii* or *N. cunninghamii*. *Podocarpus lawrencei* is usually a prostrate shrub in alpine and subalpine habitats in Tasmania and extends in the same habitat on mainland south-eastern Australia. It may also occur as a small tree. Costin *et al*. (1979) suggested that this species may be a pioneer following glacial or periglacial conditions. These four species can sometimes co-occur in moderately exposed sites to form coniferous heath or shrubland (Jackson 1968, Kirkpatrick 1983).

One of the very few uncut primeval stands of Huon pine (*Lagarostrobos franklinii*) in Tasmania, Australia.

Lagarostrobos franklinii and *Phyllocladus aspleniifolius* are generally found in lowland cool temperate rainforest associations, and *Athrotaxis* species are found in upland forests, scrubs, and montane heaths. The structure and floristics of the individual communities may vary considerably (Jarman *et al.* 1984, 1994). *Lagarostrobos franklinii* is largely restricted to the margins of the lowland river systems of western and southern Tasmania, although there are a few large stands away from rivers and small stands at up to 1030m in altitude (Gibson 1986, Peterson 1990, Gibson *et al.* 1991). Vegetation dominated by *L. franklinii* has been estimated as less than 2600ha (Gibson *et al.* 1991), with a total distribution of 10,600ha (Peterson 1990).

Phyllocladus aspleniifolius has the broadest ecological range of any Tasmanian conifer, occurring in a variety of rainforest types from sea level to 1200m altitude, becoming dominant on the poorest soils. *Athrotaxis cupressoides* generally occurs in open montane forests at higher elevations than *A. selaginoides*. It is most prominent on valley floors and fire-protected slopes of the Central Highlands. *Athrotaxis selaginoides* occurs from sea level to 1300m altitude (although it is most common above 400m), generally as a rainforest emergent in the west of the island.

Callitris oblonga and *C. rhomboidea* occur in the east of the island, in dry sclerophyll forest, woodland, scrub, or shrubland with *Eucalyptus* and other Myrtaceae, along with a variety of scleromorphic shrubs. Both species also have a disjunct distribution in south-eastern mainland Australia, where *C. oblonga* is restricted to two areas in New South Wales and *C. rhomboidea* is more widespread. *Callitris oblonga* typically occurs in riverine environments, but it can also grow in more xeric sites typically favoured by *C. rhomboidea* (Harris and Kirkpatrick 1991). Both species are susceptible to fire.

Evolutionary history

In comparison to angiosperms, conifers are often well-represented and well-preserved in the Tasmanian fossil record, and therefore it is possible to reconstruct the history of several of the extant species and examine reasons for their current distribution and abundance.

Lagarostrobos franklinii (Hook. f.) Quinn

The fossil history of *L. franklinii* is complex. Macrofossils (leafy twigs and cones) have been recovered from several Quaternary sites on the Tasmanian west coast with the oldest being in the Early Pleistocene Regatta Point sediments (Hill and Macphail 1985, Wells and Hill 1989a). The only other macrofossil species of *Lagarostrobos* is the Early Oligocene *L. marginatus*, which was described from a single specimen in sediment from north-west Tasmania (Wells and Hill 1989b). However, this species is morphologically distinct from *L. franklinii*. There is a reasonable expectation of a much more extensive macrofossil record for *L. franklinii* or its immediate ancestor in Tasmania, since it now occurs frequently alongside water courses and is ideally placed to input litter into sedimentary environments (as evidenced by the good Quaternary record). Also, pollen attributed to *L. franklinii* (*Phyllocladidites mawsonii*) is common and sometimes dominant in Tertiary sediments throughout south-eastern Australia and even further afield. Given the large amount of fossil material which has been examined, the rarity of Tertiary *Lagarostrobos* macrofossils strongly suggests that it was uncommon in the past, and *L. franklinii* may be relatively recently evolved rather than a palaeoendemic species (Hill and Orchard 1998).

Phyllocladus aspleniifolius (Labill.) Hook. f.

Phyllocladus has two types of phylloclades - simple in *P. aspleniifolius* and *P. alpinus* (suggesting a close phylogenetic relationship) and pinnately compound in the other species. *Phyllocladus* was once more widespread across the Southern Hemisphere than it is today, with fossil pollen extending into West Antarctica (Florin 1963). During the Tertiary, *Phyllocladus* pollen and macrofossils occurred throughout south-eastern Australia (Hill 1989), and there are isolated occurrences of the pollen in western Australia (e.g. Cookson and Pike 1954) suggesting that it was a common component of the flora of mainland Australia as well as Tasmania. However, these fossil occurrences are for the genus as a whole, not necessarily *P. aspleniifolius* or its immediate ancestors. So far there is no direct evidence for the past occurrence of *P. aspleniifolius* on mainland Australia.

In Tasmania, there are several Tertiary macrofossil species of *Phyllocladus*. *Phyllocladus aspleniifolius* has been recorded from several Quaternary sites on the west coast (Hill 1989), and *P. aberensis*, which has been recovered from Eocene to Early Oligocene sediments, is morphologically very similar to *P. aspleniifolius* and is interpreted as representing an immediate ancestor to it (Hill 1989).

Thus *P. aspleniifolius* has a long history in Tasmania, and it has survived to the present day while at least two other *Phyllocladus* species have become extinct there. This species or its immediate ancestors have never been recorded as fossils outside Tasmania and its history there is uncertain. However, the presence of a closely related species in New Zealand (*P. alpinus*) also suggests a long history, although relatively recent (Tertiary) long-distance seed dispersal between New Zealand and Tasmania or vice versa cannot be ruled out (Hill and Orchard 1998). It is clear that *P. aspleniifolius* fits well within the definition of a palaeoendemic species. The survival of *P. aspleniifolius* in Tasmania while other *Phyllocladus* species have become extinct cannot yet be explained, but its absence from mainland Australia may be due to a combination of unsuitable climate and higher fire frequency.

Microcachrys tetragona (Hook.) Hook. f.

Despite the limited extant distribution of *Microcachrys tetragona*, it has a significant and widespread fossil record. Its pollen is very distinctive and grains with a similar morphology are common as fossils. These fossil pollen grains were first described by Cookson (1947) from the Kerguelen Archipelago, as *Microcachrydites antarcticus*. Later, Cookson and Pike (1954) noted the common occurrence of this species in Australian Tertiary deposits. Palynologists generally accept that this pollen type matches *M. tetragona*, but this causes some obvious ecological problems. Hill and Macphail (1983) noted that *Microcachrydites antarcticus* occurs with other species which have their nearest extant affinities in extant subtropical or temperate rainforests and that the simplest explanation of this is that the living species represents only a fraction of the Tertiary ecological range. *M. antarcticus* has a widespread distribution in both time and space, occurring as far back as the Jurassic, and as far away as India (Cookson and Pike 1954). It is also possible that *Microcachrys tetragona* represents the last remnant of a previously diverse group of podocarps which produced the *Microcachrydites antarcticus* pollen type. Unlike the angiosperms, which have radiated greatly during the Late Cretaceous and Tertiary, many coniferous groups have become extinct, and thus pollen which was in the past representative of a diverse group may now be restricted to a small remnant (Hill and Orchard 1998). If this is the case here, then many of the taxa which produced this pollen type in the past may have had little in common with *M. tetragona* either morphologically or ecologically.

The only pre-Quaternary macrofossil record of *Microcachrys* is a leafy twig from the Oligocene-Miocene Morwell Open Cut coal mine in Victoria (Blackburn 1985) which is very similar to extant *M. tetragona*. These specimens occur at low altitude with a mixture of species with living affinities ranging northwards to subtropical rainforests. If it is accepted that morphology to some degree at least reflects the physiological response of the plant, then this fossil appears to be ecologically out of place (Hill and Orchard 1998). However, the presence of fossil shoots which strongly resemble *M. tetragona* at Morwell provide strong supporting evidence for the hypothesis that this genus has become very restricted ecologically in the relatively recent past and was once much more widespread, and thus it can be considered as a palaeoendemic species.

Microstrobos niphophilus J. Garden and L. A. S. Johnson

The fossil record of *Microstrobos* is sparse. The fossil pollen species *Podosporites erugatus*, which ranges from the Late Eocene onwards in New Zealand, probably represents *Microstrobos niphophilus* (e.g. Hill and Macphail 1983). However, in Australia this species has only been recorded in Tasmania where it occurs from the Oligocene onwards (Hill and Macphail 1983,1985).

Macrofossils of *Microstrobos* are known from three localities in Tasmania. *Microstrobos sommervillae*, (Townrow 1965a) from the Early Eocene Buckland sediments in southeastern Tasmania, is intermediate between the two extant species. The other fossil species, *M. microfolius*, has been recovered from two localities spanning the Oligocene-Early Miocene (Wells and Hill 1989b) and is virtually identical in leaf

morphology with the extant Tasmanian species *M. niphophilus*. The Early Oligocene specimens are associated with rainforest species which now have their affinities in forests up the east coast of Australia and into the highlands of New Guinea. These species suggest a relatively high temperature and *M. microfolius* appears out of place in such an environment. However, the Late Oligocene-Early Miocene specimens tie in well with the ecology of the extant species, since they are considered to be part of an embryonic sub-alpine flora (Macphail *et al*. 1991). The full ecophysiological significance of these macrofossil records is not yet understood, but extant *M. niphophilus* may only be occurring in a fraction of its past ecological range. *Microstrobos niphophilus* can clearly be considered as a palaeoendemic species (Hill and Orchard 1998).

Podocarpus lawrencei Hook. f.

Podocarpus leaves and occasional cones are common fossils within south-eastern Australia, but very little critical research has been carried out on them. In the Early Tertiary, the vegetative fossils are extremely variable, with a range of size from very large (similar to many extant tropical species) down to very small (within the range of *P. lawrencei*). Given the abundant evidence for a reduction in leaf size in response to declining temperature through the Tertiary in Tasmania (e.g. Hill 1995), it is likely that *P. lawrencei* is the result of this process and represents a palaeoendemic species.

Diselma archeri Hook. f.

Li (1953) considered *Diselma* to be part of the subfamily Callitroideae of the Cupressaceae, allying it with several other southern genera. However, the past history of *Diselma* is unknown, since there is no certain fossil record. The pollen of Cupressaceae is well known in the Australian fossil record, but resolution below the family level is poor and macrofossils of *Diselma* are unknown. The similarity in leaf morphology of *D. archeri*, *Microcachrys tetragona*, and *Microstrobos niphophilus* and their broadly similar distribution suggests that similar factors may have affected all three species. While it is probable that *D. archeri* is a palaeoendemic species, this cannot be demonstrated with certainty.

Alpine 'heath' with scattered clumps of *Diselma archeri* in Western Tasmania, Australia.

Athrotaxis D. Don

The two *Athrotaxis* species are best considered together, since the fossil record applies to both of them. The fossil pollen record is of little assistance since the pollen is of a general cupressaceous type and hardly distinct at the species level. However, leafy twigs of *Athrotaxis* have been reported from the Early Cretaceous of Canada and Argentina; Miller (1977) notes that the latter record has cuticle structure preserved which supports the identification. Miller (1977) also mentions impressions of foliage and cones like those of modern *Athrotaxis* from the Early Cretaceous of the eastern United States of America. Species of *Athrotaxis* have also been described from Tertiary sediments in New Zealand, South America, and Tasmania (Townrow 1965b, Hill *et al.* 1993). However, Hill and Carpenter (1991) noted that some macrofossils previously given affinity with *Athrotaxis* have not withstood critical re-examination. It is now also clear that other genera with similar gross vegetative morphology to *Athrotaxis* have occurred in Australasia in the past (e.g. *Austrasequoia*, see Peters and Christophel (1978), Hill *et al.* (1993)). There are macrofossil records of *Athrotaxis* from mainland Australia, but they are either hardly determinable or in need of revision and could represent a number of genera in other families. Hill and Carpenter (1991) concluded that none of the fossil species from outside Tasmania should be considered as unambiguous records of *Athrotaxis* at this stage.

A stand of ancient Pencil pines (*Athrotaxis cupressoides*) in Tasmania, Australia.

Within Tasmania, Townrow (1965b) reported specimens of *Athrotaxis ungeri* (originally described from South American specimens) from the Early Eocene. This species is distinct from all extant species, although in leaf size is closest to *A. cupressoides*. It is probable that the Tasmanian specimens are distinct from the South American specimens of *A. ungeri* (Hill and Carpenter 1991). Hill *et al.* (1993) described *Athrotaxis* foliage and reproductive structures from several Oligo-Miocene Tasmanian sites, and erected the new species, *A. mesibovii*, to accommodate most specimens. *A. mesibovii* has foliage reminiscent of extant *A. selaginoides*. They also transferred the fossil species *Mesibovia rhomboidea* to *Athrotaxis*, although this species is very distinct from all extant species. Therefore, the reliable fossil record of *Athrotaxis* is confined to post-Cretaceous sediments in Tasmania. *Athrotaxis* represents an enigma - it is the survivor of a more diverse cupressaceous flora in Australia in the past, but it is still relatively common and widespread in Tasmania. We do not know whether it ever occurred outside the Tasmanian region, and if so when it became extinct there. Its continued presence in Tasmania remains a puzzle for biogeographers and palaeobotanists, but *A. selaginoides* and *A. cupressoides* at least can be considered as palaeoendemic species.

Callitris Vent.

Callitris has a very poor fossil record, with only two macrofossil sites known (Hill 1995). One of these is in Tasmania (Jordan 1995), but the fossils concerned are not phylogenetically close to the two extant Tasmanian species. In the absence of evidence it is difficult to account for the presence of the extant Tasmanian species.

Conservation of Tasmanian conifers

The main conservation issues for Tasmanian conifers now come from conversion of native vegetation for agriculture or plantation forest establishment in eastern Tasmania, and from fire in western Tasmania. The only species directly affected by land clearance are the two *Callitris* species, and the plans in place to deal with the risks from this practice are outlined below for the individual species. The habitats of the other conifers are largely contained within reserves, and the main issue for their continued survival is the development and implementation of appropriate fire regimes. Below there are some examples of regeneration failure due to grazing and unexplained dieback in *Athrotaxis cupressoides,* but in general conservation of the conifers in western Tasmania is a problem of fire management rather than resource extraction.

Aborigines have occupied Tasmania for at least 30,000 years (Cosgrove 1989), and fire has been in continuous use during that time. Fire has had a considerable effect on the distributions of the Tasmanian conifers, most of which are extremely fire sensitive, because they lack the adaptations seen in some conifers of the Northern Hemisphere and in the Australian autochthonous sclerophyll vegetation (Regal 1979, Beadle 1981). At European settlement in the early

1800s, Tasmania was extensively forested but there were many open areas also - of montane vegetation in central Tasmania, grassland and grassy woodlands in the east and north-west, coastal heaths and scrubs and importantly about 1 million ha of pyrogenic buttongrass moorlands in the high rainfall, oligotrophic environments of the west. These moorlands are the edaphic climax on poorly drained low nutrient soils but have expanded far beyond these situations because of anthropogenic firing of the vegetation both by Aborigines and subsequently by Europeans (Plomley 1966, Jackson 1968, Jones 1969, Brown and Podger 1982, Bowman and Brown 1986, Cosgrove 1989). These expansions have been at the expense of the forests and in particular of the conifers. Thus some current buttongrass plains retain stems and dead wood of *Phyllocladus* and sub-fossil wood (c. 2000 years old) of *Athrotaxis* (Podger *et al.* 1989, F. Podger pers. comm.).

The Tasmanian landscape now reflects the effects of nearly 200 years of European settlement. This occupancy is most obvious in the drier eastern half of the state but its effects are visible almost everywhere. In Tasmania, as elsewhere in Australia and the world, there has been a pattern of clearance of the fertile valleys and plains, the mountain tops and infertile areas have been proclaimed as National Parks or other Protected Areas, and the forests in between have been utilised for wood production (Brown 1996). Most wood production was and is from *Eucalyptus* species, the native conifers are no longer utilised except from salvage or dead and downed material for craft wood. The main conifer species used for timber were *Athrotaxis selaginoides* and *Lagarostrobos franklinii*. The latter species grows in riparian situations and was much prized for boat building. Logging of the species was fairly benign, in that only intermediate size classes were targeted, and then only within easy reach of the river bank, so that most logged stands today appear intact. In the wetter western parts of the state and in the Central Highlands there has been considerable hydroelectric development, which has resulted in the inundation of many of the river valleys and low-lying plains. Mining has also been a major industry in Tasmania and has resulted in the past in loss of conifer habitat, particularly in the later part of the 19th century and early 20th century in western Tasmania. The fires of mineral prospectors in the same period have also depleted conifer stands. Despite all of these incursions, forests still occupy 82% of the forested area that was present at European settlement of Tasmania (Brown 1996). Until recently most of the public interest and disputes about logging, mining, and hydroelectric development have been about wilderness and visual or aesthetic values and have not addressed biodiversity conservation (Brown and Hickey 1990). Because of the bias towards western Tasmania, this interest has resulted in a high proportion of the forest and montane coniferous vegetation being placed in legislated Protected Areas, particularly the Western Tasmania Wilderness World Heritage Area (WTWWHA).

Fires are a natural part of the overall ecosystem process in the WTWWHA; the area of the total ecosystem is rela-

A burnt stand of ancient *Athrotaxis* killed by the fire, being replaced by other vegetation, Tasmania, Australia.

tively large (1.4 million ha), but the area occupied by conifers is small, dispersed and restricted to areas topographically protected from fire. Thus two of the most fire sensitive Tasmanian endemic conifers, Huon pine (*Lagarostrobos franklinii*) and King Billy pine (*Athrotaxis selaginoides*) are now restricted to river courses and fire shadow areas on mountain slopes. These species are killed outright by fire and have no recovery mechanisms other than step-wise recolonisation from adjacent unburned areas. *A. selaginoides* previously occupied about 50,000ha but approximately one third of its population by area has been killed by fire in the past 100 years (Brown 1988). The ages of the oldest trees in sampled stands are 800+ (-1200) years, and this rate of attrition by fire is clearly not ecologically sustainable. Huon pine lives for 2000+ years, and its populations are restricted largely to riverine situations, again in areas protected from fire (Peterson 1990). Both species are found in specialised habitats and are not able to migrate in the landscape on timetables that accord with likely fire regimes. The ecotone between the very old conifer stands and the flammable buttongrass moorlands can be as little as 10-30m wide (Gibson 1986). Thus, maintenance of these species will require active management of fires; a simple model of benign neglect and of letting wildfires take their course is not sufficient to ensure the survival of these species (Brown 1996). Active habitat management will be needed to maintain species found on the buttongrass plains, and active suppression of fires will be needed in and near the conifers. Such management is not assisted by the non-random nature of fires and the fact that the patterns of anthropogenic fire that prevail are not those of the past.

Conservation status of individual species

In undertaking a review of the status of individual species, it soon became apparent to us that the current IUCN guidelines are misleading if applied rigidly to the Tasmanian conifers, and we suspect to any long lived tree species. The problem arises from having to determine decline over three generations, when generation time is defined in terms of "average

age of parents in the population". In the case of *Lagarostrobos* for example, three generations could take us back to the commencement of the Holocene, and it could be argued (and demonstrated via the pollen record) that the species has in fact expanded its range since that time, not declined. Most of its problems have arisen in the last 200 years and its population is almost entirely reserved. Of more immediate relevance is the fact that *Athrotaxis selaginoides* is nearly all within Protected Areas, the last major fire events that significantly affected stands were 30-60 years ago, and fire management techniques are now far better developed. There are no other actions that can be taken to improve the outlook for the species, yet it is still listed as Vulnerable under the current guidelines. We are far more comfortable with the alternative treatment proposed by Farjon and Page in which a maximum of 50 years be used for a generation, and that two generations (or this century) be used to calculate decline. In the treatment below we have used both sets of guidelines.

Athrotaxis cupressoides D. Don

This species is rated as Vulnerable under IUCN criteria A1a+c. The species is extremely fire sensitive and much of the total population was fire-killed mainly in widespread fires on the Central Plateau in 1960/61. All remaining areas of the species (and much of the fire-killed area) are now within IUCN Category I-IV reserves. Regeneration of the species is limited by grazing by introduced and native animals, mainly sheep and rabbits. Stock are no longer a problem, but the threat from rabbits remains. Some stands of this species show symptoms of a high-altitude dieback, which has an as yet unconfirmed association with a species of *Phytophthora,* a root rotting fungal pathogen.

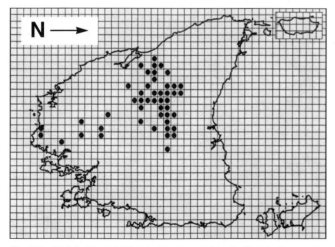

Fig 3.3. Distribution of *Athrotaxis cupressoides* in Tasmania.

Athrotaxis x *laxifolia* Hook.

This putative hybrid is Vulnerable under the IUCN criterion D1. Because it is probably a hybrid, it is only found in areas of overlap of the two parental species, usually as solitary individuals (Cullen and Kirkpatrick 1988) but occasionally as hybrid swarms. Nearly all known individuals are in reserves.

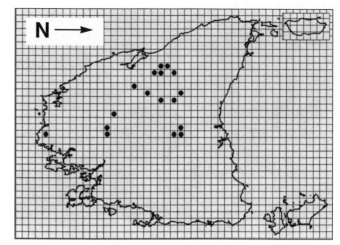

Fig 3.4. Distribution of *Athrotaxis x laxifolia* in Tasmania.

Athrotaxis selaginoides D. Don

This species is rated as Vulnerable under IUCN criteria A1a+c, but would be LRlc or LRcd under the proposed amendments of Farjon and Page, a status which accords with our own perceptions of the risk to the species. The species is fire sensitive and about 1/3 of its habitat has been burned in the past century or so, primarily in the 19th century (Brown 1988). The species habitat protection is now stabilised with 84% of forests in reserves. Tasmanian Government policy precludes logging of the remainder, which is found in informal reserves in small, widely dispersed stands.

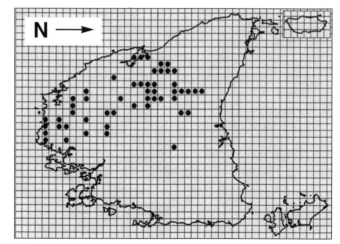

Fig 3.5. Distribution of *Athrotaxis selaginoides* in Tasmania.

Callitris oblonga Rich. and A. Rich.

This species is rated as Vulnerable under the IUCN criterion A1c and is also Vulnerable under the Farjon and Page criteria. It has been in decline mainly from land clearance, which remains a problem on private land. Regeneration success is limited by inappropriate fire regimes combined with invasion by gorse and by stock grazing. A recovery plan for the species is under way and entails active liaison with land owners, active stand rehabilitation and reservation where possible. The species is listed as vulnerable under State legislation.

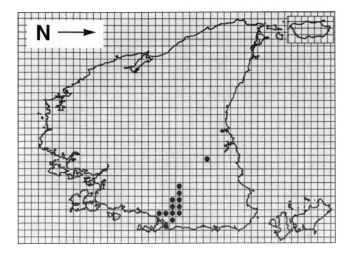

Fig 3.6. Distribution of *Callitris oblonga* in Tasmania.

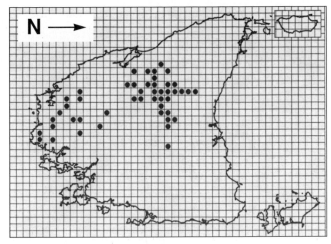

Fig 3.8. Distribution of *Diselma archeri* in Tasmania.

Callitris rhomboidea R. Br. ex Rich. and A. Rich.

This species is not threatened under either set of criteria. It is widespread and locally common. However closed stands of the species that were reported as abundant at European settlement are now rare. There are many stands of the species in IUCN Category I-IV Reserves. The main future threats to stands outside reserves come from agriculture and expansion of human habitation.

Lagarostrobos franklinii (Hook. f.) Quinn

This species is not threatened under either set of criteria, but can be listed as LRcd. An estimated 15% of its habitat has been lost through inundation for hydroelectric schemes and to fire over the past 100 years or so. The construction of such schemes in Tasmania has now ceased, and 86% of the remaining area of Huon pine is in legislated reserves. One stand of pine has been made available for access to craft wood from dead and downed timber, but there is no cutting of green Huon pine. Management of fire is the main priority for ensuring its continued conservation under the currently prevailing policies.

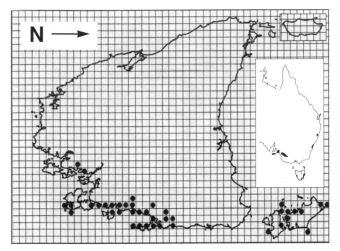

Fig 3.7. Distribution of *Callitris rhomboidea* in Tasmania and Australia.

Diselma archeri Hook. f.

This species is not threatened under either set of criteria. It is fire sensitive but has a wide distribution on Tasmanian mountains, where it is almost entirely reserved within the WTWWH.

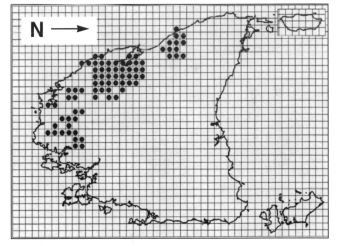

Fig 3.9. Distribution of *Lagarostrobos franklinii* in Tasmania.

Microcachrys tetragona (Hook.) Hook. f.

This species is locally abundant and widely distributed on Tasmania mountains, and its populations are all within Protected Areas. It is not at risk under any of the IUCN criteria but in common with all montane vegetation requires protection from fire.

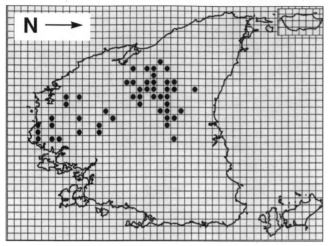

Fig 3.10. Distribution of *Microcachrys teragona* in Tasmania.

Microstrobos niphophilus J. Garden and L. A. S. Johnson

This species is locally common but widespread on mountains where it is potentially at risk from fire across its range. However, it does not meet any of the IUCN criteria for listing. Its habitats are almost entirely within IUCN Category I-IV Protected Areas.

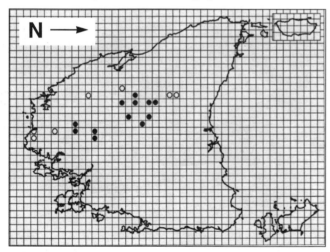

Fig 3.11. Distribution of *Microstrobos niphophilus* in Tasmania.

Phyllocladus aspleniifolius (Labill.) Hook. f.

This species is widespread and frequent in wet eucalypt forests and in rainforest. It is found in many reserves and regenerates freely in logged and burned forests. It does not meet any of the criteria for listing under the IUCN guidelines.

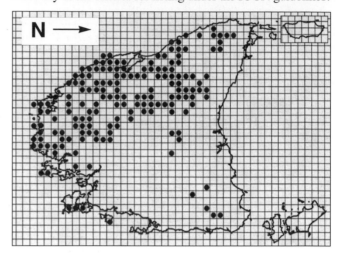

Fig 3.12. Distribution of *Phyllocladus aspleniifolius* in Tasmania.

Podocarpus lawrencei Hook. f.

This species is widespread and abundant in appropriate habitats across its range and is not at risk. Most of its habitat in Tasmania and all of its known populations on the Australian mainland are within IUCN Category I-IV Protected Areas.

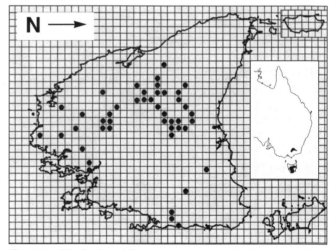

Fig 3.13. Distribution of *Podocarpus lawrencei* in Tasmania and Australia.

References

Beadle, N. C. W. 1981. *The Vegetation of Australia*. Cambridge University Press, Cambridge.

Blackburn, D. T. 1985. Palaeobotany of the Yallourn and Morwell coal seams. *Palaeobotanical Project - report 3. SECV.*

Bowman, D. M. J. S. and M. J. Brown 1986. Bushfires in Tasmania : a botanical approach to anthropological questions. *Archaeology in Oceania* 21: 166-171.

Bowman, D. M. J. S. and S. Harris 1995. Conifers of Australia's dry forests and open woodlands. In: N. J. Enright and R. S. Hill (eds.). *Ecology of the Southern Conifers*. pp. 252-270. Melbourne University Press, Melbourne.

Brown, M. J. 1988. *The Distribution and Conservation of King Billy Pine*. Forestry Commission, Tasmania.

Brown, M. J. 1996. Benign neglect and active management in Tasmania's forests: a dynamic balance or ecological collapse? *Forest Ecology and Management* 85: 279-289.

Brown, M. J. and J. E. Hickey 1990. Tasmanian forest - genes or wilderness? *Search* 21: 86-87.

Brown, M. J. and F. D. Podger 1982. Floristics and fire regimes of a vegetation sequence from sedgeland - heath to rainforest at Bathurst Harbour, Tasmania. *Austral. J. Bot.* 30: 659-676.

Cookson, I. C. 1947. Plant microfossils from the lignites of Kerguelen Archipelago. *B.A.N.Z. Antarctic Research Expedition 1929-1931 Reports, Series* A2: 127-142.

Cookson, I. C. and K. M. Pike 1954. The fossil occurrence of Phyllocladus and two other podocarpaceous types in Australia. *Austral. J. Bot.* 2: 60-67.

Cosgrove R. 1989. Thirty thousand years of human colonisation in Tasmania - new Pleistocene dates. *Science 243*: 1706-1708.

Costin, A. B., M. Grey, C. J. Totterdell and D. J. Wimbush 1979. *Kosciusko Alpine Flora.* CSIRO/Collins, Melbourne.

Cullen, P. J. and J. B. Kirkpatrick 1988. The ecology of *Athrotaxis* D. Don (Taxodiaceae). I. Stand structure and regeneration of *A. cupressoides. Australian Journal of Botany* 36: 547-560.

Duncan, F. and M. J. Brown 1985. Dry sclerophyll vegetation in Tasmania. Extent and conservation status of the communities. *Wildlife Division Technical Report* No. 85/1. Tasmanian National Parks and Wildlife Service.

Florin, R. 1963. The distribution of conifer and taxad genera in time and space. *Acta Horti Bergiani* 20: 121-312.

Gibson, N. 1986. The conservation and management of Huon pine in Tasmania. *Wildlife Division Technical Report* No. 86/3.Tasmanian National Parks and Wildlife Service.

Gibson, N., J. Davies and M. J. Brown 1991. The ecology of *Lagarostrobos franklinii* (Hook. f.) Quinn in Tasmania. 1. Distribution, floristics and environmental correlates. *Austral. J. Ecol.* 16: 215-229.

Gibson, N., P. C. J. Barker, P. J. Cullen and A. Shapcott 1995. Conifers of southern Australia. In: N. J. Enright and R. S. Hill (eds.). *Ecology of the Southern Conifers.* pp. 223-251. Melbourne University Press, Melbourne.

Harris, S. and J. B. Kirkpatrick 1991. The distribution, dynamics and ecological differentiation of *Callitris* species in Tasmania. *Austral. J. Bot.* 39: 187-202.

Hill, R. S. 1989. New species of *Phyllocladus* (Podocarpaceae) macrofossils from south eastern Australia. *Alcheringa* 13: 193-208.

Hill, R. S. 1995. Conifer origin, evolution and diversification in the Southern Hemisphere. In: N. J. Enright and R. S. Hill (eds.). *Ecology of the Southern Conifers.* pp. 10-29. Melbourne University Press, Melbourne.

Hill, R. S. and R. J. Carpenter 1991. Evolution of *Acmopyle* and *Dacrycarpus* (Podocarpaceae) foliage as inferred from macrofossils in south-eastern Australia. *Austral. Syst. Bot.* 4: 449-479.

Hill, R. S., G. J. Jordan and R. J. Carpenter 1993. Taxodiaceous macrofossils from Tertiary and Quaternary sediments in Tasmania. *Austral. Syst. Bot.* 6: 237-249.

Hill, R. S. and M. K. Macphail 1983. Reconstruction of the Oligocene vegetation at Pioneer, northeast Tasmania. *Alcheringa* 7: 281-299.

Hill, R. S. and M. K. Macphail 1985. A fossil flora from rafted Plio-Pleistocene mudstones at Regatta Point, Tasmania. *Austral. J. Bot.* 33: 497-517.

Hill, R. S. and A. E. Orchard 1998. Composition and endemism: vascular plants. In: J. B. Reid, R. S. Hill, M. J. Brown and M. J. Hovenden (eds.). *Vegetation of Tasmania.* ABRS, Canberra.

Jackson, W. D. 1968. Fire, air, water and earth - an elemental ecology of Tasmania. *Proc. Ecol. Soc.* Australia 3: 9-16.

Jarman, S. J. and M. J. Brown 1983. A definition of cool temperate rainforest in Tasmania. *Search* 14: 81-87.

Jarman, S. J., M. J. Brown and G. Kantvilas 1984. *Rainforest in Tasmania.* Tasmanian National Parks and Wildlife Service.

Jarman, S. J., G. Kantvilas and M. J. Brown 1994. Phytosociological studies in Tasmanian cool temperate rainforest. *Phytocoenologia* 22 (3): 355-390.

Jones, R. 1969. Fire-stick farming. *Austral. Nat. Hist.* 16: 224-248.

Jordan, G. J. 1995. Extinct conifers and conifer diversity in the Early Pleistocene of western Tasmania. *Rev. Palaeobot. Palynol.* 84: 375-387.

Kirkpatrick, J. B. 1983. Treeless plant communities of the Tasmanian high country. *Proc. Ecol. Soc. Australia* 12: 61-77.

Kirkpatrick, J. B., R. J. Peacock, P. J. Cullen and M. J. Neyland 1988. *The Wet Eucalypt Forests of Tasmania.* Tasmanian Conservation Trust, Hobart.

Li, H. L. (1953). Present distribution and habitats of the conifers and taxads. *Evolution* 7: 245-261.

Macphail, M. K., R. S. Hill, S. M. Forsyth and P. M. Wells 1991. A Late Oligocene-Early Miocene cool climate flora in Tasmania. *Alcheringa* 15: 87-106.

Miller, C. N. 1977. Mesozoic conifers. *Bot. Rev.* 43: 217-280.

Peters, M. D. and D. C. Christophel 1978. *Austrosequoia wintonensis,* a new taxodiaceous cone from Queensland, Australia. *Canad. J. Bot.* 56: 3119-3128.

Peterson, M. J. 1990. *Distribution and Conservation of Huon Pine.* Forestry Commission, Tasmania.

Plomley N. J. B. 1966. *Friendly mission: The Tasmanian journals and papers of George Augustus Robinson 1829-1834.* Tasmanian Historical Research Association, Hobart.

Podger, F. D., T. Bird and M. J. Brown 1989. Human activity, fire and change in the forest at Hogsback Plain, southern Tasmania. In: K. J. Frawley and N. Semple (eds.). *Australia's ever changing forests.* Australian Defence Force Academy, Canberra.

Regal, P. 1979. Australia's own pines. *Austral. Nat. Hist.* 19: 386-391.

R.F.A. 1997. *Tasmanian Regional Forest Agreement between the Commonwealth of Australia and the State of Tasmania.* Commonwealth of Australia, Canberra.

Townrow, J. A. 1965a. Notes on some Tasmanian pines I. Some Lower Tertiary podocarps. *Pap. Proc. Roy. Soc. Tasmania* 99: 87-107.

Townrow, J. A. 1965b. Notes on some Tasmanian pines II. *Athrotaxis* from the Lower Tertiary. *Pap. Proc. Roy. Soc. Tasmania* 99: 109-113.

Townrow, J. A. 1967. On *Rissikia* and *Mataia,* podocarpaceous conifers from the Lower Mesozoic of southern lands. *Pap. Proc. Roy. Soc. Tasmania* 101: 103-136.

Wells, P. M. and R. S. Hill 1989a. Leaf morphology of the imbricate-leaved Podocarpaceae. *Austral. Syst. Bot.* 2: 369-386.

Wells, P. M. and R. S. Hill 1989b. Fossil imbricate-leaved Podocarpaceae from Tertiary sediments in Tasmania. *Austral. Syst. Bot.* 2: 387-423.

Regional Action Plan

Conifers of the Oceanic Islands in the Insular South Pacific (Fiji, Tonga, Solomon Islands and Vanuatu)

Michael F. Doyle
Jepson and University Herbaria
University of California

Description of the area

The oceanic (volcanic) islands of the Southwest Pacific (Fiji, Tonga, Solomon Islands, and Vanuatu) are floristically poorer than the rich Indo-Malesian region to the west, and New Caledonia and New Zealand to the south, but are notable because some of their floras (esp. the high islands of Fiji and Vanuatu) have considerable endemism (c. 30-50%). Fiji represents the easternmost distribution of many Malesian genera, especially palms (Doyle and Fuller 1998) and conifers (Doyle 1998). The occurrence of gymnosperms on some of these islands (e.g. Fiji) has been construed by some biogeographers to suggest past continental connections, but all taxa present can be accounted for by long-distance dispersal (Doyle 1998). Dispersal events ranging from nearby island-hopping ("stepping stones") to moderate or long distance dispersal generally relates to the overall diversity of taxa on each island group. Predictably, the floristic richness of each island group is correlated to its geographic position in relation to source areas and geological age, combined with the availability and diversity of suitable habitats. The islands closest to the Malesian source area (Solomon Islands) have the highest diversity, and the islands farthest away (Tonga) have the lowest. However, other factors such as topography, area, bird and bat migratory routes, and sheer chance are also factors. Only Vanuatu does not fit the predicted model, and this is probably both a reflection of inadequate botanical exploration there, and other variables, as discussed above.

The vast majority of the information available for the conifers of the region is purely taxonomic and preliminary in nature; little is known about their biology and ecology. Many taxa within the region (e.g. *Acmopyle sahniana* J. Buchholz and N. E. Gray) are of particular scientific interest because of their relictual Gondwanan ancestry and are in desperate need of detailed scientific study before they are eliminated from their natural habitats by logging or other human disturbances. The region has served as a refugium for relicts; this fact makes taxon-specific conservation efforts necessary in many cases.

Summary of conifers within the region

Eighteen conifers are known to occur on the volcanic islands of the Southwest Pacific. The Solomon Islands possess the greatest number of taxa (13), followed by Fiji (8), Vanuatu (4) and Tonga (1) (Table 3.1). Within the region, the Solomon Islands have the greatest conifer diversity outside New Caledonia and New Guinea. Fiji possesses three endemic conifer species, also greater than elsewhere within the region except for New Caledonia, which has 43 endemic taxa.

The gymnosperm flora of Fiji has recently been critically reviewed by Doyle (1998), with a single taxon (*Acmopyle sahniana*) recently re-described (Bush and Doyle 1997). Several of the region's rare endemic gymnosperms are now being critically assessed for genetic diversity and conservation purposes (Doyle, unpublished data). Among the taxa occurring in the region, three are narrow endemics confined to a single island: *Acmopyle sahniana* J. Buchholz and N. E. Gray and *Podocarpus affinis* Seem.; and *P. salomoniensis* Wassch. endemic to Viti Levu (Fiji), San Cristobal (Solomon Islands), respectively. *Dacrydium nausoriense* de Laub. is confined to two islands - Viti Levu and Vanua Levu (Fiji) and *P. pallidus* N. E. Gray to the islands of 'Eua and Vava'u (Tonga). A single taxon, *Agathis macrophylla* (Lind.) Mast., is a "regional" endemic, being confined to Fiji, the Solomon Islands and Vanuatu. Of the taxa endemic to the region, it is notable that four (67%): *Acmopyle sahniana*, *Agathis macrophylla*, *Podocarpus affinis*, and *Dacrydium nausoriense*, are limited to Fiji, making this area the richest in terms of endemic taxa. Following Fiji, only the Solomon Islands and Tonga possess endemic species, *Podocarpus salomoniensis* and *P. pallidus*, respectively. Based on geological and geographical similarities of some Vanuatu islands (e.g. Espirito Santo) with Fiji's larger islands, it is surprising that more taxa are not shared between the two archipelagos. It is anticipated that additional botanical exploration in the region will reveal both new taxa and new distribution records.

Montane TMF (tropical moist forest) at Namosi, Viti Levu, Fiji. Habitat for seven native Fijian conifers - *Acmopyle sahniana*, *Agathis macrophylla*, *Dacrycarpus imbricatus* var. *patulus*, *Dacrydium nidulum*, *Podocarpus affinis*, *Podocarpus neriifolius*, and *Retrophyllum vitiense*.

Table 3.1. Conifers of the volcanic islands of the Southwest Pacific.

Species	Distribution[1]	Global Conservation status[2]	Status on each island group[3]			
			F	S	V	T
Araucariaceae						
Agathis macrophylla (Lindl.) Mast.	F, S, V (e)	LRnt	VU A2d, B2e	NE	VU A2d, B2e	-
Podocarpaceae						
Acmopyle sahniana J. Buchholz and N. E. Gray	F (e)	CR D	CR D	-	-	-
Dacrycarpus imbricatus var. *patulus* de Laub.	F, S, V	Not evaluated	LRlc	LRlc	DD	-
Dacrydium beccarrii Parl.	S	Not evaluated	-	DD	-	-
D. magnum de Laub.	S	LRnt	-	DD	-	-
D. nausoriense de Laub.	F (e)	EN A1cd, B1+2ce, C1	EN A1cd, B1+2ce, C1	-	-	-
D. nidulum de Laub.	F	Not evaluated	LRlc	-	-	-
D. xanthandrum Pilg.	S	Not evaluated	-	DD	-	-
Podocarpus affinis Seem.	F (e)	VU A1c +2c	VU A1c +2c	-	-	-
P. glaucus Foxw.	S	Not evaluated	-	DD	-	-
P. insularis de Laub.	S, V	Not evaluated	-	DD	DD	-
P. neriifolius D. Don	F, S, V	Not evaluated	LRlc	LRlc	DD	-
P. pallidus N. E. Gray	T (e)	DD	-	-	-	DD
P. pilgeri Foxw.	S	Not evaluated	-	DD	-	-
P. rumphii Blume	S	Not evaluated	-	DD	-	-
P. salomoniensis Wasscher	S (e)	Not evaluated	-	NE	-	-
P. spathoides de Laub.	S	DD	-	DD	-	-
Retrophyllum vitiense (Seem.) C. N. Page	F, S	Not evaluated	LRlc	LRlc	-	-

[1] Distribution code: F=Fiji, S=Solomon Islands, T=Tonga, V=Vanuatu; (e)=endemic to one or more of the above island groups, all other species are indigenous and occur elsewhere (e.g., Malesia).

[2] Species have been assessed using IUCN Red List Categories (IUCN 1994).

[3] Where global status is unknown, the conservation status (where known) has been provided for each geographically separated population in this region.

Distribution

Among the conifers of the region, members of the Podocarpaceae (*Acmopyle*, *Dacrycarpus*, *Dacrydium*, and *Podocarpus*) are abiotically or biotically (birds and bats) dispersed, while members of the Araucariaceae (*Agathis*) are dispersed abiotically by wind and water (Doyle 1998). Cyclones, which are common in the area during summer months, are presumably important for both local and long-distance dispersal and regeneration of the species. Many conifer taxa within the region are best developed in montane tropical rainforest habitats, and all but two species (*Dacrydium magnum* from the Solomon Islands and *Podocarpus pallidus* from Tonga) are most abundant, or limited in occurrence, above c. 400m elevation. [*Dacrydium magnum* de Laub. was described in 1969 with a type specimen from Obi Island in the Moluccas; it is also reported from the Louisiades Archipelago east of New Guinea. - the compilers]

Conservation status and recommendations

The most recent treatment of the conservation status of conifers within the region is for Fiji (Doyle 1998). Two previous world-wide reports on rare and endangered conifers and other trees (Farjon *et al.* 1993, Oldfield *et al.* 1998) include taxa from the region, but are listings with only limited information on species within the insular SW Pacific region. Some species are very poorly known, particularly under-collected species confined to remote or montane areas within the region (e.g. Solomon Islands and Vanuatu). These taxa are listed in Table 3.1 as "DD" denoting Data Deficient. All endemic Data Deficient taxa should be targeted for immediate study.

Human-induced impacts including fires, logging, mining, and land conversion have reduced the abundance of all native conifer taxa within the region. Several species (e.g., *Agathis macrophylla*, *Dacrycarpus imbricatus*, *Dacrydium nausoriense*, *D. nidulum*, *Podocarpus neriifolius*, and

Dacrydium nausoriense. Habit. Elevation c. 750 m., Nausori Highlands, Viti Levu, Fiji.

Retrophyllum vitiense) are considered excellent timber sources, with some (e.g., *A. macrophylla*) becoming scarce, or even endangered locally because of continued overexploitation. The rarest and most notable taxon within the region, *Acmopyle sahniana*, is directly endangered by proposed mining activities. A second taxon, *Dacrydium nausoriense*, is also endangered because it provides good timber; it is confined to two small declining populations in Fiji. Some planting schemes of native conifers have been attempted within the region, but in most cases more swiftly growing (and in some cases invasive) exotic species such as *Pinus caribaea* Morelet and *Swietenia mahogani* (L.) Jacq. are preferred by foresters. However, it is expected that as native conifer timbers become rare they will command significantly higher prices than exotic timbers, and re-planting schemes for native taxa should be encouraged for both ecological and economic reasons.

Detailed conservation biology work (including population genetics) has been conducted for *Acmopyle sahniana* (Bush 1997, Doyle *et al.*, unpublished data), and *Dacrydium nausoriense* (Doyle 1998, and Doyle, unpublished data) and is now underway for all endemic Fijian conifers as well as *Cycas seemanni* (Doyle 1998, and Doyle, unpublished data, and Doyle and Keppel, unpublished data, respectively). Unlike other naturally rare conifers assessed for genetic diversity, the rare Fijian endemic *Acmopyle sahniana* shows remarkable genetic variation (Bush 1997). Conservation priorities on a regional basis make Fiji the most important island group because of its larger representation of both endemic taxa (67% of the region's endemic conifers) and more widely distributed taxa (44% of the region's conifers occur in Fiji). It is expected that as more information (especially biological, genetic, and ecological) becomes available, well-designed science-based conservation programmes can be implemented for the long-term conservation of these relict plants.

References

Bush, E. W. 1997 (unpublished). *The ecology and conservation biology of Acmopyle sahniana Buchh. and N.E. Gray (Podocarpaceae).* M.Sc. Thesis. Biology Department, School of Pure and Applied Sciences, The University of the South Pacific, Suva, Fiji.

Bush, E. W. and M. F. Doyle. 1997. Taxonomic re-description of *Acmopyle sahniana* (Podocarpaceae): Additions, revisions, discussion. *Harvard Pap. Bot.* 2 (2): 229-233.

Doyle, M. F. 1998. Gymnosperms of the SW Pacific. I. Fiji's endemic and indigenous species: changes in nomenclature, key, annotated checklist, and discussion. *Harvard Pap. Bot.* 3 (1): 101-106.

Doyle, M. F. and D. Fuller. 1998. Palms of Fiji. I. Endemic and indigenous species: changes in nomenclature, annotated checklist, and discussion. *Harvard Pap. Bot.* 3(1): 95-100.

Doyle, M. F., E. W. Bush, P. Hodgskiss and C. T. Conkle. Genetic drift in a naturally small population of rare endemic conifers (*Acmopyle sahniana*) in Fiji. (unpublished manuscript).

Farjon, A., C. N Page, and N. Schellevis. 1993. A preliminary world list of threatened conifer taxa. *Biodiv. Conserv.* 2: 304-326.

IUCN 1994. *IUCN Red List Categories.* IUCN, Gland, Switzerland.

Oldfield, S., C. Lusty and A. MacKinven 1998. *The World List of Threatened Trees.* World Conservation Press, Cambridge, UK.

Regional Action Plan
Conifers of the Californian Floristic Province

Rudolf Schmid
University of California, Berkeley, USA

Description of the area

California is a topographically diverse state of 411,048km² (total land area 405,431km²), about 1300km long and 325km wide, with elevations ranging from -86m at Badwater, Death Valley, to 4418m for nearby Mt. Whitney. The Californian Floristic Province (CFP) of biogeographers involves about 70% of the state. This includes cismontane California (i.e. west of the Cascade-Sierra Nevada axis, including the eastern flanks with the montane forests, but excluding the desert woodlands), plus the offshore islands (the eight Channel Islands in the southwest and the seven Farallon Islands west of San Francisco Bay).

Transmontane California involves mostly the Great Basin Floristic Province (GBFP) in the northeast and east and the Desert Floristic Province (DFP) in the southeast; each involve about 15% of the land area of California. The CFP also extends outside California into:

(a) southwestern Oregon about 165km north along the coast to include the Coos Bay region [the usually stated northern limit, but for Messick (1997) this is Cape Blanco, which is only 100km north of the state line], and then southeast inland to include most of the Rogue River watershed, and finally east of Mount Ashland to the California line about 40km east of the Interstate 5 highway;

(b) extreme western Nevada to include the Lake Tahoe and Mt. Rose areas; and

(c) northwestern Baja California about 275km south along the coast to about 25km north of El Rosario and inland to include the chaparral and montane forests of the Peninsular Ranges (Sierra Juárez and Sierra San Pedro Mártir), but not their eastern desert flanks, plus also Guadalupe Island, but not Cedros Island.

The CFP involves about 325,300km². Raven and Axelrod (1978) and Messick (1997) estimated 324,000km², with 285,000km² in California, 25,000km² in Oregon, and 14,000km² in Baja California, although some authors (Barbour 1988, Delgadillo 1992) indicate 27,000km² for Baja. There seem to be no estimates for the very small Nevadan part, which the author estimates at 1300km².

The recently published *The Jepson Manual* (Hickman 1993, hereafter as *JM*) tallied (see also Schmid 1997: p. 193) 5867 species of vascular plants for all of California, with 1416 or 24.1% endemic. For all of the major groups of vascular plants, endemism translates into a significant number of threatened taxa.

Below, northern California (NoCal) and southern California (SoCal), are used following Hickman (1993) and especially Munz (1974).

Box 3.1. Abbreviations and conventions.

CFP = California(n) Floristic Province
CNPS = California Native Plant Society, and its inventory of threatened taxa (Skinner and Pavlik, 1994)
DFP = Desert Floristic Province
FNA = *Flora of North America North of Mexico*, vol. 2 (Flora of North America Editorial Committee 1993)
GBFP = Great Basin Floristic Province
IUCN = The World Conservation Union
JM = *The Jepson manual* (Hickman 1993)
NoCal = northern California (defined floristically, not politically—see text)
SoCal = southern California (idem)
SSC = Species Survival Commission

coastal (0-55km) versus inland (>55km) on basis of *Sequoia sempervirens* usually being 8-56km in from the coast (Olson et al. 1990)

conifers = conifers and taxads

Taxonomic distribution of conifers of conservation concern
(taxa are numbered as in tables 3.2-3.5)

The conifer flora of California is rich, with four families, 14 genera (13 if *Chamaecyparis* is included in *Cupressus*, as done by *JM*), and 53 species, including 12 endemic, and 6 additional infraspecific taxa (four endemic) (*JM*, numbers as corrected by Schmid 1997). *Sequoiadendron* is the only endemic genus. California has 31 conifer taxa of conservation concern. In California, 29 of these taxa occur entirely or partly in the CFP, with *Pinus edulis* (22) in the DFP (New York Mts.) and *P. longaeva* (23) in the GBFP (White-Inyo Range) and the DFP (Panamint Mts.). California has seven species of *Cupressus* found in scattered, relict populations; five species (as six species in *JM*) involving eight taxa are Threatened (4-10, 12). Only the relatively broadly distributed *C. macnabiana* (42) and *C. sargentii* (43) are not of conservation concern.

Because of the well-known diversity and high endemism of conifers and other groups in California, efforts to promote their conservation are considerably more advanced in this state than in most other areas. The California Native Plant Society (CNPS; www.calpoly.edu/~dchippin/cnps_main.html) has been active in this endeavor since the late 1960s and has published five inventories of threatened taxa: 1974, 1980, 1984, 1988, and 1994 (Skinner and Pavlik, 1994; throughout CNPS refers to this edition).

75

Box 3.2. Key to tables 3.2-3.5.

Distribution abbreviations after numbers of taxa: B = Baja CA; S = SoCal; N = NoCal; O = Oregon; + = other states; * = endemic to B, S, and/or N; ! = endemic to CFP.

Latin names: Latin names of conifer taxa derive from the main "Global Red List of Conifers" (pp. 11 - 26).

Taxonomy: In brackets is noted whether the Latin name accepted by IUCN is accepted or at variance in CNPS, *JM*, and *FNA*.

CNPS conservation code and statistics (number of taxa in each category/percentage of native flora). (CNPS, 1994).
    list 1A = presumed extinct in California (34/0.5%)
    list 1B = rare or endangered in California and elsewhere (in California 857/13.6%)
    list 2 = rare or endangered in CA, more common elsewhere (in California 272/4.3%)
    list 3 = need for more information—"a review list" (in California 47/0.8%)
    list 4 = plants of limited distribution—"a watch list" (in California 532/8.4%)
    total = 1742/27.7% of 6300 native taxa (species, subspecies, varieties)

R (rarity):

1 = "rare, but found in sufficient numbers and distributed widely enough that the potential for extinction is low at this time";
2 = "distributed in a limited number of occurrences, occasionally more if each occurrence is small";
3 = "distributed in one to several highly restricted occurrences, or present in such small numbers that it is seldom reported"

E (endangerment):
1 = "not endangered"; 2 = "endangered in a portion of its range"; 3 = "endangered throughout its range"

D (distribution):
1 = "more or less widespread outside California"; 2 = "rare outside California"; 3 = "endemic to California"

Oregon has four families, 13 genera, 31 species, and four additional infraspecific taxa of conifers, none at all endemic (Flora of North America Editorial Committee 1993, hereafter as *FNA*). The IUCN/SSC Conifer Specialist Group (hereafter referred to as IUCN) lists six conifer taxa (1, 6, 16, 31, 32, 34) of conservation concern in Oregon. All these taxa occur in the CFP part of Oregon, with only *Tsuga mertensiana* ssp. *grandicona* (31) and *Taxus brevifolia* (32) extending broadly beyond it. CNPS lists five Oregonian conifer taxa (2, 6, 13, 15, 17) as threatened in California, with *Cupressus bakeri* also threatened in Oregon. This is the only conifer taxon in Oregon jointly listed by IUCN and CNPS.

Baja California has two families, five genera, 15 species, and two additional infraspecific taxa of conifers, of which four taxa are endemic (see Table 3.3); Baja has 10 species of *Pinus*, but only *P. cembroides* is common with the 34 pine species on mainland Mexico (Farjon and Styles 1997, Farjon *et al*. 1997a, b, Wiggins 1980). IUCN lists seven conifer taxa (3, 5, 10, 11, 20, 25, 26) of conservation concern in Baja, all occurring entirely in its CFP part except the endemic *P. cemboides* ssp. *lagunae* (20) outside it in the south and the endemic *P. radiata* var. *binata* (26) in the CFP on Guadalupe Island and outside the CFP on Cedros Island. *Pinus muricata* var. *muricata* is the only other threatened pine in Baja.

Four conifer taxa of conservation concern are insular: *Cupressus guadalupensis* var. *guadalupensis* (11) endemic to Guadalupe Island, Baja; *Pinus radiata* var. *binata* (26) endemic to this and Cedros Island, Baja; *P. muricata* var. *muricata* (25) native to mainland California and Baja and also to Santa Cruz and Santa Rosa Islands, California; *P. torreyana* ssp. *insularis* (28) endemic to the last isle. Island taxa are especially susceptible to being out-competed by alien plants or eaten by alien animals (Junak *et al*. 1995, Moran 1996, Thorne 1969).

Of the 35 taxa under consideration, 20 taxa are endemic to either political Baja California (3, 11, 20, 26, see Table 3.3) or political Alta California (4, 7-9, 12, 14, 18, 19, 21, 24, 27-29, 30, 33, 35). However, if endemism is considered from the perspective of a floristic province, namely, the CFP, there are seven additional endemic taxa, *Chamaecyparis lawsoniana* (1), *Cupressus arizonica* var. *stephensonii* (5), *C. bakeri* (6), *C. guadalupensis* var. *forbesii* (10), *Picea breweriana* (16), *Pinus muricata* var. *muricata* (25), and the well-known *Sequoia sempervirens* (34). In other words, there are 20 political endemics but 25 floristic (CFP) endemics (not 27 total because political endemics 20 and 26 are not CFP endemics). Moreover, while California has one endemic conifer genus, *Sequoiadendron*, the CFP has two, this and *Sequoia*.

The author considers not only the 32 taxa found entirely or partly in the CFP but also includes three others not occurring in the CFP: *Pinus edulis* (22) and *P. longaeva* (23) endemic to the western United States plus *P. cemboides* ssp.

Table 3.2. Taxa listed by both IUCN and CNPS (13 taxa).
(for codes see Boxes 3.1 and 3.2, for IUCN categories see Appendix 2)

4 N*! *Cupressus arizonica* var. *nevadensis*
Piute cypress [IUCN; CNPS, *JM* as ssp. *nevadensis*;
FNA as *C. arizonica*, var./ssp. not accepted]
Status: *IUCN* VU D2; *CNPS* list 1B, RED 2-2-3

5 BS! *Cupressus arizonica* var. *stephensonii*
Cuyamaca cypress/ Arizona cypress [IUCN; CNPS
as *C. stephensonii*; *JM* as *C. arizonica* ssp.
arizonica; *FNA* as *C. a.* var./ssp. not accepted]
Status: *IUCN* VU D2; *CNPS* list 1B, RED 3-3-3
(should be RED 3-3-1 as more common outside CA)

6 NO! *Cupressus bakeri*
Baker cypress/ Modoc cypress [IUCN, CNPS, *FNA, JM*]
Status: *IUCN* VU B1+2bd; *CNPS* list 4, RED 1-2-2

7 N*! *Cupressus goveniana* var. *abramsiana*
Santa Cruz cypress [IUCN; CNPS, *JM* as *C. abramsiana*; *FNA* as *C. goveniana* Gordon, var./ssp. not
accepted]
Status: *IUCN* EN C2a; *CNPS* list 1B, RED 3-2-3

8 N*! *Cupressus goveniana* var. *goveniana*
Gowen cypress [IUCN; CNPS, *JM* as ssp. *goveniana*;
FNA as *C. goveniana*, var./ssp. not accepted]
Status: *IUCN* VU D2; *CNPS* list 1B, RED 3-2-3

10 BS! *Cupressus guadalupensis* var. *forbesii*
Tecate cypress [IUCN, CNPS, FNA, JM as *C. forbesii*]
Status: *IUCN* VU D2; *CNPS* list 1B, RED 3-2-2
(should be RED 3-2-1 as more common outside CA)

12 N*! *Cupressus macrocarpa*
Monterey cypress [IUCN, CNPS, *FNA, JM*]
Status: *IUCN* VU D2; *CNPS* list 1B, RED 3-2-3

14 N*! *Abies bracteata*
Bristlecone fir/ Santa Lucia fir [IUCN, CNPS, *FNA, JM*]
Status: *IUCN* LRcd; *CNPS* list 4, RED 1-1-3

21 N*! *Pinus contorta* ssp. *bolanderi*
Bolander pine/ pygmy pine [IUCN, CNPS, *JM; FNA* as
P. contorta var. *contorta*, var./ssp. *bolanderi* not accept-
ed]
Status: *IUCN* LRnt; *CNPS* list 1B, RED 1-2-3

23 SN+ (not in CFP) *Pinus longaeva*
Great Basin bristlecone pine [IUCN, CNPS, *FNA, JM*]
Status: *IUCN* VU B1+2e; *CNPS* list 4, RED 1-1-1

27 N*! *Pinus radiata* var. *radiata*
Monterey pine/ insignis pine [IUCN; CNPS, *FNA, JM*
as just *P. radiata*]
Status: *IUCN* LRcd; *CNPS* list 1B, RED 3-2-2
[For taxonomy and distribution see comment under
P. radiata var. *binata* in Table 3.3]

28 S*! (insular) *Pinus torreyana* ssp. *insularis*
Torrey pine/ island Torrey pine, Santa Rosa Island
Torrey pine [IUCN, CNPS, *FNA; JM* as *P. torreyana*,
ssp. not accepted]
Status: *IUCN* EN D; *CNPS* list 1B, RED 3-2-3

29 S*! *Pinus torreyana* ssp. *torreyana*
Torrey pine/ mainland Torrey pine [IUCN, CNPS, *FNA;
JM* as *P. torreyana*, ssp. not accepted]
Status: *IUCN* EN C2b; *CNPS* list 1B, RED 3-2-3

---

lagunae (20) endemic to Baja California Sur and first described in 1981 (Farjon and Styles 1997, Passini and Pinel 1989). CNPS lists the former two taxa as threatened whereas IUCN lists the latter two. *Pinus edulis* and *P. longaeva* occurring in eastern California and beyond in the GBFP and the DFP are the only Californian conifers of conservation concern entirely outside the CFP. Even though *P. cemboides* ssp. *lagunae* is rather far from the CFP, I include it because it is the only pine (Farjon and Styles 1997), and the only threatened gymnosperm in southern Baja.

Because of the long-standing efforts of CNPS, the author has compared for each taxon the conservation status assessments provided by IUCN and CNPS. The conservation criteria of these organizations naturally differ because IUCN has a global perspective whereas CNPS has a regional (state) one. This discussion thus consists of four parts:

1) Taxa listed by both IUCN and CNPS (13), Table 3.2.

2) Taxa listed by only IUCN (16), Table 3.3.

3) Taxa listed by only CNPS (5), Table 3.4.

4) Taxa endemic to California but listed by neither IUCN nor CNPS (3), Table 3.5.

These lists are necessary for the following discussions because of different threats and measures that are considered. For instance, ozone pollution is a significant factor for some taxa listed in Table 3.3, but apparently not for any taxon listed in Table 3.2. In each group, taxa are arranged alphabetically by genus within four families (Cupressaceae, Pinaceae, Taxaceae, and Taxodiaceae) to conform with the sequencing in the Global Red List of Conifers (pp. 11-26). Taxa are sequentially numbered within genera for easier reference throughout this report.

Distribution maps

For detailed maps of taxa see: Aune (1994A), Charlet (1996A), Dunn (1987AB), Faber (1997A*), Griffin and Critchfield (1976A), Minnich (1982A, 1987B), Passini and Pinel (1989B), Willard (1995A) ["A" after the date = maps for Alta California, "B" = Baja California].

Taxa listed by both IUCN and CNPS

Possible revisions to listings

Allozyme work by Aitken and Libby (1994) suggests that *Pinus contorta* ssp. *bolanderi* is not warranted and that this is a recent edaphic (Pygmy Forest) ecotype of ssp. *contorta*. Similarly, because *Cupressus goveniana* var. *pygmaea* is "10-50m on rich soil" but only "1-2m on sterile soil" in the Pygmy Forest (*JM*, p. 112), "a remarkable example of phenotypic plasticity" (*FNA* 1993, p. 407), it may be indistinct from *C. goveniana* var. *goveniana*. Leaf monoterpene evidence also suggests this (Zavarin *et al*. 1971). IUCN does not accept *C. goveniana* var. *pygmaea*; FNA accepts neither pygmy infraspecific taxon.

Distribution and endemism

All of the 13 listed taxa are Californian, at least partly so; nine are endemic to California, seven to NoCal (4, 7-8, 12, 14, 21, 27), two to SoCal (28, 29). *Cupressus* (4, 7-8, 12) has four of these endemics. The remaining four taxa not endemic to California also occur in southwestern Oregon (*Cupressus bakeri*), northern Baja (*Cupressus arizonica* var. *stephensonii* and *Cupressus guadalupensis* var. *forbesii*), or Nevada and Utah (*Pinus longaeva*). Most taxa occur in or near coastal areas (7, 8, 10, 12, 14, 21, 27-29) with centers of extensive urban development.

Almost all of these taxa have extremely restricted ranges (especially 8, 12, 28, 29). The seven threatened taxa of *Cupressus* in California have "fewer than" 42 "native occurrences" total (CNPS, 1994); see box 3.3.

The six Pinaceae taxa of conservation concern mostly have appreciably wider distributions than the seven threatened taxa of Cupressaceae. *Pinus longaeva* is by far the most broadly distributed species of these 13 taxa. It occurs in floristic NoCal in the GBFP (White-Inyo Mts.) and floristic SoCal (Telescope Peak, Panamint Mts., omitted by *JM*; see Griffin and Critchfield 1976) in the DFP, plus also in Nevada in 20 mountain ranges in eight counties (Charlet 1996) and in Utah in 14 counties (Welsh *et al*. 1993).

Pinus torreyana (28, 29; IUCN, CNPS, and *FNA* but not *JM* accept the two subspecies) is the most restricted pine species in the United States (Evarts 1994, Griffin and Critchfield 1976, Haller 1986). It involves just two populations of "less than" 405ha (Evarts 1994) on Santa Rosa Island, Santa Barbara Co. (as ssp. *insularis*) and on the mainland in San Diego Co. (as ssp. *torreyana*). The mainland population "extends for a total 6km along the immediate coast and up to 1.6km inland" and occurs in two subpopulations that are "divided by the 1km wide Soledad Valley into a northern segment, 3.5km long, mostly within the city of Del Mar, and a southern segment, 2km long, largely within the Torrey Pines State Reserve," according to Haller (1986), who could not locate the "small outlier" that Griffin and Critchfield (1976) mapped 1.5km to the south. The smaller insular population also occurs in two subpopulations "on the northeastern shore": "the larger stand extends for c. 1km in an east-west direction" and within 300m of the shore, whereas "the smaller stand is ... c. 1.2km to the south-east, c. 0.8km inland, and extends for about 500m" (Haller 1986). The mainland population is "approximately 3400 mature trees," the insular one "about 1000 mature trees" (Haller 1986); other estimates include "about 10,000 trees" total (Evarts 1994) and "around 6,000" trees on the mainland (Griffin and Critchfield 1976). Trees planted in the 1930s have also

---

Box 3.3. Threatened *Cupressus* in California.

Taxon	Native Occurrences	Source
Cupressus arizonica* var. *nevadensis	9	Griffin and Critchfield,1976
C. arizonica* var. *stephensonii	2 (1 extinct; note that this species "has the most restricted range of any tree [taxon] in California"	Griffin and Critchfield 1976
C. bakeri	8 (plus 1 extinct)	Griffin and Critchfield, 1976
C. goveniana* var. *abramsiana	<10	CNPS, 1994
C. goveniana* var. *goveniana	2	CNPS, 1994
C. guadalupensis* var. *forbesii	<5	CNPS, 1994; Dunn 1985, 1987 map 4 populations.
C. macrocarpa	2	CNPS, 1994

Note that *C. arizonica* var. *stephensonii* and *C. guadalupensis* var. *forbesii* occur much more extensively in Baja California (Dunn 1985, 1987; Minnich 1987; Rehfeldt 1997; see Table 3.3 for the two Baja endemics of *Cupressus*).

Tecate cypress (*Cupressus guadalupensis* var. *forbesii*) in southern California, near the Mexican border.

A. Farjon

become naturalized at La Purísima Mission State Historical Park in western Santa Barbara Co. (Evarts 1994). Both picturesque species are the subjects of fine coffee-table books (respectively, Muench and Lambert 1972 and Evarts 1994).

Of the 13 taxa considered here, 10 taxa, that is, six of *Cupressus* and four of *Pinus* (all those taxa found in Table 3.2, except *A. bracteata, C. bakeri,* and *P. longaeva*), occur in closed-cone coniferous forest (see also Table 3.3 for *P. muricata*), either exclusively in this community type (*C. governiana* var. *abramsiana, C.g.* var. *goveniana, C. macrocarpa, Pinus cortorta* ssp. *bolanderi, P. radiata* var. *radiata,* and *P. torreyana* ssp. *insularis*), or also in other plant communities (*C. arizonica* var. *nevadensis, C.a.* var *stephensonii, C. guadalupensis* var. *forbesii,* and *Pinus torreyana* ssp. *torreyana*), especially Chaparral (CNPS, Holland and Keil 1995, *JM*). As discussed by e.g. Axelrod (1983) and Millar (1986), from the early Pliocene to well into the late Pleistocene closed-cone coniferous forest occupied a nearly continuous coastal strip in California. After the last glacial period (Wisconsin) ended about 12,000 years ago the subsequent warming, especially during the so-called Xerotherm (8000-4000 years ago), fragmented the community into the scattered, relict distributions of its component conifer taxa. However, in "revised evolutionary interpretations" Millar (1998) concluded that *P. radiata* appears to have existed in fragmented populations

throughout its Quaternary history in California, and thus to be adapted to small population sizes, to fluctuations in size, to colonisations of new locations, and even to local extirpations.

Three taxa endemic to coastal southern central California exemplify these narrowly distributed taxa: *Cupressus goveniana* var. *goveniana* and *C. macrocarpa* each found in two groves in Monterey Co. (Del Monte Forest and Point Lobos), but disjunctly so, the former taxon only 1.8-4.5km inland from the latter; *Pinus radiata* var. *radiata* found in three areas in San Mateo and Santa Cruz Cos. (Año Nuevo), Monterey Co. (Monterey Peninsula), and San Luis Obispo Co. (Cambria) (Coffman 1995, Griffin and Critchfield 1976). The native stands occupy between 4050-6475ha (Owen 1998, about 4850ha in Faber 1997). In California, *C. macrocarpa* and *P. radiata* var. *radiata,* the famous and picturesque Monterey cypress and Monterey pine, are widely planted and indeed naturalized outside their natural range.

Conservation status and threats

Conservation Status of the 13 taxa considered here is summarized in Table 3.2. Threats to taxa mostly result, directly or indirectly, from humans and include a broad litany (mainly from CNPS): agriculture or alteration of fire regimes (*Cupressus goveniana* var. *abramsiana*,7), grazing and mining (*C. arizonica* var *nevadensis*, 4), frequent wildfires (*C. a.* var *stephensonii*, 5 and *C. guadalupensis* var. *forbesii*, 10), lack of grazing (*Pinus torreyana* ssp. *insularis*, 28—see below), fire suppression (*C. bakeri*, 6), or development (*C. goveniana* var. *abramsiana, C. g.* var. *goveniana,* 8, *C. guadalupensis* var. *forbesii, Pinus contorta* ssp. *bolanderi,* 21, *P. radiata* var. *radiata,* 27, and *P. torreyana* ssp. *torreyana,* 29). Off-road vehicles are a threat to *Pinus contorta* ssp. *bolanderi* in the Pygmy Forest of Mendocino Co. Most of these threats relate to the 10 taxa occurring in or near heavily populated coastal urban areas (5, 7, 8, 10, 12, 14, 21, 27-29) as opposed to the three taxa occurring more inland (4, 6, 23). Previously, Little (1970) discussed "preservation of cypress groves." CNPS also regarded one taxon, *C. bakeri,* as threatened in Oregon but gave no details.

Closed-cone coniferous forest is adapted to fire (Holland and Keil 1995) in that most of its conifer species require fire for their serotinous cones to open and release their seed. Chaparral, of course, is also a fire-adapted community. Development usually means associated fire suppression. Because prescribed burns are still controversial, especially in populated areas, fire suppression and concomitant wildfire are probably more important than noted by CNPS for just four taxa (5-7, 10), one of which *C.bakeri* is in relatively unpopulated, inland areas of extreme NoCal.

Two intensively studied species illustrate the threat from wildfire: CNPS noted (p. 119) that *Cupressus arizonica* var. *stephensonii* is "threatened by frequent wildfire; the 1950 Conejo fire extirpated plant [i.e., the species] over part of its range." According to Rehfeldt (1997), in Alta California this taxon currently consists of about "800 individuals dispersed across 207ha in six spatially isolated subpopulations." In the past century three fires occurred in its area, the 1950 fire reducing the population to about 12 individuals (Rehfeldt 1997); another fire occurred in 1970. Earlier, Little (1970) had mentioned "seed germination after the 1950 fire" but warned that "the number of trees could [be] reduced by successive fires in reproduction too small to bear cones." Frequent wildfires also threaten *C. guadalupensis* var. *forbesii,* which occurs in 11 populations in Baja California (from near San Quintín north) and four populations in SoCal, including the Tecate Peak area in Baja and especially Alta California (Dunn 1985, 1987). According to Dunn (1987), this taxon does not achieve full reproductive maturity until 35-40 years of age; thus fire at 1-25 year intervals would permanently eliminate the taxon, fire at 26-39 year intervals would probably eliminate it after several fire intervals, and fire at longer intervals should maintain populations at present levels. Unfortunately, fire has variously burnt the Tecate Peak area of Alta and Baja California c. 1880 and in 1911, 1928, 1945, 1965, 1970, and 1975, and since 1928 and especially since 1945 the extent of the taxon has decreased from 105 to 31ha. Currently, there is perhaps 1ha of reproductively mature cypress; it will not be until 2015 before the rest of the population becomes mature (Dunn 1985, 1987). Zedler (1995) has similar data and conclusions; he notes that senescence "is certainly greater than 100 years," with "survival in good condition to 200 or more years ... likely." In "Proposed conservation actions" (see below), both taxa receive further attention from a management perspective.

Some threats to taxa are due to natural phenomena other than wet or dry lightning strikes. CNPS regards *Pinus radiata* var. *radiata* as threatened from genetic contamination of native trees by planted trees as well as range fragmentation into native populations that are not self-sustaining over the long-run. "Introgression from planted *Cupressus macrocarpa*" possibly threatens *C. goveniana* var. *abramsiana* as these taxa are not naturally sympatric (CNPS). Native pathogens also pose potential threats. Various species of native beetles (bark beetles and other types) threaten *P. torreyana* ssp. *torreyana* (see below) and *P. radiata* var. *radiata.*

A recent alien threat "with potentially disastrous consequences" and "no known cure" (Faber 1997) now threatens *Pinus radiata* var. *radiata.* The pitch canker fungus, *Fusarium subglutinans* forma specialis *pini,* which apparently is indigenous to Mexico and the southeastern United States, turned up on *P. radiata* var. *radiata* in Santa Cruz and Alameda counties in 1986 and has now spread rapidly to all three native populations in California as well as to many planted trees. Currently in California infestation involves 17 coastal counties from San Diego Co. to Mendocino Co. and all three native stands (Owen 1998, see maps in Dallara *et al.* 1995 and Storer *et al.* 1995). At least 12 native species of beetles are the vectors for the fungus (see lists in Dallara *et al.* 1995, Storer et al. 1994, 1995). The seven-year drought of the late 1980s and early 1990s in California exacerbated beetle attacks on many individuals of both threatened and non-threatened conifer species. Moreover, the fungus has also invaded *Pseudotsuga menziesii* and other species of *Pinus* in California, in all three alien and eight native species, including *P. muricata* (see Table 3.3), considered of conservation concern by IUCN and *P. torreyana* (Table 3.2), considered threatened by IUCN and CNPS, plus *P. attenuata* x *radiata.* Laboratory seedling tests report susceptivity of yet additional pines—three alien and three native species (data from Storer *et al.* 1994, 1995; Storer, pers. comm. 1 July 1997, adding *P. monophylla*; Dallara *et al.* 1995, adding *P. mugo).*

Pinus radiata var. *radiata* has been intensively studied from many other perspectives. Faber's (1997) symposium proceedings and Millar (1998) give status reports on its conservation.

A brief discussion of *Pinus torreyana* ssp. *insularis* and ssp. *torreyana* (see above for its distribution and population size) will illustrate the multiplicity of threats that can involve a species of very limited distribution: CNPS did not list any threats for the insular population (28) but for the mainland population mentioned "development" and a threat from a native bark beetle, which "biological control apparently has contained." The CNPS synopsis actually minimizes the threats. Evarts (1994) discusses various threats, most of which are now more severe than the "development" one:

a. In the c. 710ha Torrey Pines State Reserve on the mainland in "the winter of 1988, fierce winds toppled several dozen trees. The freshly downed trees helped attract and nurture populations of the California five-spined ips, a native bark beetle. By the following spring, the tiny beetles had invaded the recently killed trees and were breeding in earnest. Once established, they moved to neighboring live trees and within a few years had spread throughout portions of the Reserve's drought-stressed woodlands. ... Under normal conditions, healthy pines can repulse the invaders..." About 15% of the drought-weakened trees were lost by late 1992, when "pheromone lures," "pheromone-baited traps," and "anti-aggregation pheromone release devices" successfully ended the threat.

b. On the mainland "decades of fire suppression have probably hindered pine regeneration and created a population in which old trees far outnumber saplings." The threat from wildfire is obvious. "Plans to encourage ... regeneration with [prescribed burns] have been postponed until further studies are completed".

c. In the mainland Reserve possibly the "current number of trees is artificially high, perhaps as a result of tree planting earlier this century." Competition could lead to "stressed stands that are vulnerable to beetle infestations".

d. Compared to the mainland population, the number of insular Torrey pines "has dramatically increased within the past 100 years," perhaps because "grazing by sheep and cattle ... has served as something of a substitute for fire" in that the animals preferentially ate "competitive grasses and herbs while leaving pine seedlings uneaten." Sheep grazing was eliminated in the early 1900s, and cattle grazing is to be eliminated within 20 years. After "the groves' native understorey is expected to become reestablished ..., the pines' reproduction rate may gradually decrease".

e. Actually, "the greatest obstacle to the long-term survival" of both the insular and the mainland population is their "lack of genetic diversity" that makes them "extremely vulnerable" to various natural threats.

f. Too recent for Evarts (1994) to have noted is the aforementioned threat from the alien pitch canker fungus.

Pinus longaeva is currently not appreciably of conservation concern due to its occurrence in Subalpine Coniferous Forest in remote areas [in California c. 2200-3700m (*JM*), but as low as 2060m in Nevada (Charlet 1996)]; on mostly calcareous, low nutrient, basic substrates (dolomite) supportive of little other vegetation; and in many protected areas (Bailey 1970, Schmid and Schmid 1975). Forest fire, grazing, logging, mining (historically some occurred in the past), etc. thus are not current threats. Range fragmentation, of ourse, is a factor.

In recent decades in northwestern Baja, the population and land area developed for agriculture have increased dramatically, especially in the coastal areas (see Minnich and Franco-Vizcaino 1997a). Increased development here would most severely impact *Cupressus guadalupensis* var. *forbesii* and especially, from Table 3.3, *Pinus muricata* var. *muricata*.

Northern Baja has a forest reserve established in 1951 and two national parks: the 5000ha Parque Nacional Constitución de 1837 established in 1962 in the central Sierra Juárez and the 63,000ha Parque Nacional de Sierra de San Pedro Mártir established in 1947 in the northern part of that mountain range. However, these parks "are not fully protected from grazing and timber extraction"; moreover, in Baja "relatively few laws are available to support biodiversity protection" (Messick 1997). Delgadillo (1992) discussed conservation in northern Baja but gave no specifics on its threatened conifers.

Farjon and Styles (1997) discussed conservation of Mexican pines and gave the usual litany of threats—grazing, fire, and especially logging. However, so far these threats mostly do not apply to northern Baja. According to Minnich and Franco-Vizcaino (1997a), "except in the mountain meadows, livestock grazing was limited by the low value and inaccessibility of vegetation. ... In the Sierra Juárez pine forests were logged during the mining booms ... [but] with little lasting impact on the forest. ... The forests of the Sierra San Pedro Mártir have never been logged," although "due to the spotted owl controversy" in California, American interests are seeking logging concessions in Baja. In montane northern Baja "fire control is practically nonexistent because much of the Peninsular Ranges are still accessible only by foot or horseback." Wildfire thus is not much of a threat in northern Baja. Analyses by Minnich (1995, see also Minnich and Franco-Vizcaino 1997a, b) reveal that between 1920-72 the Peninsular Ranges of Baja and SoCal experienced extensive burning, with a total of 537,000ha of chaparral consumed. However, in Baja burns were many (2011 burns > 15ha) but rather small (none > 2300ha) whereas in SoCal burns were few (373) and often large (several > 20,000ha). In Baja "fire suppression is not a high priority. ... The Mexican pattern is closer to the pre-European or natural pattern, whereas the U.S. pattern of fires reveals the bad effects of fire suppression, which sets up the vegetation for large catastrophic fires" (quotes from Zedler 1995, citing an 1989 work by Minnich).

Of these 13 Californian taxa only two also occur in northern Baja: *Cupressus guadalupensis* var. *forbesii* in the west coastal foothills at 200-1200m elevation, *C. arizonica* var. *stephensonii* in the southern Sierra Juárez at 1200-1545m elevation, plus in this complex the Baja endemic *C. arizonica* var. *montana* (see Table 3.3) to the southeast in the northern Sierra San Pedro Mártir at 1400-3095m (Minnich 1987). According to Minnich and Franco-Vizcaino (1997a), *Cupressus guadalupensis* var. *forbesii* and the unthreatened closed-cone species *Pinus attenuata* "have fared well under a regime of stand-replacement burns during the present century. ... The greatest threat to the [montane] closed-cone forests of Baja California may be from wood cutting and gathering," although "most stands appear to be protected by impenetrable chaparral. ... Perhaps the greatest value of both threatened and unthreatened "closed-cone conifers is as a genetic resource."

Taxa listed by only IUCN

Possible revisions to listings

Pinus radiata var. *binata* as circumscribed above is regarded as endemic to Guadalupe and Cedros Islands. Populations on the latter island have been regarded as var. *cedrosensis* by Millar (1986), Millar *et al.* (1988), Moran (1996), and other workers (e.g., Delgadillo 1992, Minnich 1987) on the basis of morphological and chemical (allozyme) evidence.

Distribution and endemism

Of the 16 taxa considered here, 12 are Californian, at least partly so; 10 taxa are endemic, six to California, five to NoCal (18, 19, 24, 33, 35), one to SoCal (*Pseudotsuga macrocarpa*), plus three to Baja Norte (*Cupressus arizonica* var. *montana*, *C. guadalupensis* var. *guadalupensis,* and *Pinus radiata* var. *binata*); and, outside the CFP, one to Baja Sur (*Pinus cemboides* ssp. *lagunae*). *Pinus* has five of these endemics (18-20, 24, 26). The remaining six taxa not endemic to California also occur in south-western Oregon (*Chamaecyparis lawsoniana, Picea breweriana,* and *Sequoia sempervirens*); Baja (*Pinus muricata* var. *muricata*); and Oregon and points north (*Tsuga mertensiana* ssp. *grandicona* and *Taxus brevifolia*). Some of these taxa have fairly broad ranges (1, 24, 25, 30-34), including for the Californian part (1, 24, 25, 30-34). In this group the most widespread species in California is the SoCal endemic *Pseudotsuga macrocarpa*, which does not occur in Baja (Minnich 1982, 1987). Occurring scattered over a broader area is *Torreya californica*. "This California endemic is not really rare": its "range is fairly extensive but localities are few in number and trees few in a given locality" (Griffin and Critchfield 1976). Only three mainland taxa (*Pinus muricata* var. *borealis, P.m.* var. *muricata,* and *Sequoia sempervirens*)

Table 3.3. Taxa listed by only IUCN (16 taxa).

(For codes see Boxes 3.1 and 3.2, for IUCN categories see Appendix 2)

1 NO! *Chamaecyparis lawsoniana*
Port Orford cedar, Lawson cypress [IUCN, *FNA*; CNPS, *JM* as *Cupressus lawsoniana*]
Status: *IUCN* VU A1de+2e; *CNPS* "Considered but rejected: Too common"

3 B*! *Cupressus arizonica* var. *montana*
San Pedro Mártir cypress [IUCN; syn.: *C. montana*]
Status: *IUCN* VU D2

11 B*! (insular) *Cupressus guadalupensis*
var. *guadalupensis*
Guadalupe cypress [IUCN, Moran 1996]
Status: *IUCN* CR B1+2c

16 NO! *Picea breweriana*
Brewer spruce/ weeping spruce [IUCN, CNPS, *FNA, JM*]
Status: *IUCN* LRnt; *CNPS* "Considered but rejected: Too common"

18 N*! *Pinus balfouriana* ssp. *austrina*
foxtail pine [IUCN, CNPS, *JM; FNA* as *P. balfouriana*, ssp. not accepted]
Status: *IUCN* LRcd; *CNPS* "Considered but rejected: Too common"

19 N*! *Pinus balfouriana* ssp. *balfouriana*
foxtail pine [IUCN, CNPS, *JM; FNA* as *P. balfouriana*, ssp. not accepted]
Status: *IUCN* LRcd; *CNPS* "Considered but rejected: Too common"

20 B* (not in CFP) *Pinus cemboides* ssp. *lagunae*
Mexican pinyon [IUCN; syn. *P. lagunae*]
Status: *IUCN* VU A1c

24 N*! *Pinus muricata* var. *borealis*
Bishop pine [IUCN; *FNA, JM* as just *P. muricata*]
Status: *IUCN* LRnt

25 BSN! (including insular S)
Pinus muricata var. *muricata*
Bishop pine [IUCN, including *P. remorata; FNA, JM* as just *P. muricata*]
Status: *IUCN* LRnt

26 B* (insular CFP + Cedros I.)
Pinus radiata var. *binata*
Guadalupe Island pine [IUCN, including *P. muricata* var. *cedrosensis, P. radiata* var. *cedrosensis* from Cedros I.; Millar 1986, Millar *et al.* 1988, Moran 1996, excluding var. *cedrosensis* on Cedros I.]
Status: *IUCN* EN C1

30 S*! *Pseudotsuga macrocarpa*
bigcone Douglas fir [IUCN, *FNA, JM*]
Status: *IUCN* LRnt

31 NO+ (CFP +) *Tsuga mertensiana* ssp. *grandicona*
mountain hemlock [IUCN; no ssp. in *FNA, JM* accepted or in syn.]
Status: *IUCN* LRcd [ssp. *mertensiana* is not in California, occurring in eastern and central Oregon and points north.]

32 NO+ (CFP +) *Taxus brevifolia*
Pacific yew [IUCN, CNPS, *FNA, JM*]
Status: *IUCN* LRnt; *CNPS*: "Considered but rejected: Too common"

33 N*! *Torreya californica*
California nutmeg, *California torreya* [IUCN, *FNA, JM*]
Status: *IUCN* LRcd

34 NO! (genus endemic to CFP)
Sequoia sempervirens
coast redwood, sequoia [IUCN, *FNA, JM*]
Status: *IUCN* LRcd

35 N*! (genus endemic to California and CFP)
Sequoiadendron giganteum
giant sequoia/ big tree, Sierra redwood [IUCN, CNPS, *FNA, JM*]
Status: *IUCN* VU A1c+d; *CNPS*: "Considered but rejected: Too common"

Foxtail pine (*Pinus balfouriana*) in the Sierra Nevada, California, USA.

A. Farjon

are truly coastal. The remaining 11 mainland taxa are coastal and mainly inland (1, 16, 30-33) or strictly inland (18, 19, 35; plus 3, 20 in Baja).

Conservation status and threats

IUCN category breakdown for the 16 conifer taxa in Table 3.3 is as follows:

Critically Endangered:	*11*!
Endangered:	*26*
Vulnerable:	1!, *3*!, 20*, 35*!
Lower Risk:	16!, 18*!, 19*!, 24*!, 25!, 30*!, 31, 32, 33*!, 34!

("*" = Endemic to California or Baja;
"!" = Endemic to CFP; Baja taxa italicised)

Bristlecone fir (*Abies bracteata*) in the Santa Lucia Mountains.

A. Farjon

ly Santa Cruz Co.) and mill the logs up north (*San Francisco Examiner*, 20 July 1997). For the current controversy about the Headwaters area see under Proposed conservation actions below. Continued logging also threatens *Chamaecyparis lawsoniana*; "as logs, mostly exported to Japan, it brings higher prices than almost any other conifer in the United States. ... Old-growth forests are being depleted rapidly" (Zobel 1990).

Ozone pollution is a second threat to taxa in Table 3.3. The following paragraph abstracts the excellent summary by Miller *et al.* (1997): "California is the only state in the western United States where ozone damage to montane conifer forests is a significant problem," affecting "mixed conifer forests on distant mountain ranges" "as far as 300-350km downwind from urban source areas". Conifers in the inland montane areas, especially in the Sierra from Lake Tahoe and south and in the Transverse Ranges (especially in the San Bernardino Mountains) of SoCal, have been severely impacted by urban air pollution. The impact of air pollution on *Pinus jeffreyi* and *P. ponderosa* in SoCal is well-known, and indeed these extremely sensitive yellow pines "have been used as bioindicators of chronic ozone injury". This manifests itself as needle damage known as "ozone mottle." "Ozone injured trees are more vulnerable to immediate mortality from insect/disease complexes," bark beetle attack being "almost always a direct cause of mortality". Ozone pollution also decreases seedling regeneration.

The author's impression is that ozone pollution affects Pinaceae more than other families of conifers. Miller *et al.* (1997) rank species from "highest to lowest sensitive to ozone" as follows: *Pinus ponderosa = P. jeffreyi*; *Abies concolor*; *Quercus kelloggii*; *Pseudotsuga macrocarpa**; *Calocedrus decurrens*; *Pinus lambertiana – P. coulteri*; *Sequoiadendron giganteum**. IUCN and/or CNPS list the *-marked taxa as of conservation concern. "*So far*, mature sequoias have seemed to be relatively impervious to smog" (Miller *et al.* 1997; Willard 1995, for the quote, emphasis his). However, "ozone may be a selective agent, influencing the natural regeneration of giant sequoia seedlings," and possibly reducing genetic diversity (Miller *et al.* 1997).

Other threats are development and fire suppression with concomitant eventual devastating wildfire to the rather broadly distributed *Pinus muricata* (var. *borealis* and var. *muricata*) and *Pseudotsuga macrocarpa*. For instance, western Marin Co., California, did not have a significant fire for 65 years until October 1995 when a fire started by teenagers camping on Mt. Vision in the Pt. Reyes National Seashore burnt 5000ha and destroyed 45 houses. The fire burnt from Mt. Vision (390.8m) south to the ocean through several plant communities, including closed-cone coniferous forest with *P. muricata* var. *borealis*. Actually the fire was fortuitous for the pines because they were becoming senescent and the community was undergoing significant change due to the rather short life span of the pines, generally 50-100 years. Of course, appropriate prescribed burning would have alleviated the problem. For vivid pictures see Parfit's (1996) excellent *National Geographic* article, "The essential element of fire."

CNPS did not systematically deal with the 12 Californian taxa. Indeed, CNPS "considered but rejected" six of these taxa (1, 16, 18, 19, 32, 35) because they are "too common," including *Sequoiadendron*, the only conifer genus endemic to California, and *Sequoia*, endemic to CFP. The same verdict would apply to the other six Californian taxa (24, 25, 30, 31, 33, 34). Naturally, the four endemic Baja taxa (3, 11, 20, 26), two of them insular (11, 26), are out of the province of CNPS. Thus it is hard to evaluate the threats to taxa, as done in the manner for Table 3.2, treating "Taxa listed by both IUCN and CNPS." Relevant here, however, are the distinctions that taxa listed in Table 3.3 (no taxa listed by CNPS) tend to be inland, more northern (i.e., not in SoCal), and more broadly distributed compared to the more coastally located, more southern (i.e., SoCal), and more narrowly distributed taxa listed in Table 3.2 (taxa listed by both IUCN and CNPS).

Analysis of CNPS's 19 listings for conifers in Tables 3.2 and 3.4 shows logging as a threat to only one taxon (17, in Table 3.4) and air pollution as a threat to no taxa. With regard to taxa in Table 3.3, however, logging is a continued threat to the coastal redwoods (34). In recent times due to high wholesale prices for lumber ($801 per 1000 board feet, nearly double that of ten years ago) northern lumber mills find it economically feasible to lumber even in the Bay Area (specifical-

83

Chamaecyparis lawsoniana has "an uncertain future" and is severely threatened by an alien root-rot fungus, *Phytophora lateralis*. Introduced about 1952 into Coos Co., Oregon, this has now reached northern Del Norte Co., California. This "has decimated many stands in the area where Port-Orford-cedar grows best," and management "has become impossible in much of its range" (Zobel 1990).

IUCN lists both *Sequoia sempervirens* and *Sequoiadendron giganteum* as, respectively, Lower Risk, conservation dependent and Vulnerable (A1cd). CNPS lists neither, only mentioning the latter as "Considered but rejected: Too common". The same verdict would apply to *S. sempervirens*. Willard (1995) estimated this to occur in over 607,000ha whereas *S. giganteum* "has a very limited, non-continuous distribution of" 14,600-15,400ha extending about 420km "in a narrow strip less than" 32km wide. Aljos Farjon (pers. comm. 20 June 1997) wrote: "The Redwoods are listed because they meet the IUCN criteria. These have mostly to do with past rates of decline through logging and in case of *S. sempervirens* with ongoing threat, problems with regeneration and management (*S. giganteum*), air pollution threats, and the undeniable fact that they are conservation dependent."

Sequoiadendron giganteum is the subject of a separate species report (pp. 92-94) as well as a recent symposium (Aune 1994) and an invaluable, privately published "reference guide" by Dwight Willard (1995). He recognises 66 groves (detailed in 245 pages; Willard, pers. comm. 28 July 1998, informed me that there is a small 67th grove, an out-lier from one of those previously recognised) ranging in size from about 1.2-2ha for the Placer County Grove containing six living trees and two logs to the Redwood Mountain Grove, with over 1629ha "within a perimeter," the "actual [hectareage] of sequoia occurrence" about 975ha. Willard concluded: "It can now finally be said that all the groves of giant sequoia in the Sierra Nevada have been identified and their outer boundaries mapped. More than 90% of the sequoia grove area is in some form of public ownership." Willard (1995) estimated that fewer than 25,000 trees are 3m or more dbh, with fewer than 5000 4.6m or more dbh and fewer than 300 6m or more dbh. About a third of the old growth hectareage was logged, mostly before World War II (Aune 1994; see Willard 1995 for details). Earlier, Rundel (1972) listed 75 groves, including isolated clusters, and concluded that "more than 95% of the area of existing groves [is] in publicly owned preserves." Willard also discussed the fire threat, including prescribed burning. "Probably most [trees] will survive even an intense wildfire." Whether they will survive the air pollution (ozone) threat noted above perhaps is less certain.

Regarding the five threatened Baja taxa listed above, four taxa (3, 11, 20, 26) are endemic to Baja. The insular endemics *Cupressus guadalupensis* var. *guadalupensis* and *Pinus radiata* var. *binata* are under threat from grazing by feral goats (Farjon and Styles 1997; Moran 1996). Moran's (1996) section on "goats and plants" on Guadalupe Island gives many details. Even after years of attempts to control the goats, per-

haps 7000 remain. Farjon and Styles (1997) and Passini and Pinel (1989) say nothing about threats to *P. cemboides* ssp. *lagunae*, which is endemic to a remote 20,000ha area between 1200-2000m elevation in southern Baja California Sur.

Taxa listed by only CNPS

Table 3.4. Taxa listed by only CNPS (6 taxa). (for codes see Boxes 3.1 and 3.2)

2 NO+ (CFP +) *Chamaecyparis nootkatensis*
Alaska cedar, yellow cypress
[FNA; CNPS, *JM* as *Cupressus nootkatensis*]
Status: *CNPS* list 4, RED 1-1-1

9 N*! *Cupressus goveniana* var. *pygmaea*
pygmy cypress, Mendocino cypress/ "pygmy cypress and dwarf cypress are misleading" because edaphically unrestricted plants can be 10-50 m —*JM*; Little 1970, for the quote)
[CNPS as ssp. *pigmaea*, JM as ssp. *pigmaea*; FNA as *C. goveniana*, var./ssp. not accepted]
Status: *CNPS* list 1B, RED 1-2-3

13 NO+ (CFP +) *Abies amabilis*
Pacific silver fir/ silver fir
[CNPS, *FNA, JM*]
Status: *CNPS* list 2, RED 2-1-1

15 NO+ (CFP +) *Abies lasiocarpa* var. *lasiocarpa*
subalpine fir/ alpine fir
[CNPS, *JM; FNA* as *A. lasiocarpa*, var. not accepted]
Status: *CNPS* list 2, RED 2-1-1

17 NO+ (CFP +) *Picea engelmannii* var. *engelmannii*
Engelmann spruce
[*FNA*; CNPS, *JM* as just *P. engelmannii*]
Status: *CNPS* list 2, RED 2-2-1

22 S+ (not in CFP) *Pinus edulis*
Colorado pinyon/ pinyon
[IUCN, CNPS, *FNA, JM*]
Status: *CNPS* list 3, RED 3-1-1

Distribution and threats

This section reflects CNPS's regional bias. Five of these taxa have very restricted ranges in California but are more broadly distributed in Oregon (2, 13, 15, 17), Nevada (15, 17, not 22; see Charlet 1996), Arizona (17, 22), and states adjacent to these. *Pinus edulis* is in the GBFP and the DFP, but not in the CFP. CNPS mentions a specific threat, logging, for only one taxon (17). See also the discussions on logging in previous sections. [Cupressus goveniana *var.* pygmaea, *though recognized by JM at subspecies rank is most likely an edaphically determined depauperate form of* C. goveniana *which is not accepted as a taxon by IUCN and FNA.* - the compilers]

Taxa endemic to California but listed by neither IUCN or CNPS

Table 3.5. Taxa endemic to California but listed by neither IUCN nor CNPS (3 taxa).

(for codes see Boxes 3.1 and 3.2)

42 N*! *Cupressus macnabiana*
MacNab cypress [*FNA, JM*]

43 SN*! *Cupressus sargentii*
Sargent cypress [*FNA, JM*]

44 N ͯ! *Pinus sabiniana*
ghost pine, grayleaf pine [*FNA, JM*]

Distribution and threats

The previous discussion identifies 16 taxa of endemic conifers of California as of conservation concern (4, 7-9, 12, 14, 18, 19, 21, 24, 27-30, 33, 35), plus four in Baja (3, 11, 20, 26). California has three other endemic taxa of conifers, two (*Cupressus macnabiana* and *C. sargentii*) rather narrowly distributed, one (*Pinus sabiniana*) very broadly distributed. Currently these do not appear to be of significant conservation concern. However, in recent decades numerous trees of *P. sabiniana* have been lost due to the appreciable development in the cismontane Sierran foothills.

Current conservation measures

Currently in California there is an aggressive conservation agenda for plant and animal species by various agencies, including: California Fish and Game, California Native Plant Society (CNPS), Save the Redwoods League, Sierra Club, and The Nature Conservancy. Threatened species also have appropriate federal, state, and local status through endangered species acts and various other codes and regulations (e.g., National Forest Management Act, California Environmental Quality Act). However, these "protective measures are too often uncoordinated, slow, overly bureaucratic, poorly or unevenly implemented, under-funded, and weakened by loopholes" (Messick 1997). For a detailed discussion of the various social, legal, and scientific barriers to advancing conservation in California see Jensen *et al.* (1993).

Despite these barriers and the fact that some habitats in California have been severely impacted, significant parts of California are under some form of biodiversity protection. Messick (1997) estimated approximately 2.9 million ha in sites devoted primarily to biodiversity protection and approximately 0.7 million ha protected in mixed-management sites for a total of about 3.6 million ha, or 11% of the CFP.

Proposed conservation actions

As is well-known, much of the vegetation of California, especially cismontane California, is historically adapted to fire (Zedler 1995; Keeley 1995 for bibliography). However, fire has been officially suppressed by the U.S. Forest Service beginning in 1905 and by the California Department of Forestry beginning in 1924 as an evil phenomenon due to a Bambi/Smoky-the-Bear mentality (both critters date from the 1940s). Prescribed burns for fire-dependent taxa are important (see discussion above) and should be done before the fuel load increases to intolerable levels and/or the population of the critical species becomes senescent (the "senescence risk" of Zedler 1995). However, too frequent fires can eliminate trees before they achieve reproductive maturity (the "immaturity risk" of Zedler 1995) or even lead to intense inbreeding in small populations (e.g., *Cupressus arizonica* var. *stephensonii*, see Rehfeldt 1997).

Destructive wildfires are inevitable in many areas. When wildfires occur, saving life and buildings has taken priority over saving vegetation. The question should be addressed whether some houses should be sacrificed to save a population of a threatened species. For instance, if a wildfire threatens La Jolla with its super-valuable residences, will the Torrey Pines State Reserve be used as a fireline to save the town?

Rehfeldt (1997) quantitatively analysed the genetic structure of *Cupressus arizonica* var. *montana*, var. *nevadensis* and var. *stephensonii*, all threatened and the unthreatened var. *arizonica* and var. *glabra*. He concluded that the two primary human roles most likely will be to assist migration by maintaining the appropriate habitat and providing the genotypes appropriate to those habitats. This may include crossing of inbred lines to redistribute genetic variability, and planting such individuals in both the natural population and in *ex situ* reserves. This naturally assumes proper management of the local fire regime. Dunn (1987) concluded for *C. guadalupensis* var. *forbesii* that all fire management proposals should be geared toward maintaining fire frequencies at intervals of 40 years or longer, when significant numbers of individuals of this serotinous species are reproductively mature. For its Tecate Peak population, "the immaturity risk is significant" but "the senescence risk ... is not a problem now" (Zedler 1995). For this site, unfortunately, fire protection is nearly impossible due to the steep terrain and the additional "curse" of proximity to a highway and Tecate, Mexico (Dunn 1987).

Zedler (1995) aptly states for SoCal: "A biologically desirable fire regime may not be compatible with the socioeconomic regime. The two could be brought closer together except for one key difficulty: wildfire destructiveness is worse than it would need to be because of poor land use planning and unrealistic expectations for fire protection. The general public refuses to accept that catastrophic wildfires are inevitable and that where shrublands meet human development, disaster is a likely result. ... Those of us with a biologically-driven agenda hope that more sensible land use patterns will be adopted, but history tells us not to expect it. For the future, the public will probably demand a level of fire protection that is incompatible with what is best for natural ecosystems. It will therefore probably be necessary to utilise a combination of brush reduction and clearance and controlled burning along the urban/wildland interface. There may be no need, however, to impose this socio-economic regime everywhere. Efforts should be made to exempt more remote areas from short-rotation controlled burning and perhaps from controlled burning of any kind." (However, see comments above about lack of fire suppression in Baja.)

California torreya (*Torreya californica*) in cultivation at the Royal Botanic Gardens, Kew, England.

For the narrow endemics such as *Pinus radiata* var. *radiata*, *P. torreyana*, and the various taxa of *Cupressus*, a potential problem is range fragmentation into populations that are not self-sustaining over the long-run. Checking the new and recent threat by the alien pitch-canker fungus is vital, and not only for *P. radiata*, because other conifer species are also affected (see above). Dallara *et al.* (1995), Faber (1997), Owen (1998), and Storer *et al.* (1994, 1995) give recommendations for the removal of dead and dying trees as well as their proper disposal. Owen (1998) notes that "a tree should not be removed just because it has pitch canker—it could be a tolerant tree and therefore valuable." Storer *et al.* (1994, 1995) specifically recommend against new landscape plantings of *P. radiata* in California and, because most species of pine, both native and exotic, are known to be susceptible, no pines at all should be planted in close proximity to sensitive species such as *P. torreyana*. Breeding for disease resistance is clearly a future goal (Faber 1997; Owen 1998). Biological control may ultimately be feasible, as it has been for infestations of native insect species (see above on *P. torreyana*).

In this report, four conifer taxa of conservation concern are partly (*Pinus muricata* var. *muricata*) or entirely insular (*Cupressus guadalupensis* var. *guadalupensis*, *Pinus radiata* var. *radiata*, and *P. torreyana* ssp. *insularis*). The flora and fauna of the islands of California and Baja have experienced two centuries of devastation from introduced cattle, sheep, burros, pigs, goats, rabbits, dogs, cats, and rodents (Junak *et al.* 1995; Moran 1996; Thorne 1969). There has been appreciable success at controlling these pests on the Channel

Islands of SoCal. However, unless their removal is complete, relapses will occur. On Santa Cruz Island, California, sheep and pig populations are now rapidly recovering. The threat of overgrazing will exist until all introduced herbivores are removed (Junak *et al.* 1995). On Guadalupe Island, Baja, goats have obliterated all seedlings of the endemic palm *Brahea (Erythea) edulis* as well as most trees, namely: *Quercus tomentella*, *Juniperus californica*, *Pinus radiata* var. *binata*, and the endemic *Cupressus guadalupensis* var. *guadalupensis*, with the endemics *Hesperelaea palmeri* and *Heteromeles arbutifolia* var. *macrocarpa* being completely gone (Moran 1996; Thorne 1969). The situation on Guadalupe Island remains acute, as "perhaps 7,000" goats remain despite all the attempts to control them. "It is crucial to the ecology of the island, and even to the survival of the goats themselves, that [very sturdy] fences be built and maintained, to rebuild the forest and to sustain and extend the springs. The ideal, however, would be to remove all goats, as well as dogs, cats, and mice, and to preserve all the native plants..." (Moran 1996).

Giving preserve status to remaining populations of threatened taxa is critical. Currently, there is an intensive, 12-year campaign to prevent logging in extreme north-western California in the Headwaters area, which represents the largest (3035ha) private holding of old-growth *Sequoia sempervirens*. The idea is for the state and federal governments to purchase the area from Pacific Lumber Co. for $380 million and also to protect the surrounding watersheds. [*A settlement was reached early in 1999, whereby a reserve and buffer zone for this important old growth forest of Coast Redwood can now be created* - the compilers]

Recently, Jensen *et al.* (1993) in a book subtitled *A strategy for conserving California's biological diversity* focused not on specific tactical solutions (e.g., see Dunn 1987) but rather on a conservation strategy for the whole state, an approach that has been relatively neglected. They elaborated ten recommendations that include not only the obvious "acquire and protect significant natural areas" but also proposed changes in legislation, establishment of various new laws and advisory boards, reduction of "environmental illiteracy," etc. Messick (1997) lists these and succinctly notes: "Little action has been taken yet on any of these recommendations." In essence even in a rich state or country there are always the political realities of increasing the limited funding for conservation activities in a society with other, often more immediate social concerns such as schools, crime, inner-city blight, and so forth.

Minnich and Franco-Vizcaino (1997a, b) note that in northern Baja the "nearly pristine" Sierra San Pedro Mártir, which has "never been logged," "is currently at risk from inappropriate fire management, as well as increased commercial interests in the area, chiefly logging concessions," partly in relief from the "spotted owl controversy" in California. Minnich and Franco-Vizcaino (1997b) suggest that the Sierra is an ideal site for the establishment of a biosphere reserve under UNESCO's Man and the Biosphere (MAB) program and Mexico's national committee for this program (MAB-

Mexico). A reserve would be "a mechanism for conserving the Sierra's biological resources and cultural heritages by strengthening its traditional land use systems as a basis for a 'let go' fire policy" that maintains the uncontrolled fire regime that has existed in the Sierra since prehistory.

References

Aitken, S. N. and W. J. Libby. 1994. Evolution of the pygmy-forest edaphic subspecies of *Pinus contorta* across an ecological staircase. *Evolution* 48: 1009-1019.

Aune, P. S. (technol. coordinator). 1994. Proceedings of the symposium on giant sequoias: Their place in the ecosystem and society, June 23-25, 1992, Visalia, California. Albany: Pacific Southwest Research Station (series: *USDA Forest Service, Pacific Southwest Research Station, general technical report* PSW-GTR-151).

Axelrod, D. I. 1983. New Pleistocene conifer records, Coastal California. *Univ. Calif. Publ. Geol. Sci.* 127: i-x-[xi], 1-108.

Bailey, D. K. 1970. Phytogeography and taxonomy of *Pinus* subsection Balfourianae. *Ann. Missouri Bot. Gard.* 57: 210-249, 1 foldout.

Barbour, M. G. 1988. Californian upland forests and woodlands. Pp. 131-164 *in* M. G. Barbour and W. D. Billings (eds.), *North American terrestrial vegetation*. Cambridge University Press, Cambridge, UK.

Charlet, D. A. 1996. *Atlas of Nevada Conifers: A Phytogeographic Reference*. University of Nevada Press, Reno.

CNPS: See entry for Skinner and Pavlik (1994).

Coffman, T. 1995. *The Cambria Forest: Reflections on its Native Pines and its Eventful Past*. Coastal Heritage Press, Cambria, California.

Dallara, P. L., A. J. Storer, T. R. Gordon and D. L. Wood. 1995. Current status of pitch canker disease in California. *Calif. Dept. Forest. Fire Protection Tree Notes* 20: 1-4.

Delgadillo [Rodríguez], J. 1992. *Florística y ecología del norte de Baja California*. Mexicali: Universidad Autónoma de Baja California (series: *Textos*, unnum.).

Dunn, A. T. 1985. The Tecate cypress. *Fremontia* 13 (3): 3-7, cover.

Dunn, A. T. 1987. Population dynamics of the Tecate cypress. In: T. S. Elias (ed.), *Conservation and management of rare and endangered plants: Proceedings of a California conference on the conservation and management of rare and endangered plants*. Pp. 367-376. California Native Plant Society, Sacramento.

Evarts, B. 1994. *Torrey pines: Landscape and Legacy*. Torrey Pines Association, La Jolla, California.

Faber, P. M. (ed.). 1997. [Special symposium (held Oct. 1996 in Carmel) issue on Monterey pine, *Pinus radiata* var. *radiata*.] *Fremontia* 25 (2): 1-36.

Farjon, A., J. A. Pérez de la Rosa and B. T. Styles. 1997a. *A Field Guide to the Pines of Mexico and Central America*. The Royal Botanic Gardens, Kew, Richmond, UK.

Farjon, A., J. A. Pérez de la Rosa and B. T. Styles. 1997b. *Guía de Campo de los Pinos de México y América Central*. The Royal Botanic Gardens, Kew, Richmond, UK.

Farjon, A. and B. T. Styles. 1997. *Pinus* L. (Pinaceae). (*Flora neotropic monograph* 75). The New York Botanical Garden, Bronx, New York

[*FNA*] Flora of North America Editorial Committee (ed.). 1993. *Flora of North America north of Mexico*. Vol. 2. *Pteridophytes and gymnosperms*. Oxford University Press, New York. [Cited in text as *FNA*.]

Griffin, J. R. and W. B. Critchfield. 1976. *The distribution of forest trees in California*. Berkeley: Pacific Southwest Forest and Range Experiment Station (series: *USDA Forest Service, Pacific Southwest Research Station, research paper*, PSW-82). [Reprint of 1972 paper with 1976 suppl., pp. 115-118.]

Haller, J. R. 1986. Taxonomy and relationships of the mainland and island populations of *Pinus torreyana* (Pinaceae). *Syst. Bot.* 11: 39-50.

Hickman, J. C. (ed.). 1993. *The Jepson Manual: Higher Plants of California*. University of California Press, Berkeley. [Also March 1996 "third printing with corrections." Cited in text as *JM*.]

Holland, V. L. and D. J. Keil. 1995. *California Vegetation*. Kendall/Hunt Publishing Co, Dubuque, California.

Jensen, D. B., M. S. Torn and J. Harte. 1993. *In Our Own Hands: A strategy for Conserving California's Biological Diversity*. University of California Press, Berkeley.

JM: See entry for Hickman (1993).

Junak, S., T. Ayers, R. Scott, D. Wilken and D. Young. 1995. *A Flora of Santa Cruz Island*. Santa Barbara Botanic Garden, Santa Barbara.

Keeley, J. E. (ed.). 1995. *Bibliography on Fire Ecology and General Biology of Mediterranean-type Ecosystems*. Vol. 1. [*California*]. International Association of Wildland Fire, Fairfield, Maine. [With 5684 references]

Little, Jr., E. L. 1970. Names of New World cypresses (*Cupressus*). *Phytologia* 20: 429-445.

Messick, T. 1997. California Floristic Province: California and Oregon, USA and Baja California, Mexico. In: S. D. Davis, V. H. Heywood, O. Herrera-MacBryde, J. Villa-Lobos and A. C. Hamilton (eds.), *Centres of plant diversity: A guide and strategy for their conservation*. Vol. 3: 63-73. [*The Americas*]. IUCN Publications Unit Cambridge, UK.

Millar, C. I. 1986. The Californian closed cone pines (subsection *Oocarpae* Little and Critchfield): A taxonomic history and review. *Taxon* 35: 657-670.

Millar, C. I. 1998. Reconsidering the conservation of Monterey pine. *Fremontia* 26 (3): 12-16.

Millar, C. I., S. H. Strauss, M. Thompson Conkle and R. D. Westfall. 1988. Allozyme differentiation and biosystematics of the Californian closed-cone pines (*Pinus* subsect. *Oocarpae*). *Syst. Bot.* 13: 351-370.

Miller, P. R., M. J. Arbaugh and P. J. Temple. 1997. Ozone

and its known and potential effects on forests in western United States. In: H. Sandermann, A. R. Wellburn and R. L. Heath (eds.), *Forest decline and ozone: A comparison of controlled chamber and field experiments*. Pp. 39-67. (series: *Ecological studies*, vol. 127). Springer, Berlin.

Minnich, R. A. 1982. *Pseudotsuga macrocarpa* in Baja California? *Madroño* 29: 22-31.

Minnich, R. A. 1987. The distribution of forest trees in northern Baja California, Mexico. *Madroño* 34: 98-127.

Minnich, R. A. 1995. Fuel-driven fire regimes of the California chaparral. In: J. E. Keeley and T. Scott (eds.), *Brushfires in California: Ecology and resource management*. Pp. 21-27. International Association of Wildland Fire, Fairfield, Maine.

Minnich, R. A. and Franco-Vizcaino, E. 1997a. Mediterranean vegetation of northern Baja California. *Fremontia* 25 (3): 3-12.

Minnich, R. A. and Franco-Vizcaino, E. 1997b. Protecting vegetation and fire regimes in the Sierra San Pedro M·rtir of Baja California. *Fremontia* 25 (3): 13-21, cover.

Moran, R. 1996. *The flora of Guadalupe Island*, Mexico. California Academy of Sciences, San Francisco. (series: *Memoirs of the California Academy of Sciences*, no. 19). [See also summary in Fremontia 26 (3): 3-11 (1998).]

Muench, D. (photos) and D. Lambert (text). 1972. *Timberline ancients*. Charles H. Belding, Portland.

Munz, P.A. 1974. *A Flora of Southern California*. University of California Press, Berkeley.

Olson, D. F., Jr., D. F. Roy and G. A. Walters. 1990. *Sequoia sempervirens* (D. Don) Endl. Redwood. In: R. M. Burns and B. H. Honkala (technical coordinators), *Silvics of North America*. Vol. 1: 541-551. [*Conifers*]. (series: *U.S.D.A. Forest Service Agr. Handb.*, No. 654). United States Forest Service, Washington, D.C.

Owen, D. R. 1998. Health concerns for California's native Monterey pine forests. *Fremontia* 26(3): 17-19, cover.

Parfit, M. 1996. The essential element of fire. *National Geographic* 190 (3): 116-130.

Passini, M.-F. and N. Pinel. 1989. Ecology and distribution of *Pinus lagunae,* in the Sierra de la Laguna, Baja California Sur, Mexico. *Madroño* 36: 84-92.

Raven, P. H. and D. I. Axelrod. 1978. *Origin and relationships of the California flora*. (series: *University of California publications in botany,* vol. 72). University of California Press, Berkeley.

Rehfeldt, G. E. 1997. Quantitative analyses of the genetic structure of closely related conifers with disparate distri-

butions and demographics: *The Cupressus arizonica* (Cupressaceae) complex. *Amer. J. Bot.* 84: 190-200.

Rundel, P. W. 1972. An annotated check list of the groves of *Sequoiadendron giganteum* in the Sierra Nevada, California. *Madroño* 21: 319-328.

Schmid, R. 1997. Some desiderata to make floras and other types of works user (and reviewer) friendly. *Taxon* 46: 179-194.

Schmid, R. and M. J. Schmid. 1975. Living links with the past. *Nat. Hist.* 84 (3): 38-45, 84. [on bristlecone pines]

Skinner, M. W. and B. M. Pavlik. 1994. *California Native Plant Society's Inventory of Rare and Endangered Vascular Plants of California*. 5th ed. (series: *Special publication*, no. 1, 5th ed.). [eds. 1-4 1974, 1980, 1984, 1988; cited in text as CNPS]. California Native Plant Society, Sacramento.

Storer, A. J., T. R. Gordon, P. L. Dallara and D. L. Wood. 1994. Pitch canker kills pines, spreads to new species and regions. *Calif. Agr.* 48 (6): 9-13, cover.

Storer, A. J., T. R. Gordon, D. L. Wood and P. L. Dallara. 1995. Pitch canker in California. *Calif. Forest. Note* 110: 1-14.

Thorne, R. F. 1969. The California Islands. *Ann. Missouri Bot. Gard.* 56: 391-408.

Welsh, S. L., N. D. Atwood, S. Goodrich and L. C. Higgins (eds.). 1993. *A Utah Flora*. 2nd ed. Print Services, Brigham Young University, Provo.

Wiggins, I. L. 1980. *Flora of Baja California*. Stanford University Press, Stanford.

Willard, D. 1995. *Giant Sequoia Groves of the Sierra Nevada: A reference guide*. 2nd ed. The Author, Berkeley. [ed. 1: 1994].

Zavarin, E., L. Lawrence and M. C. Thomas. 1971. Compositional variations of leaf monoterpenes in *Cupressus macrocarpa, C. pygmaea, C. goveniana, C. abramsiana* and *C. sargentii. Phytochemistry* 10: 379-393.

Zedler, P. H. 1995. Fire frequency in southern California shrublands: Biological effects and management options. In: J. E. Keeley and T. Scott (eds.), *Brushfires in California: Ecology and resource management*. Pp. 101-112. International Association of Wildland Fire, Fairfield, Maine.

Zobel, D. B. 1990. *Chamaecyparis lawsoniana* (A. Murr.) Parl. Port-Orford Cedar. In: R. M. Burns and B. H. Honkala (technical coordinators), *Silvics of North America*. Vol. 1: 88-96. [*Conifers*]. (series: *U.S.D.A. Forest Service Agr. Handb.*, No. 654). United States Forest Service, Washington, D.C.

Chapter 4

Species Accounts

A total of 43 species have been short-listed (Table 2.1); these occur in a total of 27 genera and their distribution is virtually world-wide. Of these, there follow accounts for nine species representing nine genera and many parts of the world (Chile, California, Mediterranean, Mexico, South Africa, China, Vietnam and Fiji). Additionally, we present an account of a species from the main list: *Cedrus libani*, which represents the commonly encountered issue of a species considered threatened in parts of its range (e.g. a country) while it is of less conservation concern elsewhere. We acknowledge that in many countries such species are of high conservation concern. Further detailed assessment, especially on the remaining short-listed species, is to be greatly encouraged for the future. The Conifer Specialist Group is committed to this objective.

One of three mature trees surviving in the wild of *Abies beshanzuensis*.

Abies beshanzuensis, probably the rarest conifer in the world, Zhejiang Province, China.

Clanwilliam cedar
(*Widdringtonia cedarbergensis* J. A. Marsh)

N. Schellevis and J. Schouten
Pinetum Blijdenstein, Hilversum and Faculty of Biology,
University of Amsterdam

Family	Cupressaceae
Status	Endangered
Criterion	A1cd
Historic range	South Africa, Western Cape Prov., Cederberg Mts.

Description (Dallimore *et al.* 1966)

Habit: a widely branched evergreen tree of 6-18m height. Most specimens on rocky sites are much branched from the base (Taylor 1976).

Bark: on larger trees dark grey-brown and flaky, fissured into squares of about 2.5cm diameter (Taylor 1976).

Leaves: of juvenile plants spirally arranged, spreading, acicular, 12.5-19mm long, flattened, glaucous green. Those of long and leading shoots of older trees also spirally, acicular but shorter. Other leaves appressed, small, scale-like, ultimately in opposite-decussate pairs, apex obtuse.

Male strobili: c. 4-5mm long, terminal on branchlets, consisting of tiny decussate scales bearing pollen sacs.

Female cones: solitary or more often several clustered together, on short, lateral shoots or nearly sessile, globose, 8.5-20mm long and wide before opening, scales normally four (occasionally six), woody, warted, strongly spurred with the protruding bract near the apex.

Seeds: up to 12-14 per cone, to 8.5mm long, angular, resinous, narrowly winged, the wings forming a notch near the seed apex.

Biology (Manders *et al.* 1990)

The Clanwilliam cedar grows very slowly. It may be 30 years or more before a plant bears a significant crop of seeds, while it is still a very small tree. Both male and female cones occur on the same trees. The very small male (pollen) cones appear at the apex of leafy branchlets in autumn. Female cones, after pollination, develop in April, and remain closed for almost three years before ripe seeds are released. They persist on the tree thereafter. Vigorous large trees carry many clusters of female cones producing 3000 or more seeds per year. If cedars do not succumb to fire, they may live up to 400 years.

Distribution and habitat

The Clanwilliam cedar is an endemic tree, confined to the Cederberg Mountains in the Western Cape Province of South Africa (Manders 1986). It has three closely related species occurring elsewhere in southern Africa, two of which are also threatened. The Cederberg range lies between latitudes 32°00' and 32°45' S and longitudes 18°50' and 19°25'E, within the winter rainfall region of South Africa. The cedars are found on cliffs, rocky outcrops, and very rocky slopes of the Table Mountain Group, predominantly the sandstones of the Peninsula Formation. The altitude range of the species is 1050m to 1650m above sea level, with isolated specimens at lower altitudes. In 1937, the Clanwilliam cedar was estimated to occur discontinuously in an area of c. 25.000ha in a zone of varying width and nearly 50km long (Hubbard 1937). The populations have since been reduced much further due to destruction by fire. The cedars grow mainly on eastern slopes in the northern areas of the range, but are not obviously limited to any aspect elsewhere (Manders 1986). The dominant vegetation of the Cederberg is mesic mountain fynbos. This is a low sclerophyllous shrub vegetation, characterised by the abundance of plants belonging to or resembling members of the Proteaceae, Ericaceae and Restionaceae (Taylor 1976). It is likely that this fire-prone vegetation, which is the result of climate change and more recently human intervention, represents a replacement ecosystem where once a more fire-resistant woodland of cedars existed.

A gnarled, fire-damaged specimen of Clanwilliam cedar (*Widdringtonia cedarbergensis*) in the Western Cape, South Africa.

History and conservation

Given the fact that natural woodland is scarce in the predominant shrub lands of the Cape, it is not surprising that the discovery of the Clanwilliam cedar on the Cederberg Mountains led to ruthless exploitation, especially in the time of the first European settlers, as their society was extremely dependent on wood and overgrazing by their livestock prevented sufficient regeneration. From the beginning of the eighteenth century, when the cedars were first identified as a useful source of general purpose timber (being both rot resistant and beautiful), until late in the nineteenth century, when the first serious conservation attempts were made, uncontrolled exploitation took place (Smith 1955). The decline was very substantial. An area of 60-70,000 densely populated hectares of woodland was reduced to 25,000ha of scattered trees. Contrary to the beginning of the twentieth century, when it was still possible to collect 2700kg of seed in a single year, it is now difficult to collect even a few kilograms (Manders 1986). Although palynological evidence suggests that even before any human exploitation took place, the ecological situation of the cedar had been fragile for some time due to climatic changes (Meadows 1991), these majestic trees are well worth preserving in their natural habitat.

In July 1973 most of the state forest area where the cedar occurs was therefore proclaimed a wilderness area, under which status grazing is no longer allowed. But cedar numbers continued to decline in extensive wildfires and regeneration was and is low due to granivory and herbivory by rodents. Conservation of this species has proven to be difficult. In order to save the existing adult, seed bearing trees it is important to prevent large scale, high intensity fires, but for natural cedar regeneration light fires periodically burning the fynbos are essential. However, it seems that the seed bank of the natural stands has been reduced to such an extent that after the fire in 1989/90 regeneration was very low (Mustart et al. 1995). An accidental fire early in 1998 is also likely to have further reduced the chances of natural population recruitment (Hilton-Taylor 1998). The only option open to increase cedar numbers is now found to lie in a large-scale planting scheme of nursery-grown seedlings in newly burnt areas and careful management of the burning regimes (Manders et al. 1990, Mustart et al. 1995). During the last seven to eight years several attempts have been made to re-establish cedar populations. If future wildfires are prevented until this current seedling cohort has reached reproductive maturity to produce sufficient seed and attain some resistance to fire (15-30 years) then the Clanwilliam cedar might have a chance. However, financial constraints are already threatening the perpetuation of the planting schemes for the duration of this period (Wilderness manager Van Dyk in pers. comm. to C.S.G. chair A. Farjon, November 1995). Without it, there seems to be little hope of stopping the decline and eventual extinction of this remarkable tree.

Propagation *ex situ*

The most economic method of propagating this species is by sowing. The seeds will germinate after a period of two to six weeks. It takes a few months before the seedlings can be transplanted to small containers. The total period in the nursery before planting out in its natural habitat is 9-14 months. A second method is by taking cuttings from the first year twigs. Propagation by rooting these increases the chance that the plant bears cones after a few years to produce further seed, which is of course genetically identical with the mother plant.

Cones of *Widdringtonia*, plant in cultivation at the Botanic Garden Berlin-Dahlem, Germany.

A. Farjon

References

Dallimore, W., A. B. Jackson and G. Harrison (rev.). 1966. *A Handbook of the Coniferae and Ginkgoaceae*. Edward Arnold, London.

Farjon, A., C. N. Page and N. Schellevis 1993. A preliminary world list of threatened conifer taxa. *Biodiv. Conserv.* 2: 304-326.

Hilton-Taylor, C. 1998. *Widdringtonia cedarbergensis*. In: Oldfield, S., C. Lusty and A. MacKinven (comp.) *The World List of Threatened Trees*, p. 570. World Conservation Press, Cambridge.

Hubbard, C. S. 1937. Observations on the distribution and rates of growth of Clanwilliam cedar *Widdringtonia juniperoides* Endl. *South African J. Sci.* 33: 572-586.

Manders, P. T., S. A. Botha, W. J. Bond and M. E. Meadows 1990. The enigmatic Clanwilliam cedar. *Veld and Flora* 76: 8-11.

Manders, P. T. 1986. An assessment of the current status of the Clanwilliam cedar (*Widdringtonia cedarbergensis*) and the reasons for its decline. *South African Forest. J.* 139: 48-53.

Meadows, M. E. 1991. A vegetation history of the last 14.000 years on the Cederberg, Southwestern Cape Province. *South African J. Sci.* 87: 34-43.

Mustart, P., J. Juritz, C. Makua, S. W. van der Merwe & N. Wessels 1995. Restoration of the Clanwilliam cedar *Widdringtonia cedarbergensis*: the importance of monitoring seedlings planted in the Cederberg, South Africa. *Biol. Cons.* 72: 73-76.

Smith, C. A. 1955. Early 19th century records of the Clanwilliam cedar (*Widdringtonia juniperoides* Endl.). *J. South African Forest. Assoc.* 25: 1-8.

Taylor, H. C. 1976. Notes on the vegetation and flora of the Cederberg. *Veld and Flora* 62: 28-30.

Giant Sequoia
(*Sequoiadendron giganteum* (Lindl.) Buchholz)

N. Schellevis and J. Schouten
Pinetum Blijdenstein, Hilversum and Faculty of Biology,
University of Amsterdam

Family   Taxodiaceae (Cupressaceae *s.l.*)
Status   Vulnerable
Criterion   A1cd
Historic Range   USA, California, Sierra Nevada

Description (Dallimore *et al.* 1966)

Habit: a giant evergreen tree 45-100m tall, with a massive tapering trunk up to 12m in diameter above the buttressed base, clear of branches for half or more than half of its height with a dense, rounded crown, much broken in aged trees. Young trees are of a conical outline. Branches are often drooping suddenly at the trunk.

Bark: 15-60cm thick, deeply furrowed, fibrous, bright reddish-brown, fire-resistant.

Foliage and leaves: young shoots glabrous, green by reason of attached leaf bases, turning brown; buds minute, without scales, hidden by late leaves. Leaves persisting c. four years, spirally arranged, crowded, scale-like or needle-like, the flat base adhering to the branch, decurrent, the free tip 3-5mm long, acute, stomata present on both surfaces.

Male strobili: terminal, 6-9mm long, arising in abundance at the apex of the lateral shoots.

Female cones: terminal, solitary, ovoid, 5-7.5cm long, 2.5-4cm wide, reddish-brown when mature, maturing in the second autumn, persisting some time after seed dispersal; scales 30-40 in number, spirally arranged, peltate, four-sided, 2-2.5cm wide, woody with a central depression revealing the bract tip.

Seeds: numerous, flattened, thin, oblong, 3-6mm long, margined by a membranous wing.

Biology

The Giant Sequoia (also known as 'Big tree' in California) grows to great size and age, individuals exceeding 2000 years are not very rare and trees of over 3000 years are known. Male and female cones are borne on the same tree. Pollination takes place between December and March, or sometimes as late as May. The cones form in late May and early June and continue to grow until the autumn, resuming the following spring. Seed distribution starts in the autumn of the year following maturi-

ty but it may take several years for a tree to shed all seeds of a cone crop, depending on weather conditions.

The Giant Sequoia is remarkably resistant to natural disasters and pathogens, although it is not immune from them. It is also very storm resistant, while the very thick and pitch or resin free bark is highly resistant to fires, which are therefore seldom capable of killing the larger trees. This resistance may also be due to the presence of tannin, which gives both the bark and the heartwood a reddish colour. The trees seem to be quite free from serious infection by fungi or insect attacks, the former even when the tree has been standing dead for centuries. Little is known of effects in younger stages of growth (Piirto 1994). However, this species does not compete successfully with other conifers, especially firs, which in the absence of major disturbance have been seen to prevent seedling or tree establishment in most of the protected groves. It is therefore dependent on episodal disturbance which removes these competitors, so that the big trees can reseed the space left vacant (Stephenson 1994).

The small seeds, virtually lacking reserve tissue, demand highly favourable soil conditions in order to germinate. Layers of litter and humus prevent germination. When, however, the soil is cleared of this layer, for instance by the uprooting of trees, landslides, erosion or forest fires, it is not uncommon to find hundreds of seedlings springing up (Fry and White 1948). In the most northern groves, the species does not reproduce, probably because the soil is too dry to favour the germination of seeds. In the southern groves reproduction is more abundant, especially in Sequoia National Park (Hewes 1981). In Converse Basin, on National Forest land, numerous young trees have become established after the clear cutting of a century ago.

Distribution and habitat

The Giant Sequoia grows on the western slopes of the Sierra Nevada in California (USA) at elevations between 1500m and 2500m, some trees have been found at 1000m and a few at 2550m. It occurs in c. 65 groves, which become increasingly disjunct towards the north (Rundel 1972,Willard 1994) and stretch over a distance of c. 400km in a belt at most 25km wide. The total area of occupancy is c. 14,200ha (Rundel 1972). The trees grow in favourable or protected locations where the soil is deep, rich and moist, usually on glacial moraine or till, and thrive in a belt where the annual precipitation ranges between 1100-1500mm. Much of this occurs in the form of snow which stays on the ground for 3-

'Young' trees of Giant Sequoia (*Sequoiadendron giganteum*) in the Sierra Nevada, California, USA.

6 months. Giant Sequoias in these groves are usually found in association with White fir, Incense cedar, Sugar pine and Yellow pine.

History and conservation

(Hewes 1981, Aune 1994)

The present disjunct distribution of the groves represents the remnants of what was once a relatively continuous Giant Sequoia forest along the western slopes of the Sierra Nevada. This forest became dissected by successive Pleistocene glaciations, culminating at the Wisconsin glaciation which largely determined the present distribution (Rundel 1972). Apparently, the other conifer species were more successful in re-establishing themselves more widely, restricting the Giant Sequoias to montane sites characterised by mesic soil moisture conditions throughout the summer drought periods.

The Giant Sequoia was first discovered in 1852 by a hunter and reported in the 'Sonora Herald' of San Francisco. The fact that yet another giant tree species was found, even larger than the previously discovered Coast redwood (*Sequoia sempervirens*) was hard to believe for most people.

Soon after this was verified, however, a 'pilgrimage' began from all parts of the world. The last grove was discovered in 1933. Also soon after discovery, lumbering operations began, the fire- and rot resistant wood being ideal building material. In this way about 34% of the total acreage was consumed, but only one grove (Converse Basin) was virtually obliterated, cutting some 8000 Giant Sequoias and leaving more than 1000ha of wasteland (Aune 1994). It was later estimated that less than one-fifth of what was commercially valuable timber had actually been salvaged from this site, mainly due to the destructive methods of felling the giant trees. The wood was found to be more brittle than that of the Coast redwood and often shattered on impact into unmerchantable lengths, despite attempts to prevent this. Presumably this tendency to shatter, as well as prohibitive costs of transporting the wood, slowed down the cutting and averted wholesale exploitation of many other groves before public opinion, aroused by famous conservationists like John Muir, helped to protect the first substantial groves. In 1890 the first National Parks in California were created in which many Giant Sequoia groves were put under federal protection. In 1926 the National Park areas were substan-

The 'Boole Tree' is one of the largest of Giant Sequoia and was the only large tree left when the 'Converse Basin' was clearcut a century ago.

tially enlarged, while most other groves came under protection on National Forest and State lands, so that at present virtually all Big trees are in public ownership.

Due to nearly a century of forest fire prevention in many of the protected groves, the density of other coniferous trees has greatly increased and it is now widely accepted that this prevents the Giant Sequoia from regenerating successfully (Aune 1994). Despite the longevity of the mature trees, the balance may have been upset as fires would now be much more destructive with the accumulation of fuel wood. For this reason, managers are seeking methods to rid the groves of excessive numbers of competitors, by controlled burning (National Park Service) but also by logging (on other lands), which is more controversial (Aune 1994). In the future, we need to learn more about natural disturbance regimes in these forests and enlarge protected areas to allow nature to take its course unimpaired by short-term human considerations.

Propagation *ex situ*

Giant Sequoias have become widely cultivated and are planted in many countries, especially in Europe. The most economic way of propagation will be sowing. The seeds will germinate after a period of 3-10 months. Symbiosis with mycorrhizae is essential for development of the seedlings, which after a few months can be transplanted to small containers. Total stay in the nursery varies between 18-36 months. A second method is provided by rooting cuttings from the first year twigs. By using this method we can expect the trees to bear cones after a few years. A third method is making grafts (side or whip grafts) either in August-September or in January-February. The USDA Forest Service has implemented a programme of planting nursery-grown Giant Sequoias to extend its occurrence within the natural range.

References

Aune, P. S. (tech. coord.) 1994. Proceedings of the Symposium on Giant Sequoias: their place in the ecosystem and society. (series: *General Technical Report* PSW-GTR-151). Pacific Southwest Research Station, Albany, California

Dallimore, W., A. B. Jackson and G. Harrison (rev.). 1966. *A Handbook of the Coniferae and Ginkgoaceae*. Edward Arnold, London.

Fry, W. and J. R. White 1948. *Big Trees*. Stanford University Press, Stanford.

Hewes, J. J. 1981. *Redwoods, the World's Largest Trees*. New York.

Piirto, D. D. 1994. Giant Sequoia insect, disease, and ecosystem interactions. In: P. S. Aune (tech. coord.). Proceedings of the Symposium on Giant Sequoias: their place in the ecosystem and society. (series: *General Technical Report* PSW-GTR-151). Pacific Southwest Research Station, Albany, California.

Rundel, P. W. 1972. An annotated check list of the groves of *Sequoiadendron giganteum* in the Sierra Nevada, California. *Madroño* 21: 319-328.

Stephenson, N. 1994. Long-term dynamics of Giant Sequoia populations: implications for managing a pioneer species. In: P. S. Aune (tech. coord.). Proceedings of the Symposium on Giant Sequoias: their place in the ecosystem and society. (series: *General Technical Report* PSW-GTR-151). Pacific Southwest Research Station, Albany, California.

Willard, D. 1994. The natural Giant Sequoia (*Sequoiadendron giganteum*) groves in the Sierra Nevada, California - an updated annotated list. In: P. S. Aune (tech. coord.). Proceedings of the Symposium on Giant Sequoias: their place in the ecosystem and society. (series: *General Technical Report* PSW-GTR-151). Pacific Southwest Research Station, Albany, California.

Alerce
(*Fitzroya cupressoides* (Molina) I. M. Johnston)

N. Schellevis and J. Schouten

Pinetum Blijdenstein, Hilversum and Faculty of Biology,
University of Amsterdam

Family	Cupressaceae
Status	Endangered
Criteria	A1cd + 2cd
Historic Range	Southern Chile and adjacent Argentina (Southern Andes)

Description

Habit: a large evergreen tree 40-55m tall and up to 5m dbh, but reduced to a bush at high elevations. Trunk free of branches for 2/3 to 4/5 in old trees, crown dense, top rounded.

Bark: furrowed, fibrous, peeling in long strips, reddish-brown.

Branchlets: flexible, pendulous, green because of the covering scale leaves, turning reddish-brown.

Buds: minute, without scales, covered by terminal leaves of branchlet tip.

Leaves: in alternating whorls of three, their bases flattened and decurrent, the free apex spreading in young trees, more or less appressed in old trees, oblong-lanceolate to obovate, the smallest c. 3mm long with an incurved apex, concavo-convex with whitish stomata in two bands on both sides separated by a green midrib or vein.

Male strobili: small, c. 5mm long, situated on the apex of ultimate branchlets, consisting of minute scales bearing the pollen sacs.

Female cones: small, 6-8.5mm in diameter, composed of nine scales in three alternate whorls, the lowest minute and sterile, the middle sterile or each bearing a two-winged seed, the upper the largest and each bearing two to three seeds, near the apex of each scale is a protruding bract tip.

Biology

Alerce is one of the largest trees in temperate South America and probably the longest lived: ring counts of 3000-3600 years have been reported (Lara and Villalba 1993) and none of these could have been nearly complete due to rot of the heartwood. It is extremely slow growing, with average increment rings of only 0.39mm (Bonnemann 1973) and its wood is dense, durable and almost indestructible to decay. Like many large and long-lived conifers, its regeneration is correlated with episodal disturbances such as fire and in this case also volcanic activity (Lara 1991). It will not readily regenerate in shady conditions and hence in old 'alerzales' or woods with alerces, broad-leaved angiosperm trees predominate but the alerce holds its ground as an emergent tree 'waiting' for the next fire to eradicate the other trees. In spite of ample seed production, its rate of natural regeneration is poor (Lara 1991), which is another characteristic of very long-lived trees. In the coastal Cordillera Pelada, trees have been found to regenerate by 'root-suckering' on exceptionally podzolised soils (Veblen and Ashton 1982). In this way they form dense thickets, evading competition from other trees.

Distribution and habitat

The Alerce occurs in Southern Chile from Valdivia along the coastal mountains to Puerto Montt, on parts of Chiloë Island and on the mainland coast along the Andes in Chile and Patagonia (Argentina) south to c. 43°S in scattered and mostly disjunct populations (Golte 1996). Its altitudinal range is between 500-1200m in the coastal mountains and Cordillera foothills. Within its range, it is adapted to very high rainfall, between 2000-6000mm annually. It seems to be limited by a line demarcating episodal summer drought of one month or longer along its northern distributional margin (Golte 1996). Often Alerce occurs on poorly drained, peaty, or sandy and podzolised soils with a low pH less suitable for many other tree species. It can grow in pure stands, but more commonly it is associated with trees such as *Nothofagus*, *Podocarpus*, *Drymis winteri*, *Laurelia philippiana*, *Desfontainea spinosa*, *Philesia magellanica* etc. (Schmithüsen 1960).

History and conservation

Fossil, ecological, and historical evidence indicate that Alerce was much more widespread in southern South America, especially in lowland areas down to sea level, from where it has now virtually disappeared, in part by natural causes probably active in the last 4500 years (Veblen and Ashton 1982). No other tree species in the Andes has been exploited so long and so intensively (Golte 1996). Since the end of the 16th century logging has taken place at an ever increasing rate and by the end of the 19th century timber exploitation had eliminated *Fitzroya cupressoides* from nearly all the accessible lowland sites (Golte 1996, Veblen *et al.*

1976). At higher altitudes, where the trees are still found, 'alerzales' have been logged and burnt to the extent that the species can be classified as Endangered on criterion A1 alone; its present area of occupancy is estimated at 20,000ha, only c. 15% of what it was when Europeans first arrived (Golte 1996). In addition, in many of the logged areas natural regeneration is poor: in the large lowland area north of Puerto Montt the European alien shrub *Ulex europaeus* has become invasive and may hinder *Fitzroya* regeneration (Golte 1996). Recent climatic changes, involving longer dry periods in summer, may have become another cause of the lack of regeneration; it has been suggested that *Fitzroya* is a relict in the sense that it is better adapted to past climatic conditions (Veblen and Ashton 1982, Schmithüsen 1960). Once removed from certain stands where climatic conditions have changed, it can no longer compete effectively with other tree species better adapted to the present climate. In other locations, however, such as in the Cordillera Pelada, its persistence was assured by its competition avoidance strategy (Veblen and Ashton 1982).

In 1941 the Convention on Nature and Wildlife Preservation was enacted and Argentina placed *Fitzroya cupressoides* on the Annex. The small Argentinean populations, about 3800 mature trees, have been protected ever since. Chile, which was also party to this convention, submitted no list of species for the Annex.

In 1969 Chile enacted a law that promised Alerce some degree of protection. Logging permits had to be obtained and management measures had to be taken to assure repopulating after logging. This failed, and the populations continued to decline. In 1976 *F. cupressoides* was declared by law a Chilean 'natural monument' and exploitation of living trees was totally banned, putting an end to some commercial operations. However, this action could not prevent the continuation of illegal exploitation on a large scale, and because the law was only published a year later, ruthless opportunists in the interim saw to it that the number of dead trees increased greatly (Golte 1996).

International measures have also been taken to reduce the pressure. In 1975 *Fitzroya* was included in Appendix II of CITES (later upgraded to Appendix I, prohibiting any international trade). In 1979 the USA listed the species as a Threatened Species of Wildlife and Plants, prohibiting the importation of its wood.

Prevention of the exploitation of existing trees alone has proved to be inadequate to save the Alerce from extinction. Regeneration has to be adequate in order to sustain a viable population. It has now become clear, that *Fitzroya cupressoides* is an outstanding example of a conifer that cannot be sustainably exploited. Slow growth (200 year old specimens reach a height of 10-12m) and critical conditions for seed germination and seedling survival make any form of timber extraction destructive (Golte 1996, Veblen *et al.* 1976). Intense fires, consuming soil peat overlaying podzolised soils, appear to destroy a moisture-holding cover assuring preferable conditions for seedling establishment (Veblen and

Ashton 1982). Colonisation of sites that have been made available after natural disturbances, e.g. deposition of volcanic ash and light forest fires killing competitive broadleaved trees, has been reported (Lara 1991). Further studies and trials are necessary to determine the ability of *Fitzroya cupressoides* to regenerate on a wide range of sites. Such studies are now being undertaken by the University of Santiago de Chile in collaboration with the Royal Botanic Garden, Edinburgh under a 'Darwin Initiative' grant. Alerce may yet be capable of sustaining itself in its natural habitat provided that any future exploitation is prevented.

Propagation *ex situ*

The most economic method of propagation is from seed. The seeds will germinate after a period of two to four months. After another few months the seedlings can be transplanted to small containers; the total period in the nursery before planting out in the wild should be 20-24 months. Cuttings can be made from first year twigs and rooted. With this method one can expect the plant to bear cones after a few years, but the seeds are genetically identical with the parent cuttings. A third method is to make grafts (side or whip grafts) on rootstock taken from *Cupressus* or *Thuja*, with results as in cuttings.

The Alerce (*Fitzroya cupressoides*) is Chile's 'national tree' and listed on Appendix 1 of CITES.

References

Bonnemann, A. 1973. *El Alerce* (Fitzroya cupressoides *(Mol.) Johnston) y su madera.* Inst. Tecnol. de la Madera, Univ. Austral de Chile, Valdivia.

Golte, W. 1996. Exploitation and conservation of *Fitzroya cupressoides* in southern Chile. In: D. Hunt (ed.). *Temperate trees under threat.* Proceedings of an IDS symposium on the conservation status of temperate trees, University of Bonn, 30 September - 1 October 1994. International Dendrology Society, Morpeth, England.

Lara, A. and R. Villalba 1993. A 3620 year temperature reconstruction from *Fitzroya cupressoides* tree rings in southern South America. *Science* 260: 1104-1106.

Lara, A. 1991. *The dynamics and disturbance regimes of Fitzroya cupressoides forests in the south-central Andes of Chile.* Thesis..for the degree of Doctor of Philosophy, Dept. of Geography, University of Colorado, Boulder.

Schmithüsen, J. 1960. Die Nadelhölzer in den Waldgesellschaften der südlichen Anden. *Vegetatio* 9: 313-327.

Veblen, T. T. and D. H. Ashton 1982. The regeneration status of *Fitzroya cupressoides* in the Cordillera Pelada, Chile. *Biol. Conserv.* 23 (2): 141-161.

Veblen, T. T., R. J. Delmastro and J. E. Schlatter 1976. The conservation of *Fitzroya cupressoides* and its environment in southern Chile. *Environ. Conserv.* 3: 291-301.

Sicilian fir
(*Abies nebrodensis* (Lojac.) Mattei)

N. Schellevis and J. Schouten
Pinetum Blijdenstein, Hilversum and Faculty of Biology,
University of Amsterdam

Family	Pinaceae
Status	Critically Endangered
Criterion	D
Historic range	Northern Sicily, Italy

Description (Farjon 1990)

Habit: an evergreen tree with a maximum height of 10-15m on Sicily at present but it may grow taller, diameter at breast height (dbh) 40-60cm, with spreading branches and a broad conical crown.

Bark: smooth, light grey in young trees, rough and scaly in larger trees.

Branchlets: glabrous, yellowish-green, grooved, densely set with short, upturned leaves; buds slightly resinous.

Leaves: spirally arranged, densely set, the lower leaves pectinately spreading, the upper leaves directed forward or slightly upturned to assurgent on shoots with cones, 10-22mm long, 2-3.5mm wide, with two greenish-white bands of stomata below, dark lustrous green above, apex variable but not emarginate.

Male strobili: crowded, 1.5-2cm long, greenish-yellow.

Female cones: erect, on short peduncles, cylindrical, 8-10cm long, 3-4cm wide, green, ripening towards brown; bracts exserted beyond the scales and recurved. Cones will appear near the top on small trees.

Seeds: 6-8mm long, with a broad wing.

Some doubts have been expressed regarding the species-status of the Sicilian fir; it is undoubtedly closely related to *A. alba* and *A. cephalonica*; however, it has been recognised at species rank in most modern treatments of the genus (e.g. Farjon 1990, Liu 1971, Schutt 1991) which we will follow here.

Biology

Obviously the present very small population is a relict from a substantially more abundant population which existed in the past. Due to its size, as well as limited occurrence in a very small area, levels of inbreeding can be expected to be high. Natural regeneration, which in this genus occurs exclusively by seed, is poor due to erosion, exposure to drought, and grazing of livestock (Uotila 1984). Existing trees are mostly stunted, those that produce cones and good seed are hardly in a position for successful seed dispersal. Competition, especially by *Fagus sylvatica*, with which it once must have formed a mixed forest, is also limiting the possibilities for this tiny population to regenerate and expand on its own.

Distribution and habitat

Abies nebrodensis is found on Monti Nebrodi in the northern part of Sicily in Italy near or in the small village of Polizzi Generosa on Le Madonie Mountain. There is one old tree (in the village) and 20-25 stunted, younger trees on the mountain slope, which is all that is left of the naturally occurring population (Uotila 1984, Morandini 1969). The altitudinal range is 1400-1600m, where it grows on rocky, calcareous soil among limestone crags and on slopes. The annual precipitation (mostly winter rains) is 700-800mm. It is at present associated with secondary vegetation (maquis), in which *Quercus ilex* dominates; *Fagus sylvatica* occurs mostly higher on Monti Nebrodi (Uotila 1984, Morandini 1969) where it forms a krummholz vegetation.

History and conservation

When the Sicilian fir was discovered by Italian botanists at the beginning of the 20th century, it had already been reduced more or less to its present relict state. Mattei (1908), who recognised this fir as a distinct species, speculated that it had formed extensive forests in the past, not only on higher mountains in Sicily, but also in the Apennines of Calabria. It seemed to have been relatively frequent in Sicily at the beginning of the 18th century, but it was already scarce before 1750. In 1908 Mattei located only a single tree, which grows in the village of Polizzi Generosa. Later investigations revealed the other, much smaller trees, more or less hidden on the scrubby and rocky slopes a short distance from the village.

It is not clear what causes led to such a strong decline of *Abies nebrodensis*. Climatic changes may have played a major role leading to a disadvantage for the fir in relation to beech (*Fagus sylvatica*). Disappearance of deep soils following deforestation probably aggravated the distress. Beeches dominate to the treeline in many mountains of south-western Europe especially on limestone, indicating their greater adaptability to adverse conditions (Ellenberg 1988).

Attempts have recently been made to allow *Abies nebrodensis* to regenerate naturally. The area in which the trees grow has been fenced (enclosed) to prevent grazing, but local farmers have repeatedly destroyed the fence. At present, attention is entirely focused on rearing Sicilian fir seedlings in nurseries for a replanting scheme (Uotila 1984). Besides livestock grazing, fire is a very real potential hazard which needs attention. A protection plan for the species, comprising both *in situ* and *ex situ* actions, has recently been proposed (Venturella *et al.* 1997).

Propagation *ex situ*

The most economic method of propagation is from seed. The seeds will germinate after a period of two to three months. It takes a further two years before these seedlings can be transplanted to small containers. The total period required in the nursery before planting out will be four to five years. Trees planted in sheltered places and in gardens in north-western Europe are doing quite well, indicating that the decline of the natural population is not caused by genetic or auto-ecological factors. A second method of propagation is making grafts (side or whip grafts) in December-February. As rootstock we can use *Abies alba* and *A. cephalonica*.

References

Ellenberg, H. 1988. *Vegetation Ecology of Central Europe.* 4th ed. (English transl. of *Vegetation Mitteleuropas mit den Alpen*). Cambridge University Press, Cambridge.

Farjon, A. 1990. Pinaceae. Drawings and Descriptions of the Genera *Abies, Cedrus, Pseudolarix, Keteleeria, Nothotsuga, Tsuga, Cathaya, Pseudotsuga, Larix* and *Picea.* (series: *Regnum Vegetabile* Vol. 121). Koeltz Scientific Books, Königstein, Germany.

Liu, T. S. 1971. *A Monograph of the Genus Abies.* National Taiwan Univ., Taipei.

Mattei, G. E. 1908. *Abies nebrodensis* in: *Boll. Reale Orto Bot. Giardino Colon. Palermo* 7: 59-69.

Morandini, R. 1969. *Abies nebrodensis* (Lojac.) Mattei inventario 1968. *Pubbl. Ist. Sper. Selvicoltura Arezzo* 8: i-iv + 1-93.

Schutt, P. 1991. *Tannenarten Europas und Kleinasiens.* Basel.

Uotila, P. 1984. *Abies nebrodensis. Sorbifolia* 15: 35-39.

Venturella, G., P. Mazzola and F. M. Raimondo 1997. Strategies for the conservation and restoration of the relict population of *Abies nebrodensis* (Lojac.) Mattei. *Bocconea* 7: 417-425.

Fiji acmopyle
(*Acmopyle sahniana* J. Buchholz and N. E. Gray)

Michael F. Doyle
Jepson and University Herbaria
University of California

Family Podocarpaceae
Status Critically Endangered
Criterion D
Historic range Fiji, Viti Levu, mountains of Namosi and Mt. Koroyanitu (Mt. Evans Range)

Description

(Bush 1997, Bush and Doyle 1997)

Habit: monopodial evergreen tree up to 12m tall.

Bark: greyish-brown, thin, smooth to slightly pustulate on older trees.

Leaves: of two types (foliage and scale); foliage leaves green, thin, leathery, flattened, distichous, arising from stem spirally but curving around stem to form two rows in a single plane, 1.7-24.0mm x 0.6-4.8mm, linear and bilaterally flattened, falcate with acute apex and decurrent base. Scale leaves adpressed, spirally and imbricately arranged, 1.2-3.8 x 0.6-1.5mm wide, deltate to narrowly triangular with acuminate apex and decurrent base, occurring at bases of female cones, on unfoliated stems, and regions of recent growth.

Male strobili: terminal and lateral, single or paired, 1.5-7.3 x 1.0-2.1mm, with numerous microsporangia, pollen grains bisaccate, 44-55μ.

Female cones: terminal or lateral, solitary, borne on curved peduncle up to 6mm long, the cone consisting of a fleshy, warty receptacle 7-8mm in diameter and 7-9mm long, bearing a single erect seed.

Seeds: 7-9mm long, with irregular longitudinal striations, greenish-grey at maturity.

Biology (Bush 1997)

The Fiji acmopyle appears to be moderately slow growing (c. 15cm/yr.) based on measurements from Namosi (Bush 1997). Of 64 known wild individuals, 46 are probably reproductively mature trees, which range from 1-12m in height, the majority being less than 4.5m tall. However, relatively few female cones seem to be produced, and even less reach maturity on the tree. Cone and seed maturation period is still unknown, but probably less than one year. Recruitment appears to be poor, with only one population exhibiting signs of recent seedling establishment. Although we have no knowledge concerning the longevity of the trees, it appears that they are susceptible to wind damage from cyclones and competition from other more aggressive species (both native and exotic) which probably impede their growth and recruitment. The species appears to be declining based on the apparent extinction of the one disjunct population at Mt. Koroyanitu, and the small number of individuals now comprising the species.

Distribution and habitat

Acmopyle sahniana is an extremely rare endemic tree which occurs in three tiny populations in montane tropical rainforest on Viti Levu, Fiji. Less than 100 individuals are known, and all are restricted to low, reduced-canopy forest on ridgetops from 375-800m. The climate is warm and super-humid (generally 3800-5000mm/yr.) with little or no dry season. The trees grow in acidic humic latisols derived from volcanic andesite. Nodules are present on the roots (Bush and Doyle 1997).

Acmopyle sahniana. Habit. Elevation c. 700m., Namosi, Viti Levu, Fiji.

History and conservation

The species was first collected from the Namosi area in the late 1800's, but not formally described until 1947. In the same year A. C. Smith discovered it on Mt. Koroyanitu, thus extending the range of the species to the eastern side of the island. Because of both its rarity and generally inaccessible habitat, the species was seldom observed or collected. In an attempt to elucidate evolutionary processes of naturally rare plants on islands, an ecological and biosystematic study on *A. sahniana* was initiated by Michael Doyle in1993 and later completed by his graduate student Elizabeth Bush in 1997. Extensive field surveys from 1993 to 1996 were conducted in both the Namosi and Mt. Koroyanitu areas, resulting in the discovery of some new small populations in Namosi, but also the discovery of the apparent extinction of the population at Mt. Koroyanitu. A genetic analysis of the entire species (all 64 known individuals) utilising isozymes revealed remarkable genetic variation; 50% of total loci polymorphic, mean number of alleles $=1.3$-1.4, and heterozygosity $=0.105$ (Bush 1997, Doyle *et al*. unpublished). In addition, significant inter-populational gene differentiation was detected; 21% between populations, and greatest between the most widely separated populations. The genetic data obtained from this species provide a textbook example of genetic drift in a small natural population.

New population genetics information, combined with the documented fossil history of the genus in the Southern Hemisphere, now makes it one of the scientifically most significant conifers, and worthy of special conservation efforts. At present, the species appears to be afforded a natural measure of protection by occurring in generally remote inaccessible montane areas. However, a proposed large copper mining project now threatens some of the Namosi populations which comprise more than 50% of all the known individuals. In a recent review of Fijian gymnosperms by Doyle (1998), *Acmopyle sahniana* was listed as Critically Endangered (CR), which superseded its previous status as Vulnerable (VU) reported by Farjon *et al*. (1993).

The species is currently not formally protected by law in Fiji, and future protection is unlikely because no formal regulations are in place concerning rare and endangered plant species within the country.

Propagation *ex situ*

Attempts at propagating the species by seed and cuttings have thus far been unsuccessful, except for a sole specimen at Otway Ridge Arboretum in Australia, which was apparently cultivated from seed collected from Namosi in 1989 (Bush 1997).

References

Bush, E. W. 1997. *Ecology and conservation biology of Acmopyle sahniana* (Podocarpaceae). M.Sc. Thesis, Biology Department, School of Pure and Applied Sciences, The University of the South Pacific, Suva, Fiji.

Bush, E. W. and M. F. Doyle. 1997. Taxonomic re-description of *Acmopyle sahniana* (Podocarpaceae): Additions, revisions, discussion. *Harvard Pap. Bot.* 2 (2): 229-233.

Doyle, M. F., E. W. Bush, P. Hodgskiss, and C. T. Conkle. Genetic variation and drift in naturally small populations of the rare endemic conifer (*Acmopyle sahniana*) in Fiji. (unpublished manuscript).

Doyle, M. F. 1998. Gymnosperms of the SW Pacific. I. Fiji's endemic and indigenous species: changes in nomenclature, key, annotated checklist, and discussion. *Harvard Pap. Bot.* 3(1): 101-106.

Farjon, A., C. N. Page, and N. Schellevis. 1993. A preliminary world list of threatened conifer taxa. *Biodiv. Conserv.* 2: 304-326.

Bigcone Pinyon pine
(*Pinus maximartinezii* Rzed.)

Aljos Farjon
Herbarium, Royal Botanic Gardens, Kew

Family   Pinaceae
Status   Endangered
Criteria   B1 + 2bc
Historic Range Mexico, Zacatecas, Sierra de Morones

Description (Farjon and Styles 1997)

Pinus maximartinezii forms a small, bushy tree with a short, often contorted trunk and long, irregularly spaced and wide spreading branches, forming a rather open, rounded crown. It usually reaches only 5-10m and occasionally 15m in height and the short bole may be up to 50cm in diameter. The bark is dark brown and tesselated into square plates about 10cm in diameter. Most trees have distinctly glaucous foliage, but greener individuals do occur. The leaves (needles) are in fascicles of five, slender and flexible, 7-11cm long. In these characters it is similar to some other, more distantly related Pinyons or "nut pines" and from a distance this tree certainly looks like them. The most remarkable feature of this species is its huge cone, on a par with the largest and heaviest cones in the entire genus of more than 100 species, such as Coulter pine (*P. coulteri*) and Digger pine (*P. sabiniana*), both from California. The cones vary from (10-) 15-25cm in length and 10-15cm in width, with thick, woody scales variable in shape but often strongly recurved. The wingless seeds are similarly amongst the largest in the genus, 20-28mm long and 10-12mm wide and 3 - 4 x the weight of the common Mexican pinyon pine (*P. cembroides*).

Its nearest relatives appear to be *Pinus nelsonii* and *P. pinceana*, both Mexican pinyons with restricted ranges and limited to sceletal, often calcareous soils over bare rock. Its 'wingless' seeds (in reality the wing, as part of the inner surface of the seed scale, is rudimentary and remains with the scale) are similar, but this is undoubtedly a result of convergent evolution. It is much less closely related to the pinyon pines with small cones of Mexico and the American Southwest, and may even have affinities with the Asian 'nut pine' *P. gerardiana* of the western Himalayas (Malusa 1992, Farjon 1996).

Biology (Farjon and Styles 1997)

The cones take 2 to 2.5 years to ripen and hang like woody pineapples (piñas as the local villagers call them) from pendulous branches up to one year after seed dispersal. This dispersal is by animals but little is known of the species involved (squirrels, ravens?). The large seeds are protected in cup-like cavities on the inner side of the seed scales and difficult to dislodge from the cones which have very hard woody apophyses (the outer part of pine cone scales). The young seedling has 18-24 cotelydons, this is the highest number known in any seed plant. Seedlings apparently only grow up in the protection of (thorny) shrubbery where grazing animals cannot reach them (ill. on p.57).

Distribution and habitat

Pinus maximartinezii occurs in just one locality in Mexico, near the village of Pueblo Viejo in southern Zacatecas, about 100km NNE of Guadalajara and 10km south-west to a few km west of the town of Juchipila. The trees occupy a range of between 5 and 10km^2 on the eastern flanks of the Sierra de Morone in an area aptly named Cerro de Piñones. This pine grows on dry, rocky sites on eroded limestones and sandstones or metamorphic rocks at altitudes between 1800-2400m. The annual precipitation in this area is between 700-800mm, mainly restricted to June-August; occasional winter frosts occur. Bigcone pinyon pine is virtually the only species of pine on this mountain, but it is abundantly accompanied by deciduous oaks (e.g. *Quercus macrophylla*) which shed their leaves in the long dry season. The local people are well-informed about the distribution of this pine due to their interest in harvesting the edible seeds. Within this area, the stands are now very degraded, reduced to scattered trees and small denser stands in gullies or other inaccessible 'cliff' areas, and the total population must be somewhere between a few thousand and perhaps 10,000 trees. Due to limited botanical exploration of this part of Mexico and the likelihood that similar ecological conditions occur on other 'mesas' in the region, future finds of other populations cannot be ruled out, however searches by botanists from Guadalajara have not had any results so far (J. Pérez de la Rosa, pers. comm.).

History and conservation

It is remarkable, given the long history of accumulated knowledge of pines, that this extraordinary species was only discovered in 1964, by Dr. J. Rzedowski (Rzedowski 1964). It appears, that Dr. Rzedowski's attention was first drawn to the huge pine seeds offered for sale in a local market where he recognised them to be very different from the commonly displayed 'pinyon nuts'. Villagers led him to the trees, some two hours walk from the nearest road. Exploitation of the seeds as a minor food source appears to make a heavy impact on the total seed crop, but collection (by knocking down and breaking up of ripe cones) is far from complete and many cones remain on the trees. However, observed regeneration is extremely sparse. Fires are frequent and prevalent across most of the area and appear to be the main constraint on regeneration; in 1986 an extensive burn devastated a large area, burning mature trees as well as seedlings and saplings. Additional pressure is imposed by grazing, mainly by cattle. Land tenure is complex due to the number of small private land owners; at present no part of the range is under protective management.

This unusual pine is now well-known amongst Mexican botanists and foresters and there is considerable awareness of its endangered status (Farjon 1994). The 1986 fire was fought by army personnel. Proposals for funding for *in situ* conservation measures have recently been made. Researchers of North Carolina State University (Department of Forestry) in the USA have recently re-investigated the distribution and ecology of the species and collected seeds from 80 trees in 1992 and 1993 for the purposes of *ex situ* conservation. Support and interest from and direct benefits to the local population are deemed essential for success, as the area is privately-owned and the trees are heavily used. The local interest in seed production needs to be coupled with effective land management and prevention of fires, the most acute hazard. Subsidized restraint on seed harvesting, in conjunction with localised exclosure fencing, could start off regeneration in selected sites. Increased seed production for use and sale by local people could provide the framework for their cooperation and active protection of regeneration.

Given the difficulties of *in situ* protection in this area, establishment of *ex situ* stands in protected Mexican areas as well as propagation programmes in Mexico and abroad are also recommended. Research is urgently needed and should focus on inventories of range, age structure, and genetic variation in the population, as well as fire-related ecology and population dynamics, particularly in relation to seed dispersal by animals and seedling/sapling recruitment.

Propagation *ex situ*

The very thick and hard seed coat requires special treatment to break dormancy and quicken germination. No rooting of shoots is possible in this species. After germination, the young plants retain their juvenile-type foliage for several years and are quite tender and vulnerable to attacks by herbivores and pathogens; in temperate climates they need to be protected against frost at all times. The species has only very recently been taken into cultivation, and a few young plants are present in some botanic gardens (e.g. Pinetum Blijdenstein, Netherlands); a limited propagation programme has been set up at the North Carolina State University, Department of Forestry, Raleigh, NC, USA.

References

Farjon, A. 1994. Bigcone pinyon pine — *Pinus maximartinezii*. Pages 1072-1073 in: M. Emanoil (ed.). *IUCN/SSC Encyclopedia of Endangered Species*. Gale Research, Detroit.

Farjon, A. 1996. Biodiversity of *Pinus* (Pinaceae) in Mexico: speciation and palaeo-endemism. *Bot. J. Linn. Soc.* 121: 365-384.

Farjon, A. and B. T. Styles 1997. *Pinus* (Pinaceae). *Flora Neotropica Monograph* 75. The New York Botanical Garden, Bronx, New York.

Malusa, J. 1992. Phylogeny and biogeography of the pinyon pines (*Pinus* subsect. *Cembroides*). *Syst. Bot.* 17: 42-66.

Rzedowski, J. 1964. Una especie nueva de pino piñonero del estado de Zacatecas (México). *Ciencia* 23: 17-20, t. 2.

Dawn Redwood
(*Metasequoia glyptostroboides* Hu & W. C. Cheng)

Tang Ya
Chengdu Institute of Biology
Chengdu, China

Family Taxodiaceae (Cupressaceae *s.l.*)
Status Critically Endangered
Criteria A1c, C2a
Historic Range China, border area of Hubei, Hunan and Sichuan

Description

Habit: a large deciduous tree, up to 46m tall and 2.5m dbh, trunk usually swollen (buttress) at base, crown of young trees narrow conical or cylindrical, turning broad ellipsoid on old trees.

Bark: furrowed, peeling in long strip, reddish-brown on young trees, dark grey or grey-brown on old trees.

Branchlets: current year branchlets green or brownish, glabrous, pendulous, lateral branchlets pinnately arranged, 4-15cm long, falling in winter.

Buds: Winter buds minute, c. 3mm long, ovoid or ellipsoid, scales triangular, membranaceous, longitudinally keeled.

Leaves: Pinnately arranged on branchlets, opposite, linear, flat, soft, 4-20mm long, 1-2mm wide, greenish, midrib impressed on the adaxial surface, raised on the abaxial surface, stomata bands 4-10 on each side of the midrib, grey-white.

Male strobili: solitary in axils of leaves, in raceme or panicule, 21-24(31)cm long.

Female strobili: solitary or in pairs, scattered on branchlets, scales woody, 9-12 pairs, middle scale with 5-8(9) ovules. Cones with long stipe of 1.5-4cm long, pendulous, nearly round or oblong, 1.6cm long, 1.5cm wide.

Seeds: yellowish, obovoid, flat, narrowly winged, emarginate at apex, c. 5-6mm long, 4-5mm wide. Cotyledons 2, rarely 3, germination epigeal.

Biology

The genus was first recognised as fossils and the living plants were found in a very limited area in southern Central China in 1940's. Obviously the present very small natural population is a relict of a much wider distribution in the past and a result of a natural refuge from glaciation.

Fast growth is a characteristic of the species. In the natural habitat of the species, the annual height growth is 30-80cm, and young trees up to 50 years can sustain an annual growth rate of 60-80cm. The early annual diameter increment is 1-1.75cm, after 20 years it levels off to 1.3-1.6cm per year, slowing further after 80-100 years.

Following its discovery in 1940's, *Metasequoia* was introduced to many parts of China and to other parts of the world. It can grow in a wide range of environments and has succeeded in areas with a mean temperature range of 12-20°C and a mean annual rainfall of 1000mm, though it will grow better in areas with more precipitation. Even in drier climates, with annual precipitation as low as 557mm to 631mm, it will grow well when irrigation is provided. It can endure minimum temperatures of -18.7°C to -19.9°C and grows well in e.g. southern Alaska.

Soils should be deep and fertile. It is sensitive to a deficiency in soil moisture, which usually leads to the death of the plants. However, in areas which are frequently flooded it cannot grow well. It can also tolerate slightly saline soils with salt contents up to 0.2%. In the wild, usually plants of 25-30 years old start bearing seeds and those of 40-60 years start major seed production; this can last up to at least 100 years during which time it produces seed abundantly. Natural regeneration by seeds is good if there is no soil disturbance, e.g. from agriculture.

Distribution and habitat

The wild population of *Metasequoia glyptostroboides* is limited to an area in the adjacent provinces of south-western Hubei, eastern Sichuan, and north-western Hunan (Lichuan

Dawn Redwood (*Metasequoia glyptostroboides*) cultivated at the Royal Botanic Gardens, Kew, England.

County of Hubei, Shizhu County of Sichuan (now a county of the Chongqing Municipality), and Longshan County of Hunan). The largest populations are found in the very limited areas of Xiao He and Shui Shan Ba in western Lichuan County. Its altitudinal range is between 750-1620m.

History and conservation

Fossil, ecological and historical evidence indicates that as many as about 10 species of *Metasequoia* were much more widespread in the Northern Hemisphere in the past. The oldest fossils were found in Lower Cretaceous, and in the Upper Cretaceous they were distributed as far north as 80-82°N in Europe. In the Tertiary the genus spread to most parts of Europe, Siberia, north-east China, Korea, Japan, and North America, at latitudes north of 35°N (Florin 1952). Recently, it has been found abundantly in Eocene deposits on Axel Heiberg Island in the Canadian Arctic at c. 80°N (Anderson and LePage 1995). The glaciation during the Quaternary caused the extinction of almost all the species and virtually all populations. Only the present species has been conserved in a glacial refugium of very limited extent, hence it has been widely known for a long time as fossil only.

In 1941, the same year in which Miki (1941) realised that a number of fossils from various deposits did not belong to *Sequoia,* as previously thought, but to a new genus *Metasequoia,* it was discovered to be living in China (Hsueh 1991). During the war years not much research could be done, but in 1948 it was both described in China and introduced to many countries, particularly in the USA and Europe (Bartholomew *et al.* 1983). In the early 1980's, it was listed as one of the eight species under the Category of Grade One of the Endangered and Protected Plant Species in China by the Chinese Government. This species has been widely used for afforestation and as a common ornamental tree in many parts of China (Ed. Committee).

Propagation *ex situ*

The seed bearing of *Metasequoia glyptostroboides* is usually later in life. Experience in European cultivation has been that the first female cones only begin to be produced after the trees are c. 50 years old, while male cones will then not have appeared yet. The unpollinated female cones can grow to maturity but no fertile seeds develop. Once seed production starts, it is usually abundant, but usually only around 10% of the seeds are fertile. The probable causes of undeveloped seeds lie in abnormal development of the ovule, abortion of the development of the nucellus, and abnormal development of the embryo cell and the embryo.The most economic method of propagation is from seed. The seeds will germinate after a period of 10 days. There are about 430,000-560,000 seeds/kg. The germination rate is about 8% (5-11%). Usually the seed vigour is good within one year, but the germination rate will decrease greatly after two years. The best seeding time is in spring. One year old seedlings are usually 40cm tall. Seedlings should be two to three years old to be ready for transplanting. The transplanting time is in the later part of winter. Because fertile seeds are often not available in sufficient numbers, an additional or alternative method of propagation is by cuttings, and this has become the major propagation method in China. Cuttings should be from young trees, preferably seed propagated seedlings of two to three years old. Cuttings can be carried out in spring, summer, and autumn. Treatment of cuttings with methyl a-naphthyl acetate will greatly improve rooting.

References

Anderson, K. B. and B. A. LePage 1995. Analysis of fossil resins from Axel Heiberg Island, Canadian Arctic. *In*: K. B. Anderson and J. C. Crelling (eds.). Amber, resinite, and fossil resins. *Amer. Chem. Soc. Symp. Ser.* 617: 170-192.

Bartholomew, B., D. E. Boufford and S. A. Spongberg 1983. *Metasequoia glyptostroboides*: its present status in Central China. *J. Arnold Arbor.* 64 (1): 105-128.

Editorial Committee of Woody Flora of China. *Afforestation Method on Principal Tree Species in China. Part 1.* Agriculture Press, Beijing.

Florin, C. R. 1952. On *Metasequoia*, living and fossil. *Bot. Not.* 1 (105): 1-29.

Hsueh, C. J. 1991. Reminiscences of collecting the type specimen of *Metasequoia glyptostroboides*. *Arnoldia* 51 (4): 17-21.

Miki, S. 1941. On the change of flora in Eastern Asia since Tertiary Period (I). The clay or lignite beds' flora of Japan, with special reference to the *Pinus trifolia* beds in Central Hondo. *J. Japan. Bot.* 11: 237-303.

Krempf's Pine
(*Pinus krempfii* Lecomte)

Claire Williams*
Faculty of Genetics, Forest Science
Texas A&M University
313 Horticulture Building, College Station
Texas 77843-2153 USA

Family   Pinaceae
Status   Vulnerable
Criteria   B1+2c
Historic Range   The Da Lat Plateau in central Vietnam

Description

Habit: Large evergreen tree 40-50m tall and up to 4m dbh. Crown dense, becoming typically umbellate (top rounded) in old trees.

Branchlets: Leaves in pairs on dwarf shoots towards tip of branchlets.

Leaves: Pairs of stiff, flat 4-5(-7) x 0.15-0.40cm, narrowly lanceolate, acute leaves, loosing the fascicular sheath early especially in older trees. Seedlings and saplings bear longer, thinner leaves retaining fascicular sheaths longer.

Male strobili: small, oblong catkins 7mm in length when shedding pollen, individually and alternately arrayed along indeterminate branch. Pollen with two large air sacs as in other pines. Pollen sheds in January and possibly in other months.

Female strobili: dark pink and 4mm in length when fully receptive, two strobili appear paired per branchlet. Mature cones ovoid, 5 x 4cm, with thin woody scales and dorsal umbo, opening at maturity.

Seeds: winged, maturing within two years of cone initiation during the wet season.

Biology

Pinus krempfii was discovered by the French botanist Lecomte (1921). Chevalier (1944) elevated *P. krempfii* to a monotypic genus and renamed it *Ducampopinus krempfii*. De Ferré (Ferré 1948) considered this to be premature but she hypothesised the species to be a close relative of the 'primitive' Pinaceae genera *Keeteleria* and *Pseudolarix*. In 1960 Gaussen suggested to classify this pine in a third subgenus, which was taken up and validly published by Little and Critchfield (1969). In all cases, *Pinus krempfii* has been long believed to be a 'living fossil' relict based on its unique morphology and similarity to some pine fossils. *P. krempfii* is the only pine with flattened needles, phenolic compounds not previously reported for any modern pine species, and unique wood characteristics (Buchholz 1951).

By 1989, molecular phylogeny work on Southeast Asian pines was reported for the few species accessible through arboreta. The Vietnamese endemic *P. krempfii* was not included in these molecular phylogeny studies. The first molecular phylogeny study including *Pinus krempfii* was recently published as an abstract (Liston *et al.* 1996). Their nuclear ITS data support *P. krempfii* as *Ducampopinus krempfii* but their rbcL data support *P. krempfii* as a member of the primitive pine section *Parrya*. Other, as yet unpublished molecular work involving this species is currently underway (A. Farjon, pers. comm. June 1998) and it supports retaining the species within *Pinus*. A recent cladistic analysis based on morphological data affirms that Krempf's pine is a basal clade to all other *Pinus* species classified in the section *Parrya* (Seitz 1997).

Habitat

The Da Lat Plateau has a fire-based ecological history which corresponds to ancient human occupation by the Lat tribe. Its flora is a part of the eastern Asia-eastern U.S. parallel. The biogeography and flora of the Da Lat Plateau has been documented by Professor Le Cong Kiet, College of Natural Resources, Vietnam National University, Ho Chi Minh City (unpublished data). Mixed hardwoods, tree ferns and ancient pines are representative species in the vegetation along steep slopes in the temperate highlands (Campbell and Hammond 1989). Hundreds, possibly thousands, of *Pinus krempfii* are found at three locations. The predominant soil type is a well-drained, low-pH lateritic clay. The wet season occurs from August to November.

History and conservation

During the 1960's and 1970's, some *Pinus krempfii* stands survived defoliating herbicides, land-clearing and high-explosive munitions (Westing and Westing 1981) followed by oleoresin-tapping until 1984 (Stephen and Tien 1986). Agricultural clearing in the area is increasing the human population pressure. There is a successful national *in situ* programme for *Pinus krempfii* conservation, supervised by

Dr. Nguyen Hoang Nghia of the Forest Institute of Vietnam, Hanoi. Conservation research to determine levels of genetic diversity is also underway. Repeated *ex situ* measures have not been successful outside of Da Lat. The trees readily reproduce from seed and the seedlings are transplanted to the central highlands. No arboretum plantings outside the Da Lat area have been successful to date. It would be desirable to try this species for cultivation in some well-known botanic gardens in mild temperate climates to study its biology in more detail.

References

Buchholz, J. T. 1951. A flat-leaved pine from Annam, Indo-China. *Amer. J. Bot.* 38: 245-252.

Campbell, D. G. and H. D. Hammond. 1989. *Floristic Inventory of Tropical Countries.* New York Botanical Garden, Bronx, New York.

Chevalier, A. 1944. Notes sur les conifères de l'Indochine. *Rev. Bot. Appl. Agr. Trop.* 24: 7-34.

Ferré, Y. de. 1948. Quelques particularités anatomique d'un pin Indo-Chinois: *Pinus Krempfii. Bull. Soc. Hist. Nat. Toulouse* 83: 1-6.

Lecomte, H. 1921. Un pin remarquable de l'Annam, *Pinus krempfii. Bull. Mus. Nation. Hist. Nat. Paris* 27: 191-192.

Liston, A., W. A. Robinson, E. R. Alvarez-Buylla and D. Pinero. 1996. Pine trees: a comparison of internal transcribed spacer region and chloroplast phylogenies of *Pinus* (Pinaceae). *Amer. J. Bot. Suppl.* (abstract). p. 175.

Little, Jr., E. L. and W. B. Critchfield. 1969. Subdivisions of the genus *Pinus.* (Pines). *USDA-Forest Service Misc. Publ.* 1144. Forest Service, Washington, D.C.

Seitz, V. 1997. The genus *Pinus* L.: a *cladistic analysis using morphological and molecular data.* Diplomarbeit im Fach Biologie an der Freien Universität Berlin, unpublished presentation, 25 Juli 1997.

Stephan, G. and L. V. Tien 1986. Development of pine resin production in Vietnam (in German). *Soz. Forst.* 36 (4): 120-121.

Westing, A. H. and C. E. Westing. 1981. Endangered species and habitats of Vietnam. *Environ. Conserv.* 8 (1): 59-63.

* Dr. Claire Williams wrote this species account at the request of the Chairman of the Conifer Specialist Group, of which she is not a member.

White berry yew
(*Pseudotaxus chienii* (W. C. Cheng) W. C. Cheng)

Lin Jin-xing, He Xin-qiang, and Hu Yu-shi
Institute of Botany
Chinese Academy of Sciences, Beijing, China

Family	Taxaceae
Status	Endangered
Criteria	A1c
Historic Range	SE China: Guangdong, Guangxi, Hunan, Jiangxi, Zhejiang

Description

Habit: a dioecious evergreen shrub or small tree, branches subopposite or nearly whorled.

Bark: smooth, exfoliating in flakes.

Leaves: spirally arranged, linear-lanceolate, 1.0-2.5 x 0.25-0.45 cm, with two white stomatal bands on the underside and prominent midribs on both surfaces, apex acuminate.

Male strobili: single in the axils of the leaves, sessile, globose at maturity, bracteate at base or the microsporophylls vertically separated by broad, interposed, sterile bracts.

Female strobili: solitary in the axils of the leaves, with 12-16 decussate bracts at the base and a single, terminal, erect ovule, developing into a nut-like, ovoid and slightly compressed seed surrounded by a fleshy, cup-shaped, white aril.

Biology

White berry yew grows rather slowly to a shrub or small tree; no data are available on its ultimate size or longevity. Plants in the wild usually begin vegetative growth in March and end it in October. Female reproductive growth requires an accumulated temperature of 1736° C and an accumulated light period of 7545hrs; for seed maturation these figures are 2213° C and 9574hrs respectively. Male strobili appear in September and release pollen through September and October. Female buds generally emerge in August of the first year and the seeds mature in November of the second year. Female plants have a low fruiting percentage and bear seeds infrequently. The seed has a rather long dormant period and germinates after a year's interval.

Distribution and habitat

Pseudotaxus chienii is sporadically distributed in five provinces in SE China. In Guangdong it occurs in Ruyuan County, in Guangxi it is found on Dayao Mountain, Daming Mt. and Tiuwan Mt., in Hunan it grows on Hupin Mountain, Badagong Mt., Zhangjiajie Mt., Mang Mt. and in Suoxiyu and Qianjiadong. In Jiangxi it occurs on Jinggan Mountain and on Yujing Mt., and in Zhejiang it is found on Fengyang Mountain, Mao Mt., Jiulong Mt., Dayang Mt., Dayuanwei Mt., and at Ruoliaoguan. This distribution, although covering a large geographical area between 23°30'N and 30°N and 108°E and 121°E is nevertheless restricted: the plant occurs only sporadically in dense forest gullies or on cliffs at elevations from 900-1400m. The number of its individuals is consequently very low (Ying and Li 1981). The species grows in forests in the subtropical middle-altitude mountains, where the climate is temperate, cool, humid, cloudy, and foggy. There is a mean annual temperature of 12-15°C, an annual precipitation of 1800-2000mm, and a mean relative humidity of over 80% (Fu and Jin 1992). The mean annual evapotranspiration is 1071mm and the annual sunshine duration is 1457hrs. The soils are mainly mountain yellow earth, strongly acidic (pH 4.2-4.5), rather fertile (organic matter 5.4-18.4%) (Zhang 1992). In the northern limits of its range (Jiulong Mountain) it grows in mixed coniferous and broad-leaved forest and at the southern limits (Daming Mt.) in evergreen broad-leaved forest.

History and conservation

Pseudotaxus chienii was first described by Cheng under *Taxus* in 1934 but subsequently recognised and named as a distinct genus by Cheng (1947) and Florin (1948); the latter named the genus *Nothotaxus* but published a year later than Cheng. It is the only species recognised in the genus, which is probably a Tertiary relic. Due to its scattered distribution and deterioration and/or destruction of its forest habitat, slow growth and poor regeneration, this species is declining rapidly both in numbers and in range. The wood has been in demand for furniture and artistic carving; over-exploitation of timber, including the wood of various yews, has con-

tributed to the threatened status. In recent years, many nature and forest reserves have been established, in which *in situ* conservation has functioned particularly well. For *Pseudotaxus chienii*, some localities are in nature reserves or forest parks, where rare and endangered plant species are under protection. In 1992, *Pseudotaxus chienii* was included as a threatened species in the China Plant Red Data Book (Fu and Jin 1992).

Propagation *ex situ*

Additional *ex situ* conservation of *Pseudotaxus chienii* is desirable. Individual plants have been cultivated in Lushan Botanical Garden (Jiangxi), Wuhan Botanical Garden (Hubei), Guilin Botanical Garden (Guangxi), Changsha Botanical Garden (Hunan) and Hangzhou Botanical Garden (Zhejiang). [*We are not aware, however, of its cultivation in any botanic garden outside China. - the compilers*]. The species can be propagated from seed sown under canopy shade similar to that of its natural habitat. Seedlings require shade and moisture for growth and large root balls should be kept when the seedlings are transplanted. Propagation by cuttings is also feasible and these can have a survival rate of up to 85%. Conservation priorities should focus both on *in situ* and *ex situ* measures. Thus the study of its biology and conservation, including *in vitro* micropropagation, has important significance in both theory and practice.

References

Cheng, W. C. 1947. New Chinese trees and shrubs. *Notes Forest. Inst. Nat. Centr. Univ. Nanking, Dendrol. Ser.*, 1: 1-?

Florin, R. 1948. On *Nothotaxus*, a new genus of the Taxaceae from eastern China. *Acta Horti Berg.* 14 (9): 385-395.

Fu, L. K. and J. M. Jin 1992. *China Plant Red Data Book.* Science Press, Beijing, New York.

Ying, T. S. and L. Q. Li 1981. Ecological distribution of endemic genera of taxads and conifers in China and neighboring area in relation to phytogeographical significance. *Acta Phytotax. Sin.* 19 (4): 408-415.

Zhang, G. X. 1992. *Pseudotaxus chienii* may cultivate in large scale. *Plants* 19 (3): 4.

Cedar of Lebanon
(*Cedrus libani* A. Rich.)

S. Khuri[1] and S. N. Talhouk[2]
[1]University of Reading, UK
[2]American University of Beirut, Lebanon

[*The following account differs from the preceding ones in that it concerns a species considered Endangered in one country, but Lower Risk in the remainder of its range.* - the compilers]

Family	Pinaceae
Status	Lower Risk (Endangered in Lebanon)
Criteria	(Lebanon: A1d)
Historic Range	Lebanon, Syria, Turkey

Description

Habit: evergreen tree, 25-40m in height with very thick trunk. Pyramidal when young, branches flatten and crown broadens as tree gets older. Branches horizontal and stout on older trees, leading shoots can be upright. Numerous branches spread out table-like from the main branches. Buds small and ovoid.

Bark: dark grey, smooth becoming fissured in older trees.

Leaves: spirally arranged and scattered on long shoots, very crowded forming pseudowhorls on short shoots, acicular, triangular, rigid, and pointed green or glaucous.

Cones: solitary and erect. Male cones cylindrical, 3-5cm long, grey-green. Young female cones ovoid, 1-2cm long, purple green. Mature cones terminal on short shoots, ovoid to ellipsoid, blunt or notched at apex, average size 6 x 9cm, brown, seed scales very broad, each with two seeds.

Seeds: irregularly triangular, broad, with a membranous orange-brown wing; seedlings with 9-10 cotyledons.

More detailed descriptions can be found in Farjon, 1990.

Biology

The Cedar of Lebanon is a slow growing monoecious tree, maturing at approximately 40 years. Male cones shed pollen in the autumn, pollination is by wind. Female strobili close once fertilised. Fertilised cones mature in the second or third year, breaking up with the scales falling from the central axis. Cedar of Lebanon can live up to 700 years.

Distribution and habitat

Cedrus libani is restricted to Lebanon, Syria and Turkey, with a close relative on the mountains of Cyprus (*C. brevifolia*) and another on the Atlas mountains of Morocco (*C. atlantica*). The fourth member of the genus is found in the western Himalayas (*C. deodara*). The phylogenetic affinities between these species awaits clarification. *C. libani* is a very common amenity tree found in many parks and gardens throughout northern Europe and the Mediterranean.

In Lebanon, it is found in 15 fragmented populations covering a total of approximately 2300ha on the western slopes of the western mountain range, between 1,050-1,925m. These are either pure cedar populations or mixed forest with pine, oak and juniper (Khouzami 1994). There is a small isolated population on the east side of Jabal an-Nusayriya in north-west Syria. The main populations, covering a total of 99,325ha, are on the Taurus mountains of eastern Turkey at elevations between 530-2000m, of which approximately one third are in a degraded state (Boydak 1996). They are reported as pure *Cedrus libani* forests, with some more occurrences of the species in larger areas of mixed forest. There are also two small remnant populations in the Black Sea region of Turkey, at elevations of 700-1400m (Boydak 1996).

History and conservation

The Cedar of Lebanon is mentioned in the oldest recorded legend, the Epic of Gilgamesh, as well as in several Books of the Old Testament. It is the Lebanese national tree and holds pride

Cedar of Lebanon (*Cedrus libani*) is relatively widespread in southern Turkey, where it is often mixed with Junipers (*Juniperus* spp.).

M. P Frankis

of place on the Lebanese flag. However, the quality of the timber (mainly in terms of water-retention and resistance to woodworm), massive human population increase on the Lebanese mountain ranges and over-exploitation of timber resources have all lead to the disappearance of any lowland forests from Lebanon and severe loss of the highland forests (Meiggs 1982). The extent of clearance is such that estimates of original forest cover in lowland Lebanon and Syria are now nearly impossible to gauge, and only an estimated 5% of the original upland forest cover remains (WWF and IUCN 1994).

The problem has been exacerbated after the cessation of the war in Lebanon (1974-1990) by further population increase on the Levantine mountain slopes concomitant with an increase in spending power leading to land speculation (e.g. new housing and ski resorts). These uplands fall within the Centre of Plant Diversity (CPD) site SWA 17 (WWF and IUCN 1994), however only 5 of the 15 known cedar forest fragments were listed, leaving out two of the larger populations. Since the CPD was published in 1994, two cedar forests, Horsh Ehden and Jabal El-Barouk in Shouf have attained protected status as National Heritage Sites, and some others, e.g. Quammoua and Bsharre, have protection from Ministry of Agriculture decrees (Tohme 1996). In 1996, a GEF funded project was set up involving the Ministry of Environment in Lebanon and various NGOs, to manage three protected areas in Lebanon, two of which are cedar forests, Horsh-Ehden and Jabal El-Barouk. A number of positive steps have been taken in terms of establishing an Office of Protected Areas within the Ministry, delegating certain managerial tasks to local NGOs and the hiring of staff (Abu-Izzeddin 1997).

Public opinion in Lebanon strongly supports reforestation with numerous NGOs involved in environmental awareness (Masri 1995). However, there are a number of complications which hinder the advance of co-ordinated conservation activities. Despite laws set by the Ministry of Agriculture forbidding damage to the cedar trees (Law 558 1996), there is little supervision of some of the forests and little enforcement of the laws. As a result, several of the stands are still under threat from pillaging and housing development. The demand for ornaments made from cedar wood has not diminished and in fact is increasing with the increase in tourism; carvers claim they only use branches that have naturally fallen off, but there are reports that trees are being cut down in one area to feed the shops in another. Developers are still targeting either the protected areas themselves or land just adjacent to or above them, which raises issues such as ground water pollution and the opportunities for pillaging. There is evidence of severe damage from winter sports and goats in the reforestation sites at Bsharre and Shouf. Parts of the Shouf and Jibbe-Tannourine forests are littered with mines which were placed there during the recent war (1974-1990). This, while discouraging illegal harvesting, also restricts access to the trees for research or for management purposes. Finally, the tenure of the land on which the surviving populations of cedar grow includes the Ministry of Agriculture, local government, private ownership and religious holdings, which adds a political and time-consuming element to any integration of conservation efforts.

Another important factor to consider is the problem of insect pests currently attacking the Lebanese forests. In the Shouf, young trees are infested with the cedar shoot moth Dichelia sp. (alias Parasyndemis sp.). The moth is found in more than one of the stands and there are fears that the problem is spreading. In Tannourine the situation is more serious. A large percentage of the trees are showing a high degree of necrosis, particularly on new shoots, and this was found to be caused by a Cephalcia sp., the first to be reported on the genus Cedrus. Both these insect species have been found in the Bsharre population. The problem is being exacerbated by mild winter conditions over the last few years which allows the insects two generations per year instead of one. Academic research is already under way to study their biology and possible methods of control. In the meantime it remains unclear whether pruning, where possible, would help to control the problem.

There is therefore an urgent need for a thorough assessment of the condition of the forests to be completed and the establishment of some form of forest supervision. This will allow an integrated management system to be established in order to enforce the laws and protect not only the trees themselves but the entire habitat in which they grow.

The situation in Turkey is rather different. The difficult topography of the Taurus mountains and a long-established forestry infrastructure have helped to preserve a relatively large area of remnant forests in that region. The cedars in Turkey are found in CPD sites SWA 15, southern, and 16, south-west (WWF and IUCN 1994). Their conservation is being co-ordinated by the General Directorate of Reforestation and Erosion Control, and is managed by regional Forest Research Institutes. There are now two protected natural cedar populations, at Elmali-Çig likara and Sharkikaraagaç-Kizildag. In addition, 21 stands throughout the natural distribution in Turkey have been given 'Seed Stand' status by the Forest Tree Seeds and Improvement Institute, Ankara (Boydak 1996, Isik 1997). It is not clear, however, if a measure of genetic diversity was used in the selection of these seed stands. There have also been extensive plantings, 61,611ha of Cedrus libani was planted between the years 1983-1989, and 5750ha between 1994-1996, some of it outside the natural range of the species (Boydak 1996). However, the impact of this planting on the existing genetic architecture of the populations is as yet unassessed, and there is damage to the forests due to unregulated tourist and agricultural development.

Propagation *ex situ*

Due to an increased environmental awareness after the war and a great pride in the national tree, there are several nurseries in Lebanon, both private and public, which are successfully producing cedar seedlings. These seedlings are being planted both as amenity trees all over Lebanon, and were used at a number of reforestation sites in Bsharre and Shouf regions. In Bsharre, the seedlings were planted over a large area just above the existing Cèdres de Dieu stand, and they have been subject to high levels of mortality and exhibit unusually slow rates of growth. It is suggested that the residual stand represents the natural altitudinal limit of the species, and that planting above that limit exposes the seedlings to excessive drought and other stresses. Planting at lower altitudes might therefore meet with more success, particularly if the area is fenced and managed. Earlier reforestation efforts in the mid 1960's targeted the hills of the Shouf region. Terraces were built over a total area of over 142,000 ha and the trees planted in rows at a high density (Chaney and Basbous 1978). At the moment these look artificial and in need of proper management, but growth is good and local NGOs working with the Ministry of Environment are investigating possible strategies.

Some Lebanese nurseries are producing both *Cedrus deodara* and *C. atlantica* as well as *C. libani*. Law 558 (1996) decrees that only *C. libani* be planted for reforestation. The problem lies in the fact that at the seedling stage it is morphologically almost impossible to tell all the species apart, and again, there is no supervision or monitoring of what is being planted where. At the American University of Beirut there is now a reliable DNA-based method of identifying one species from another (PCR-RAPDs), and it is proposed that greater use be made of this facility in order to ensure that the replanted forests are of Cedar of Lebanon rather than a mixture of exotic congenerics.

In Turkey, the co-ordinated reforestation efforts have made use of foresters' observations and ensured that nurseries use seeds from the same elevation to reforest a particular area; more than 67,000ha have been planted with *C. libani* since 1983 (Boydak 1996). There have been extensive seedling trials and valuable information has been gathered on the best methods of replanting with reforestation objectives. However, most of the reports are written in Turkish and remain for the larger part untranslated.

Cedar of Lebanon (*Cedrus libani*) cultivated at Wakehurst Place (Royal Botanic Gardens, Kew), England.

Recommended actions

The governments of Lebanon, Syria and Turkey can publish Biodiversity Action Plans which will stimulate national co-ordination efforts. Current and recent work, such as reports and theses from institutes in Turkey and Lebanon, could be built on and incorporated into such documents. Ongoing collaborative projects could also feed into these plans; for example, The American University of Beirut, Lebanon, and Akdeniz University, Turkey, are involved in a European Union Integrated Co-operation for Developing Countries (INCO-DC) project co-ordinated by The University of Reading, UK, on the assessment of genetic diversity and sustainable production of *Cedrus* in Mediterranean regions (project number IC18-CT97-0177). This project, which includes partners in Morocco and Spain, will help to provide vital information on the genetic diversity of cedars which may be incorporated into more general conservation strategies in the region.

In Lebanon, the Ministry of Environment could lead an integrated strategy for conservation that identifies core areas and maintains them, perhaps within the context of a newly established World Heritage Site or Biosphere Reserve. The GEF project currently running could form the basis for such a programme. This will ensure that the stunning landscape which houses the cedars will remain, while at the same time giving leeway for some development and commercial enterprises to benefit the local communities. With Lebanon just emerging from 20 years of war and enthusiastic about what is left of its natural resources, the step into an integrated management system is ready to be taken.

Turkey, on the other hand, already has an integrated and well co-ordinated cedar conservation strategy, and this will be further strengthened by a robust assessment of diversity. It seems from the literature available that there is an awareness of the need to protect the cedar forests, but it was not apparent whether this awareness extended to the old growth stands. These forests would probably contain the greatest genetic diversity within *Cedrus libani* as well as the greatest diversity of associated species. It is thus imperative to survey all extant old growth stands and use the index to ensure legal

Cedar of Lebanon (*Cedrus libani*) in SW Turkey.

protection with adequate provision of management. There may not be a risk of *C. libani* becoming extinct in the wild, but the surviving old growth stands will soon be lost through poor regeneration and natural death, and with them the genetic diversity required for reforestation and habitat restoration.

The remnant cedar forests of the eastern Mediterranean are probably amongst the last areas of primary habitat in these countries, and are also where a large proportion of the area's threatened biodiversity survives. Due to reasons discussed earlier in this report, these remnants are diminishing in both quality and area. This leads on to the need for adopting an ecosystem approach to conservation for the whole region, whereby instead of fencing off the forests and keeping them as "museums", they are incorporated into a larger scheme of protected areas where cedar stands of varying ages are managed. The best opportunities for the establishment of viable reserves is in mountains, and it is suggested that a series of linked reserves are set up through the range of *Cedrus libani* from Turkey to Lebanon to secure what is left of the natural habitat and encourage the recovery of other elements of the Levantine biota such as the wolf and the Syrian bear.

Acknowledgements

The authors thank Mr Andy Byfield, Fauna and Flora International; Mr Sedat Kalem, Society for the Protection of Nature, Turkey; Mr Huseyin Usta and Mr Fikret Isik, Southwest Anatolia Forest Research Institute, Turkey; Dr. Naci Onus, Akdeniz University, Turkey; Mr Nabil Nimr, Lebanese entomologist; Mr Ghattas Akl, Ministry of Agriculture, Lebanon and Dr Michael Maunder, Royal Botanic Gardens, Kew, UK.

References

Abu-Izzeddin, F. 1997. First Progress Report: *Protected Areas Project*, Ministry of Environment, the Government of Lebanon, for the IUCN Regional Conservation Forum, Jordan.

Boydak, M. 1996. *Ecology and Silviculture of Cedar of Lebanon (Cedrus libani* A. Rich.) *and Conservation of its Natural Forests*. Orman Bakanligi Yayin, Istanbul.

Chaney, W. R. and Basbous, M. 1978. The Cedars of Lebanon, witnesses of history. *Economic Botany* 32:119-123.

Farjon, A. 1990. *Pinaceae*. Koeltz Scientific Books, Königstein.

The Government of Lebanon. 1996. Law number 558, *Protection of Forests*, Aljarada Alrasmiya number 34, 1 August 1996.

Khouzami, M. 1994. The Lebanese cedar forests. In *Proceedings of the First National Conference on the Cedar of Lebanon, Present and Future*. American University of Beirut, Lebanon.

Masri, R. 1995. The cedars of Lebanon, significance, awareness and management of the *Cedrus libani* in Lebanon. Seminar given by MIT, Massachussettes,USA.URL: http://www.cybercom.net/~tonyk/cedars/

Meiggs, R. 1982. *Trees and Timber in the Ancient Mediterranean World*. Clarendon Press, Oxford.

Tohme, H. 1996. *Nature Reserves in Lebanon*. Ch. 9 in Hamadeh, S., M. Khouzami and G. Tohme (eds.), *Biological Diversity of Lebanon - Comprehensive Report*. Publication no 9. Report to the Lebanese government sponsored by UNEP project GF/6105-92-72.

WWF and IUCN. 1994. *Centres of Plant Diversity, a guide and strategy for their conservation*. Volume 1. IUCN Publications Unit, Cambridge, UK.

Appendix 1

Conifer Specialist Group Members and Members/Contributing Authors(*)

Professor Juan ARMESTO. Lab. de Sistematica y Ecol. Vegetal, Dept. de Biol., Fac. de Cienc., Universidad de Chile, Casilla 653, Santiago, CHILE. Tel: 62/2/6787334; Fax:56/2/2712983; Email: jarmesto@abello.dic.uchile.cl

Dr. John BRAGGINS. Senior Lecturer in Plant Taxonomy, The University of Auckland, School of Biological Sciences, Private Bag 92019, Auckland, NEW ZEALAND. Tel: 64/9/3737599; Fax: 64/9/3737416; Email: j.braggins@auckland.ac.nz

*Mr Michael J. BROWN; Assistant Chief of Division; Forestry Tasmania; 79 Melville St.; Hobart; Tasmania 7000; AUSTRALIA; Tel: 61/3/62338202; Fax: 61/3/62338292; Email: mick.b@forestry.tas.gov.au

*Dr Prem DOGRA; I.N.S.A. Senior Scientist; Indian Council of Forestry Res. and Education, F.R.I; Forest Research Institute; I.C.F.R.E.; P.O. New Forest; Dehra Dun; 248006; INDIA; Tel: 91/1305/27021; Fax: 91/1305/28381; Telex: 585-258 FRIC-IN; 157 - Nehru Colony, Dharampur, Dehra Dun 248001, U.P., India

*Dr Michael F. DOYLE; Jepson and University Herbaria; University of California; 1001 Valley Life Sciences Bldg. #2465; Berkeley, CA 94720; USA; Tel: 1/605/994-1900; Fax: 1/510/642-2465; Email: dacrydium@aol.com

*Mr Aljos FARJON (chair); Curator of Gymnosperms; Royal Botanic Gardens, Kew; Herbarium Division; Richmond; TW9 3AB; Surrey; UNITED KINGDOM; Tel: 44/181/3325402; Fax: 44/181/3325278; Email: a.farjon@rbgkew.org.uk

Prof. FU Likuo; Director of the Herbarium; Institute of Botany; Chinese Academy of Sciences; Nan Xin Cun 20, Xiang Shan; Beijing; 100093; CHINA; Tel: 86/10/62591431; Fax: 86/10/62566099

Mr Martin F. GARDNER (secretary); Co-ordinator, Conifer Conserv. Progr.; Royal Botanic Garden, Edinburgh; 20A Inverleith Row; Edinburgh; EH3 5LR; Scotland; UNITED KINGDOM; Tel: 44/131/5527171; Fax: 44/131/5520382; Email: m.gardner@rbge.org.uk

Prof. GUAN Zhongtian; Sichuan Institute of Forestry,; Exploration and Design; 14, Section 1; of Ren Ming Bei Lu Road; Chengdu; 610081; CHINA; Tel: 86/28/333340; Fax: 86/28/3333401

*Prof. Robert S. HILL; Department of Plant Science; University of Tasmania; GPO Box 252-55 Hobart, Tasmania 7001; AUSTRALIA

*Prof. HU Yu-shi; Director of Morphology Division; Institute of Botany, Chinese Academy of Sciences; Nan Xin Cun 20, Xiang Shan; Beijing; 100093; CHINA; Tel: 86/10/62591431-6211; Fax: 86/10/62590833; Email: linjx@ns.ibcas.ac.cn

Dr Tanguy JAFFRE; Directeur de Recherche; ORSTOM, Lab. de Botanique et d'Ecologie; BP A5; Noumea; NEW CALEDONIA; Tel: 687/261000; Fax: 687/264326

*Dr Sawsan KHURI; Postdocotral Research Fellow; The University of Reading; Dept. of Agricultural Botany; School of Plant Sciences; Whiteknights P.O. Box 221; Reading; RG6 6AS; Berks; UNITED KINGDOM; Tel: 44/118/9318092; Fax: 44/118/9316577; Email: s.khuri@reading.ac.uk

Dr Marie KURMANN; Ausserdorf 29; Altbüron; CH-6147; SWITZERLAND; Tel: 41/63/591848; Fax: 41/63/591848; Email: m.kurmann@spectraweb.ch

Dr Antonio LARA; Universidad Austral de Chile; Casilla 567; Valdivia; CHILE; Tel: 56/63/221227; Fax: 56/63/221230; Email: alara@valdivia.uca.uach.cl

Prof. David de LAUBENFELS; Syracuse University, Dept. of Geography; 343 H.B. Crouse Hall; Syracuse; 13244-1060; NY; USA; Tel: 1/315/4435636; Fax: 1/315/4434227

Dr LI Nan; Herbarium, Shenzhen Fairy Lake Botanic Garden, Liantang, Shenzhen, Guangdong 518004, CHINA; Tel: 86/755/5738647; Fax: 86/755/5738430; Email: snzlibg@public.szptt.net.cn

*Dr LIN Jinxing; Director of Department; Institute of Botany; Chinese Academy of Sciences; Nan Xin Cun 20, Xiang Shan; Beijing; 100093; CHINA; Tel: 86/10/62591431-6211; Fax: 86/10/62590833; Email: linjx@ns.ibcas.ac.cn

Dr Brian P. J. MOLLOY; Research associate; Manaaki Whenua - Landcare research Ltd., Canterbury Agriculture and Science Centre; P.O. Box 69; Gerald Street; Lincoln; NEW ZEALAND; Tel: 64/3/3256700; Fax: 64/3/3252418

Mr Colin S. MORGAN; Curator; Bedgebury National Pinetum; Weald Forest District; Goudhurst; Cranbrook; Kent; TN17 2SL; UNITED KINGDOM; Tel: 44/1580/211044; Fax: 44/1580/212423

Mr Robert NICHOLSON; Greenhouse Supervisor; Smith College Botanic Garden; 15 College Lane;

Northampton; 01063; MA; USA. Tel: 1/413/5852748; Fax: 1/413/5852744

Dr Hideaki OHBA; Associate Professor; University Museum, University of Tokyo; Hongo 7-3-1; Tokyo; 113; JAPAN; Tel: 81/3/38122111; Fax: 81/3/58022995; Email: ohba@tansei.cc.u-tokyo.ac.jp

*Dr Chistopher N. PAGE; Gillywood Cottage; Trebost Lane; Stithians, Truro; Cornwall; TR3 7DW; UNITED KINGDOM; Tel: 44/1209/860671

Dr PAN Fuh-Juinn; Director of Botanic Garden; c/o Taiwan Forestry Research Institute; 53, Nan-Hai Road; Taipei 100; Taiwan; TAIWAN; new address: Heng-Chun; Ping-Tung County, 94606 TAIWAN

*Ing. Jorge A. PEREZ DE LA ROSA; Professor Investigador; Instituto de Botanica, Universidad de Guadalajara; Apartado Postal 139; Zapopan; Jalisco; 45110; MEXICO; Tel: 52/3/6820003; Fax: 52/3/6820076

Mr Keith RUSHFORTH. The Shippen, Ashill, Cullompton, Devon, EX15 3NL, UNITED KINGDOM. Tel: 44/1884/841400; Fax: 44/1884/841991

*Mr Nico SCHELLEVIS; Curator Pinetum Blijdenstein; Botanic Garden, University of Amsterdam; Van der Lindenlaan 125; PJ Hilversum; 1217; NETHERLANDS; Tel: 31/35/6232056; Fax: 31/35/6232056

*Dr Rudolf SCHMID; Lecturer; Department of Integrative Biology; University of California, Berkeley; California 94720-3140; USA. Tel: 1/510/5250439; Fax: 1/510/6436264; Email: schmid@socrates.berkeley.edu

Dr Stefan G. SCHNECKENBURGER; Curator Botanical Garden; Botanischer Garten der TU; Schnittspahnstr. 5; Darmstadt; D-64287; GERMANY; Tel: 49/6151/164630; Fax: 49/6151/164808; Email: schneckenburger @bio1.bio.tu-darmstadt.de

Ms Myrna SEMAAN; Research/ Chief Plant Officer; Friends of Nature (NGO); Jounieh 967; LEBANON; Tel/Fax: 961/9/220665; fon@sodetel.net.lb; (current mailing address: The University of Reading; School of Plant Science; Whiteknights; PO Box 221; Reading RG6 6AS; UK)

Dr Ruth A. STOCKEY; Department of Botany; University of Alberta; Edmonton; T6G 2E9; CANADA; Tel: 1/403/4925518; Fax: 1/403/4927033

*Dr TANG Ya; Head of Dept. of Botany; Chengdu Institute of Biology, Academia Sinica; P.O. Box 416; Chengdu; 610041; Sichuan; CHINA; Tel: 86/28/5581260; Fax: 86/28/5582753

Prof. P Barry TOMLINSON; Harvard University; Harvard Forest; Petersham; 01366-0068; MA; USA; Tel: 1/508/7243302; Fax: 1/508/7243595

*Mr Alistair WATT; Otway Ridge Arboretum; Chapel Vale Road; Lavers Hill; 3238; Victoria; AUSTRALIA; Tel: 61/52/373263; Fax: 61/52/374264

Dr Philippe WOLTZ; Enseignant-Chercheur; Université Aix-Marseille 3, Fac. des Sciences et Tech. de Saint Jérome, Lab. Morpho. Végétale; Service 442; Av. Escadrille Normandie-Niémen; 13397 Marseille; Cedex 20; FRANCE; Tel: 33/91/288521; Fax: 33/91/288523; Email: philippe.woltz@mv.u-3mrs.fr

Dr YANG Jenq-Chuan; Director General; Taiwan Forestry Research Institute; 53, Nan-Hai Road; Taipei; 100; Taiwan; TAIWAN; Tel: 886/2/3616491; Fax: 886/2/3319021; Email: gove410@twnmoe10.edu.tw

*Dr Thomas A. ZANONI; Research Associate; New York Botanical Garden; 200th Street at Southern Boulevard; Bronx; 10458-5126; N.Y.; USA; Tel: 1/718/8178651; Fax: 1/718/5626780; Email: tzanoni@nybg.org

Appendix 2

IUCN Red List Categories

Prepared by the IUCN Species Survival Commission
As approved by the 40th Meeting of the IUCN Council, Gland, Switzerland
30 November 1994

I) Introduction

1. The threatened species categories now used in Red Data Books and Red Lists have been in place, with some modification, for almost 30 years. Since their introduction these categories have become widely recognised internationally, and they are now used in a whole range of publications and listings, produced by IUCN as well as by numerous governmental and non-governmental organisations. The Red Data Book categories provide an easily and widely understood method for highlighting those species under higher extinction risk, so as to focus attention on conservation measures designed to protect them.

2. The need to revise the categories has been recognised for some time. In 1984, the SSC held a symposium, 'The Road to Extinction' (Fitter & Fitter 1987), which examined the issues in some detail, and at which a number of options were considered for the revised system. However, no single proposal resulted. The current phase of development began in 1989 with a request from the SSC Steering Committee to develop a new approach that would provide the conservation community with useful information for action planning.

In this document, proposals for new definitions for Red List categories are presented. The general aim of the new system is to provide an explicit, objective framework for the classification of species according to their extinction risk.

The revision has several specific aims:

● to provide a system that can be applied consistently by different people;

● to improve the objectivity by providing those using the criteria with clear guidance on how to evaluate different factors which affect risk of extinction;

● to provide a system which will facilitate comparisons across widely different taxa;

● to give people using threatened species lists a better understanding of how individual species were classified.

3. The proposals presented in this document result from a continuing process of drafting, consultation and validation. It was clear that the production of a large number of draft proposals led to some confusion, especially as each draft has been used for classifying some set of species for conservation purposes. To clarify matters, and to open the way for modifications as and when they became necessary, a system for version numbering was applied as follows:

Version 1.0: Mace & Lande (1991)
The first paper discussing a new basis for the categories, and presenting numerical criteria especially relevant for large vertebrates.

Version 2.0: Mace et al. (1992)
A major revision of Version 1.0, including numerical criteria appropriate to all organisms and introducing the non-threatened categories.

Version 2.1: IUCN (1993)
Following an extensive consultation process within SSC, a number of changes were made to the details of the criteria, and fuller explanation of basic principles was included. A more explicit structure clarified the significance of the non-threatened categories.

Version 2.2: Mace & Stuart (1994)
Following further comments received and additional validation exercises, some minor changes to the criteria were made. In addition, the Susceptible category present in Versions 2.0 and 2.1 was subsumed into the Vulnerable category. A precautionary application of the system was emphasised.

Final Version
This final document, which incorporates changes as a result of comments from IUCN members, was adopted by the IUCN Council in December 1994.

All future taxon lists including categorisations should be based on this version, and not the previous ones.

4. In the rest of this document the proposed system is outlined in several sections. The Preamble presents some basic information about the context and structure of the proposal, and the procedures that are to be followed in applying the definitions to species. This is followed by a section giving definitions of terms used. Finally the definitions are presented, followed by the quantitative criteria used for classification within the threatened categories. It is important for the effective functioning of the new system that all sections are read and understood, and the guidelines followed.

References:

Fitter, R., and M. Fitter, ed. (1987) *The Road to Extinction.* Gland, Switzerland: IUCN.

IUCN. (1993) *Draft IUCN Red List Categories.* Gland, Switzerland: IUCN.

Mace, G. M. et al. (1992) "The development of new criteria for listing species on the IUCN Red List." *Species* 19: 16-22.

Mace, G. M., and R. Lande. (1991) "Assessing extinction threats: toward a reevaluation of IUCN threatened species categories." *Conserv. Biol.* 5.2: 148-157.

Mace, G. M. & S. N. Stuart. (1994) "Draft IUCN Red List Categories, Version 2.2". *Species* 21-22: 13-24.

II) Preamble

The following points present important information on the use and interpretation of the categories (= Critically Endangered, Endangered, etc.), criteria (= A to E), and sub-criteria (= a,b etc., i,ii etc.):

1. Taxonomic level and scope of the categorisation process

The criteria can be applied to any taxonomic unit at or below the species level. The term 'taxon' in the following notes, definitions and criteria is used for convenience, and may represent species or lower taxonomic levels, including forms that are not yet formally described. There is a sufficient range among the different criteria to enable the appropriate listing of taxa from the complete taxonomic spectrum, with the exception of micro-organisms. The criteria may also be applied within any specified geographical or political area although in such cases special notice should be taken of point 11 below. In presenting the results of applying the criteria, the taxonomic unit and area under consideration should be made explicit. The categorisation process should only be applied to wild populations inside their natural range, and to populations resulting from benign introductions (defined in the draft IUCN Guidelines for Re-introductions as "..an attempt to establish a species, for the purpose of conservation, outside its recorded distribution, but within an appropriate habitat and eco-geographical area").

2. Nature of the categories

All taxa listed as Critically Endangered qualify for Vulnerable and Endangered, and all listed as Endangered qualify for Vulnerable. Together these categories are described as 'threatened'. The threatened species categories form a part of the overall scheme. It will be possible to place all taxa into one of the categories (see Figure 1).

3. Role of the different criteria

For listing as Critically Endangered, Endangered or Vulnerable there is a range of quantitative criteria; meeting any one of these criteria qualifies a taxon for listing at that level of threat. Each species should be evaluated against all the criteria. The different criteria (A-E) are derived from a wide review aimed at detecting risk factors across the broad range of organisms and the diverse life histories they exhibit. Even though some criteria will be inappropriate for certain taxa (some taxa will never qualify under these however close to extinction they come), there should be criteria appropriate for assessing threat levels for any taxon (other than micro-organisms). The relevant factor is whether any one criterion is met, not whether all are appropriate or all are met. Because it will never be clear which criteria are appropriate for a particular species in advance, each species should be evaluated against all the criteria, and any criterion met should be listed.

4. Derivation of quantitative criteria

The quantitative values presented in the various criteria associated with threatened categories were developed through wide consultation and they are set at what are generally judgcd bc appropriate levels, even if no formal justification for these values exists. The levels for different criteria within categories were set independently but against a common standard. Some broad consistency between them was sought. However, a given taxon should not be expected to meet all criteria (A-E) in a category; meeting any one criterion is sufficient for listing.

5. Implications of listing

Listing in the categories of Not Evaluated and Data Deficient indicates that no assessment of extinction risk has been made, though for different reasons.Until such time as an assessment is made, species listed in these categories should not be treated as if they were non-threatened, and it may be appropriate (especially for Data Deficient forms) to give them the same degree of protection as threatened taxa, at least until their status can be evaluated.

Extinction is assumed here to be a chance process. Thus, a listing in a higher extinction risk category implies a higher expectation

Figure 1: Structure of the Categories

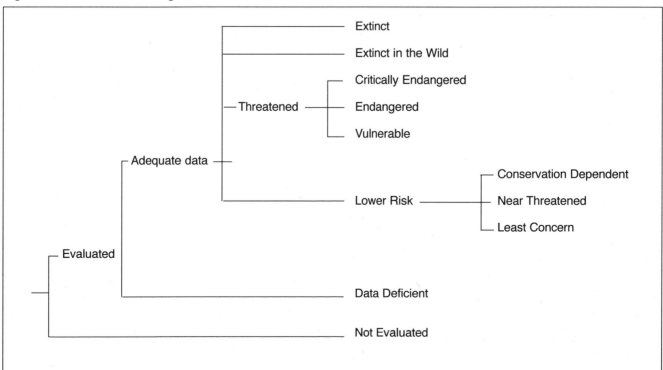

of extinction, and over the time-frames specified more taxa listed in a higher category are expected to go extinct than in a lower one (without effective conservation action). However, the persistence of some taxa in high risk categories does not necessarily mean their initial assessment was inaccurate.

6. Data quality and the importance of inference and projection

The criteria are clearly quantitative in nature. However, the absence of high quality data should not deter attempts at applying the criteria, as methods involving estimation, inference and projection are emphasised to be acceptable throughout. Inference and projection may be based on extrapolation of current or potential threats into the future (including their rate of change), or of factors related to population abundance or distribution (including dependence on other taxa), so long as these can reasonably be supported. Suspected or inferred patterns in either the recent past, present or near future can be based on any of a series of related factors, and these factors should be specified.

Taxa at risk from threats posed by future events of low probability but with severe consequences (catastrophes) should be identified by the criteria (e.g. small distributions, few locations). Some threats need to be identified particularly early, and appropriate actions taken, because their effects are irreversible, or nearly so (pathogens, invasive organisms, hybridization).

7. Uncertainty

The criteria should be applied on the basis of the available evidence on taxon numbers, trend and distribution, making due allowance for statistical and other uncertainties. Given that data are rarely available for the whole range or population of a taxon, it may often be appropriate to use the information that is available to make intelligent inferences about the overall status of the taxon in question. In cases where a wide variation in estimates is found, it is legitimate to apply the precautionary principle and use the estimate (providing it is credible) that leads to listing in the category of highest risk.

Where data are insufficient to assign a category (including Lower Risk), the category of 'Data Deficient' may be assigned. However, it is important to recognise that this category indicates that data are inadequate to determine the degree of threat faced by a taxon, not necessarily that the taxon is poorly known. In cases where there are evident threats to a taxon through, for example, deterioration of its only known habitat, it is important to attempt threatened listing, even though there may be little direct information on the biological status of the taxon itself. The category 'Data Deficient' is not a threatened category, although it indicates a need to obtain more information on a taxon to determine the appropriate listing.

8. Conservation actions in the listing process

The criteria for the threatened categories are to be applied to a taxon whatever the level of conservation action affecting it. In cases where it is only conservation action that prevents the taxon from meeting the threatened criteria, the designation of 'Conservation Dependent' is appropriate. It is important to emphasise here that a taxon require conservation action even if it is not listed as threatened.

9. Documentation

All taxon lists including categorisation resulting from these criteria should state the criteria and sub-criteria that were met. No listing can be accepted as valid unless at least one criterion is given. If more than one criterion or sub-criterion was met, then each should be listed. However, failure to mention a criterion should not necessarily imply that it was not met. Therefore, if a re-evaluation indicates that the documented criterion is no longer met, this should not result in automatic down-listing. Instead, the taxon should be re-evaluated with respect to all criteria to indicate its status. The factors responsible for triggering the criteria, especially where inference and projection are used, should at least be logged by the evaluator, even if they cannot be included in published lists.

10. Threats and priorities

The category of threat is not necessarily sufficient to determine priorities for conservation action. The category of threat simply provides an assessment of the likelihood of extinction under current circumstances, whereas a system for assessing priorities for action will include numerous other factors concerning conservation action such as costs, logistics, chances of success, and even perhaps the taxonomic distinctiveness of the subject.

11. Use at regional level

The criteria are most appropriately applied to whole taxa at a global scale, rather than to those units defined by regional or national boundaries. Regionally or nationally based threat categories, which are aimed at including taxa that are threatened at regional or national levels (but not necessarily throughout their global ranges), are best used with two key pieces of information: the global status category for the taxon, and the proportion of the global population or range that occurs within the region or nation. However, if applied at regional or national level it must be recognised that a global category of threat may not be the same as a regional or national category for a particular taxon. For example, taxa classified as Vulnerable on the basis of their global declines in numbers or range might be Lower Risk within a particular region where their populations are stable. Conversely, taxa classified as Lower Risk globally might be Critically Endangered within a particular region where numbers are very small or declining, perhaps only because they are at the margins of their global range. IUCN is still in the process of developing guidelines for the use of national red list categories.

12. Re-evaluation

Evaluation of taxa against the criteria should be carried out at appropriate intervals. This is especially important for taxa listed under Near Threatened, or Conservation Dependent, and for threatened species whose status is known or suspected to be deteriorating.

13. Transfer between categories

There are rules to govern the movement of taxa between categories. These are as follows: (A) A taxon may be moved from a category of higher threat to a category of lower threat if none of the criteria of the higher category has been met for five years or more. (B) If the original classification is found to have been erroneous, the taxon may be transferred to the appropriate category or removed from the threatened categories altogether, without delay (but see Section 9). (C) Transfer from categories of lower to higher risk should be made without delay.

14. Problems of scale

Classification based on the sizes of geographic ranges or the patterns of habitat occupancy is complicated by problems of spatial scale. The finer the scale at which the distributions or habitats of taxa are mapped, the smaller the area will be that they are found to occupy. Mapping at finer scales reveals more areas in which the taxon is unrecorded. It is impossible to provide any strict but general rules for mapping taxa or habitats; the most appropriate scale will depend on the taxa in question, and the origin and comprehensiveness of the distributional data. However, the thresholds for some criteria (e.g. Critically Endangered) necessitate mapping at a fine scale.

III) Definitions

1. Population
Population is defined as the total number of individuals of the taxon. For functional reasons, primarily owing to differences between life-forms, population numbers are expressed as numbers of mature individuals only. In the case of taxa obligately dependent on other taxa for all or part of their life cycles, biologically appropriate values for the host taxon should be used.

2. Subpopulations
Subpopulations are defined as geographically or otherwise distinct groups in the population between which there is little exchange (typically one successful migrant individual or gamete per year or less).

3. Mature individuals
The number of mature individuals is defined as the number of individuals known, estimated or inferred to be capable of reproduction. When estimating this quantity the following points should be borne in mind:

- Where the population is characterised by natural fluctuations the minimum number should be used.

- This measure is intended to count individuals capable of reproduction and should therefore exclude individuals that are environmentally, behaviourally or otherwise reproductively suppressed in the wild.

- In the case of populations with biased adult or breeding sex ratios it is appropriate to use lower estimates for the number of mature individuals which take this into account (e.g. the estimated effective population size).

- Reproducing units within a clone should be counted as individuals, except where such units are unable to survive alone (e.g. corals).

- In the case of taxa that naturally lose all or a subset of mature individuals at some point in their life cycle, the estimate should be made at the appropriate time, when mature individuals are available for breeding.

4. Generation
Generation may be measured as the average age of parents in the population. This is greater than the age at first breeding, except in taxa where individuals breed only once.

5. Continuing decline
A continuing decline is a recent, current or projected future decline whose causes are not known or not adequately controlled and so is liable to continue unless remedial measures are taken. Natural fluctuations will not normally count as a continuing decline, but an observed decline should not be considered to be part of a natural fluctuation unless there is evidence for this.

6. Reduction
A reduction (criterion A) is a decline in the number of mature individuals of at least the amount (%) stated over the time period (years) specified, although the decline need not still be continuing. A reduction should not be interpreted as part of a natural fluctuation unless there is good evidence for this. Downward trends that are part of natural fluctuations will not normally count as a reduction.

7. Extreme fluctuations
Extreme fluctuations occur in a number of taxa where population size or distribution area varies widely, rapidly and frequently, typically with a variation greater than one order of magnitude (i.e., a tenfold increase or decrease).

8. Severely fragmented
Severely fragmented refers to the situation where increased extinction risks to the taxon result from the fact that most individuals within a taxon are found in small and relatively isolated subpopulations. These small subpopulations may go extinct, with a reduced probability of recolonisation.

9. Extent of occurrence
Extent of occurrence is defined as the area contained within the shortest continuous imaginary boundary which can be drawn to encompass all the known, inferred or projected sites of present occurrence of a taxon, excluding cases of vagrancy. This measure may exclude discontinuities or disjunctions within the overall distributions of taxa (e.g., large areas of obviously unsuitable habitat) (but see 'area of occupancy'). Extent of occurrence can often be measured by a minimum convex polygon (the smallest polygon in which no internal angle exceeds 180 degrees and which contains all the sites of occurrence).

10. Area of occupancy
Area of occupancy is defined as the area within its 'extent of occurrence' (see definition) which is occupied by a taxon, excluding cases of vagrancy. The measure reflects the fact that a taxon will not usually occur throughout the area of its extent of occurrence, which may, for example, contain unsuitable habitats. The area of occupancy is the smallest area essential at any stage to the survival of existing populations of a taxon (e.g. colonial nesting sites, feeding sites for migratory taxa). The size of the area of occupancy will be a function of the scale at which it is measured, and should be at a scale appropriate to relevant biological aspects of the taxon. The criteria include values in km^2, and thus to avoid errors in classification, the area of occupancy should be measured on grid squares (or equivalents) which are sufficiently small (see Figure 2).

11. Location
Location defines a geographically or ecologically distinct area in which a single event (e.g. pollution) will soon affect all individuals of the taxon present. A location usually, but not always, contains all or part of a subpopulation of the taxon, and is typically a small proportion of the taxon's total distribution.

12. Quantitative analysis
A quantitative analysis is defined here as the technique of population viability analysis (PVA), or any other quantitative form of analysis, which estimates the extinction probability of a taxon or population based on the known life history and specified management or non-management options. In presenting the results of quantitative analyses the structural equations and the data should be explicit.

117

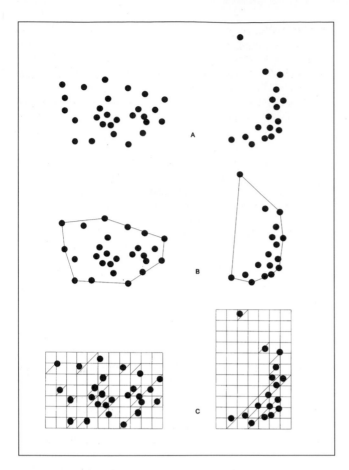

Figure 2: Two examples of the distinction between extent of occurrence and area of occupancy. (a) is the spatial distribution of known, inferred or projected sites of occurrence. (b) shows one possible boundary to the extent of occurrence, which is the measured area within this boundary. (c) shows one measure of area of occupancy which can be measured by the sum of the occupied grid squares.

IV) The categories [1]

EXTINCT (EX)
A taxon is Extinct when there is no reasonable doubt that the last individual has died.

EXTINCT IN THE WILD (EW)
A taxon is Extinct in the wild when it is known only to survive in cultivation, in captivity or as a naturalised population (or populations) well outside the past range. A taxon is presumed extinct in the wild when exhaustive surveys in known and/or expected habitat, at appropriate times (diurnal, seasonal, annual), throughout its historic range have failed to record an individual. Surveys should be over a time frame appropriate to the taxon's life cycle and life form.

CRITICALLY ENDANGERED (CR)
A taxon is Critically Endangered when it is facing an extremely high risk of extinction in the wild in the immediate future, as defined by any of the criteria (A to E) on pages 119-120.

ENDANGERED (EN)
A taxon is Endangered when it is not Critically Endangered but is facing a very high risk of extinction in the wild in the near future, as defined by any of the criteria (A to E) on page 120.

VULNERABLE (VU)
A taxon is Vulnerable when it is not Critically Endangered or Endangered but is facing a high risk of extinction in the wild in the medium-term future, as defined by any of the criteria (A to E) on pages 120-121.

LOWER RISK (LR)
A taxon is Lower Risk when it has been evaluated, does not satisfy the criteria for any of the categories Critically Endangered, Endangered or Vulnerable. Taxa included in the Lower Risk category can be separated into three subcategories:

1. **Conservation Dependent (cd).** Taxa which are the focus of a continuing taxon-specific or habitat-specific conservation programme targeted towards the taxon in question, the cessation of which would result in the taxon qualifying for one of the threatened categories above within a period of five years.

2. **Near Threatened (nt).** Taxa which do not qualify for Conservation Dependent, but which are close to qualifying for Vulnerable.

3. **Least Concern (lc).** Taxa which do not qualify for Conservation Dependent or Near Threatened.

DATA DEFICIENT (DD)
A taxon is Data Deficient when there is inadequate information to make a direct, or indirect, assessment of its risk of extinction based on its distribution and/or population status. A taxon in this category may be well studied, and its biology well known, but appropriate data on abundance and/or distribution is lacking. Data Deficient is therefore not a category of threat or Lower Risk. Listing of taxa in this category indicates that more information is required and acknowledges the possibility that future research will show that threatened classification is appropriate. It is important to make positive use of whatever data are available. In many cases great care should be exercised in choosing between DD and threatened status. If the range of a taxon is suspected to be relatively circumscribed, if a considerable period of time has elapsed since the last record of the taxon, threatened status may well be justified.

NOT EVALUATED (NE)
A taxon is Not Evaluated when it is has not yet been assessed against the criteria.

V) The Criteria for Critically Endangered, Endangered and Vulnerable

CRITICALLY ENDANGERED (CR)
A taxon is Critically Endangered when it is facing an extremely high risk of extinction in the wild in the immediate future, as defined by any of the following criteria (A to E):

A) Population reduction in the form of either of the following:
   1) An observed, estimated, inferred or suspected reduction of at least 80% over the last 10 years or three generations, whichever is the longer, based on (and specifying) any of the following:
      a) direct observation
      b) an index of abundance appropriate for the taxon
      c) a decline in area of occupancy, extent of occurrence and/or quality of habitat
      d) actual or potential levels of exploitation

[1] Note: As in previous IUCN categories, the abbreviation of each category (in parenthesis) follows the English denominations when translated into other languages.

e) the effects of introduced taxa, hybridisation, pathogens, pollutants, competitors or parasites.

2) A reduction of at least 80%, projected or suspected to be met within the next 10 years or three generations, whichever is the longer, based on (and specifying) any of (b), (c), (d) or (e) above.

B) Extent of occurrence estimated to be less than 100 km^2 or area of occupancy estimated to be less than 10 km^2, and estimates indicating any two of the following:

1) Severely fragmented or known to exist at only a single location.

2) Continuing decline, observed, inferred or projected, in any of the following:
   a) extent of occurrence
   b) area of occupancy
   c) area, extent and/or quality of habitat
   d) number of locations or subpopulations
   e) number of mature individuals.

3) Extreme fluctuations in any of the following:
   a) extent of occurrence
   b) area of occupancy
   c) number of locations or subpopulations
   d) number of mature individuals.

C) Population estimated to number less than 250 mature individuals and either:

1) An estimated continuing decline of at least 25% within three years or one generation, whichever is longer or

2) A continuing decline, observed, projected, or inferred, in numbers of mature individuals and population structure in the form of either:
   a) severely fragmented (i.e. no subpopulation estimated to contain more than 50 mature individuals
   b) all individuals are in a single subpopulation.

D) Population estimated to number less than 50 mature individuals.

E) Quantitative analysis showing the probability of extinction in the wild is at least 50% within 10 years or three generations, whichever is the longer.

ENDANGERED (EN)

A taxon is Endangered when it is not Critically Endangered but is facing a very high risk of extinction in the wild in the near future, as defined by any of the following criteria (A to E):

A) Population reduction in the form of either of the following:

1) An observed, estimated, inferred or suspected reduction of at least 50% over the last 10 years or three generations, whichever is the longer, based on (and specifying) any of the following:
   a) direct observation
   b) an index of abundance appropriate for the taxon
   c) a decline in area of occupancy, extent of occurence and/or quality of habitat
   d) actual or potential levels of exploitation
   e) the effects of introduced taxa, hybridisation, pathogens, pollutants, competitors or parasites.

2) A reduction of at least 50%, projected or suspected to be met within the next 10 years or three generations, whichever is the longer, based on (and specifying) any of (b), (c), (d), or (e) above.

B) Extent of occurrence estimated to be less than 5000 km^2 or area of occupancy estimated to be less than 500 km^2, and estimates indicating any two of the following:

1) Severely fragmented or known to exist at no more than five locations.

2) Continuing decline, inferred, observed or projected in any of the following:
   a) extent of occurrence
   b) area of occupancy
   c) area, extent and/or quality of habitat
   d) number of locations or subpopulations
   e) number of mature individuals.

3) Extreme fluctuations in any of the following:
   a) extent of occurrence
   b) area of occupancy
   c) number of locations or subpopulations
   d) number of mature individuals.

C) Population estimated to number less than 2500 mature individuals and either:

1) An estimated continuing decline of at least 20% within five years or two generations, whichever is the longer, or

2) A continuing decline, observed, projected, or inferred, in numbers of mature individuals and poplation structure in the form of either:
   a) severely fragmented (i.e. no subpopulation estiated to contain more than 250 mature individuals)
   b) all individuals are in a single subpopulation.

D) Population estimated to number less than 250 mature individuals.

E) Quantitative analysis showing the probability of extinction in the wild is at least 20% within 20 years or five generations, whichever is the longer.

VULNERABLE (VU)

A taxon is Vulnerable when it is not Critically Endangered or Endangered but is facing a high risk of extinction in the wild in the medium-term future, as defined by any of the following criteria (A to E):

A) Population reduction in the form of either of the following:

1) An observed, estimated, inferred or suspected reduction of at least 20% over the last 10 years or three generations, whichever is the longer, based on (and specifying) any of the following:
   a) direct observation
   b) an index of abundance appropriate for the taxon
   c) a decline in area of occupancy, extent of occurence and/or quality of habitat
   d) actual or potential levels of exploitation
   e) the effects of introduced taxa, hybridisation pathogens, pollutants, competitors or parasites.

2) A reduction of at least 20%, projected or suspected to be met within the next ten years or three generations, whichever is the longer, based on (and specifying) any of (b), (c), (d) or (e) above.

B) Extent of occurrence estimated to be less than 20,000 km^2 or area of occupancy estimated to be less than 2000 km^2, and estimates indicating any two of the following:

1) Severely fragmented or known to exist at no more than ten locations.

2) Continuing decline, inferred, observed or projected, in any of the following:
   a) extent of occurrence
   b) area of occupancy
   c) area, extent and/or quality of habitat
   d) number of locations or subpopulations
   e) number of mature individuals

3) Extreme fluctuations in any of the following:
   a) extent of occurrence
   b) area of occupancy
   c) number of locations or subpopulations
   d) number of mature individuals

C) Population estimated to number less than 10,000 mature individuals and either:

1) An estimated continuing decline of at least 10% within 10 years or three generations, whichever is longer, or

2) A continuing decline, observed, projected, or inferred, in numbers of mature individuals and population structure in the form of either:
   a) severely fragmented (i.e. no subpopulation esti mated to contain more than 1000 mature individuals)
   b) all individuals are in a single subpopulation

D) Population very small or restricted in the form of either of the following:

1) Population estimated to number less than 1000 mature individuals.

2) Population is characterised by an acute restriction in its area of occupancy (typically less than 100 km^2) or in the number of locations (typically less than five). Such a taxon would thus be prone to the effects of human activities (or stochastic events whose impact is increased by human activities) within a very short period of time in an unforeseeable future, and is thus capable of becoming Critically Endangered or even Extinct in a very short period.

E) Quantitative analysis showing the probability of extinction in the wild is at least 10% within 100 years.

Note: copies of the IUCN Red List Categories booklet are available on request from IUCN (address on back cover of this Action Plan). They can also be viewed on the World Wide Web at:

http://www.iucn.org/themes/ssc/iucnredlists/ssc-rl-c.htm

Definitions of the
IUCN Protected Area Management Categories

CATEGORY Ia.

Strict Nature Reserve: protected area managed mainly for science

Area of land and/or sea possessing some outstanding or representative ecosystems, geological or physiological features and/or species, available primarily for scientific research and/or environmental monitoring.

CATEGORY 1b.

Wilderness Area: protected area managed mainly for wilderness protection

Large area of unmodified or slightly modified land, and/or sea, retaining its natural character and influence, without permanent or significant habitation, which is protected and managed so as to preserve its natural condition.

CATEGORY II.

National Park: protected area managed mainly for ecosystem protection and recreation

Natural area of land and/or sea, designated to:

(a) protect the ecological integrity of one or more ecosystems for present and future generations;

(b) exclude exploitation or occupation inimical to the purposes of designation of the area; and

(c) provide a foundation for spiritual, scientific, educational, recreational and visitor opportunities, all of which must be environmentally and culturally compatible.

CATEGORY III.

Natural Monument: protected area managed mainly for conservation of specific natural features

Area containing one, or more, specific natural or natural/cultural feature which is of outstanding or unique value because of its inherent rarity, representative or aesthetic qualities or cultural significance.

CATEGORY IV.

Habitat/Species Management Area: protected area managed mainly for conservation through management intervention

Area of land and/or sea subject to active intervention for management purposes so as to ensure the maintenance of habitats and/or to meet the requirements of specific species.

CATEGORY V.

Protected Landscape/Seascape: protected area managed mainly for landscape/seascape conservation and recreation

Area of land, with coast and sea as appropriate, where the interaction of people and nature over time has produced an area of distinct character with significant aesthetic, ecological and/or cultural value, and often with high biological diversity. Safeguarding the integrity of this traditional interaction is vital to the protection, maintenance and evolution of such an area.

CATEGORY VI.

Managed Resource Protected Area: protected area managed mainly for the sustainable use of natural ecosystems

Area containing predominantly unmodified natural systems, managed to ensure long term protection and maintenance of biological diversity, while providing at the same time a sustainable flow of natural products and services to meet community needs.

For further information on the management categories, readers should consult:

IUCN (1994). *Guidelines for Protected Area Management Categories.* CNPPA with the assistance of WCMC. IUCN, Gland, Switzerland and Cambridge, UK. x + 261pp.